DISRUPTIVE CHILDREN: DISRUPTIVE SCHOOLS?

DISRUPTIVE CHILDREN~ DISRUPTIVE SCHOOLS?

Jean Lawrence, David Steed and Pamela Young

CROOM HELM
London & Sydney

NICHOLS PUBLISHING COMPANY
New York

© 1984 Jean Lawrence, David Steed and Pamela Young
Croom Helm Ltd, Provident House, Burrell Row,
Beckenham, Kent BR3 1AT
Croom Helm Australia Pty Ltd, First Floor, 139 King St.,
Sydney, NSW 2001, Australia

British Library Cataloguing in Publication Data

Lawrence, Jean
    Disruptive children; disruptive schools?
    1. Problem children—Education
    I. Title   II. Steed, David   III. Young, Pamela
    371.8'1   LC4801

    ISBN 0-7099-1442-3

First published in the United States of America 1984 by
Nichols Publishing Company, Post Office Box 96
New York, NY 10024

Library of Congress Cataloging in Publication Data

Lawrence, Jean, Ph.D.
    Disruptive children, disruptive schools?

    Bibliography: p.
    Includes index.
    1. Classroom management—Great Britain. 2. Problem
children—Education—Great Britain. 3. Teachers—Great
Britain—Job stress. I. Steed, David.   II. Young, Pamela
(Pamela E.)   III. Title
LB3013.L39   1984   371.93'0941   84-8209
ISBN 0-89397-200-2

Printed and bound in Great Britain

CONTENTS

PREFACE

It is more than 10 years since Everett Reimer wrote his book with the challenging and provocative title *School is Dead* (1971). His obsequy was premature. 30,000 schools are still alive and kicking, populated by 10 million children and an army of nearly half a million teachers (Kogan, 1975). A ritual acknowledgement however, of Illich (1976) and the Deschoolers has become *de rigueur* in any discussion of education and we are left with the uncomfortable feeling that, if school is not dead, many schools appear moribund. Institutions are no more immune than individuals to either disease or death. The apparent loss of high morale and educational purpose over time, and the failure to recognise, or respond appropriately to changed social and economic conditions, may well mean for many, that a question mark hangs over some schools as good places for children to be. It is a measure of the maturity of the teaching profession in the past ten years that there has been a growing willingness to acknowledge that many of the strains experienced both by teachers and pupils may well derive as much as much from aspects of institutional as they do from individual pathology. Illich's criticisms of hospitals as having 'iatrogenic' (1976), doctor-produced problems for patients might be applied to some schools. Can we recognise in the 'sink' schools a form of what might be termed 'Educational Nemesis'? Do such schools have 'pedagogenic', teacher-produced problems for their pupils?

Interest taken by the teacher unions (Lowenstein, 1975), was possibly influential in focussing the attention of the media and the press on the problems of a schooling system in process of change. Violence against teachers in schools became newsworthy. Television added its own contribution in a number of documentary accounts of secondary schools, none of them complimentary to the system of comprehensive education which, in the early seventies had become accepted policy by both the main political parties. Set against the background of the polemical 'Black Papers' (Cox and Dyson, 1968), such reporting seemed to confirm the impression that schools, which had promised so much in the sixties, were becoming a matter of public concern, and that the confidence in teachers to respond responsibly to the social, political and economic changes had been misplaced. Concern over experimentation with drugs, football hooliganism, violence, student disaffection and mugging all became linked with what was happening in schools. Prominence given to the Bennett (1978) research on primary schools and to what came to be called the 'Tyndale Affair' (Auld, 1976) when doubts were cast on the quality of teaching were both a further reflection of this concern.

Clearly disruption is a matter of practical and immediate concern to teachers. Most obviously they worry that disruption puts in jeopardy their intentions and efforts to teach; it is thus a threat to their *raison d'être* and an affront to their professional existence; no wonder it provokes a sense of outrage. Disruption is frustrating, irritating and stressful; in extreme cases it may lead to complete breakdown of the classroom order and, more seriously, of the teacher's health. Senior school staff worry that it may reflect on the competence of their staff, and, at a time of falling rolls and school closure, may lose them the confidence of their prospective pupils' parents. Educational administrators worry about their legal responsibility to provide appropriate education for every child and the problems which are created when school head teachers, having exhausted their coping procedures within schools, resort to the expedient of exclusion and suspension.

Parents worry that disruption will interfere with their own children's education and affect their life chances. Not least, children worry about disruption, those who are its victims, (Olweus, 1978) as well as the disrupters themselves whose behaviour, labelled disruptive, may be both a sign of alienation and disaffection from school as well as sometimes a *cri de coeur*.

When this book was in manuscript, it was objected that the researches which it reported ignored the political context and appeared to be unaware of and naive about the wider structural influence on education. The authors were invited to "come clean" about their assumptions and to acknowledge that their research was no more than a justification of existing educational arrangements.

Without conceding the pejorative implications of this criticism, we happily acknowledge a broad commitment to the value of education. It would be strange if, as professionals engaged in the training of teachers, we did not. Nevertheless it does not imply on our part an unquestioned acceptance of the present system of state schooling. If there is a single message which we would hope to convey, it is that many of the problems which are being experienced currently in schools may be as much of our own making as they are to do with the social and behavioural problems of children or with the structural contradictions in society. It is these problems of our own making which we can, and should, work on; as teachers we cannot, even if we wanted to, change families or society — at least, not quickly enough to be of benefit to the children we teach. We can change schools and the experiences which they offer to children, which precisely because of the links with and the pressures which come from the wider society, create problems for them. Whatever the intentions of planners and their protestations of commitment to notions of equalising opportunity, many schools end by generating problems; pupil failure, alienation and disruption are not to be accounted for solely, or even mainly, in terms of pupil inadequacies; they are closely linked to aspects of inadequate schools and teachers.

Our arguments support the need for structural changes in schools — in their organisation, pedagogy and curriculum; and in their relationship to the wider world of work, parents and the local community.

We claim for our account that it is structural but not structuralist. It is structural in the broad sense that all historical accounts are, where the institutions of any historical period reflect the values and ideas which are current at the time. To accord priority among the range of such influences to the force of technological advances and economic organisation is in our view to mistake the independent effects of ideas and thought.

Whilst we recognise the relationship between strains experienced by schools and wider structural and economic forces, we do not accept the further conclusion that the complete restructuring of society is either the only, nor necessarily the most desirable answer. Experience from socialist countries gives little encouragement to the belief that such changes would be wholly to the advantage of the under-privileged on whose behalf their necessity is claimed.

We believe that there is still mileage in a gradual approach and the possibilities for regeneration from within the system might be far greater than have been supposed; the resources of teachers and their inventiveness have as yet been relatively untapped. Numerous publications have highlighted and explored differences between schools and linked these to levels of problem behaviour of pupils. If our measure is the sense of outrage which greeted an article which appeared in *New Society* in 1967 (Powers) suggesting that schools might generate delinquent behaviour, then it would seem that we have come far. At one level there is a greater willingness now to acknowledge that schools do make a difference (Jencks, 1971; Rutter, 1979) and less of a defensive attitude from teachers. Early attempts to relate organisational theory to schools (Corwin, 1965; Etzioni, 1964; Shipman, 1968) appeared premature; informed opinion in the seventies appeared to favour compensatory rather than preventative models; school changes in curriculum

(Stenhouse, 1980), and streaming (Hargreaves, 1968) appeared, to radical critics, no more than tinkering with a system which was basically flawed because of its commitment to and its location within a capitalist mode of production (Young, 1976; Bowles and Gintis, 1976).

The most significant development in recent years is the development of an interest in the school as a totality and as a system of interrelated parts. Focus on the hidden messages has characterised the concern to develop a multi-ethnic approach in schools, and to examine aspects of the system which may contribute to low expectations and performance, especially of girls.

Research contributions (Rutter, 1979; Reynolds, 1976; Lawrence, 1977; 1981) have played an important role both in restoring confidence in schools and in demonstrating the possibility of generating change from within the system. The acknowledgement of the increased stressfulness of teaching has at the same time provided some assurance that changes in schools and in pedagogy might improve, rather than exacerbate, relations between pupils and teachers. Programmes of staff development, school-based action research and the renewed interest in all kinds of inservice training — all lend some encouragement to the assertion that teachers are becoming more aware of the need to find answers within the educational system. With the imminence of computer technology it may not be too fanciful to envisage a time when all schools will routinely monitor behaviour and learning and identify aspects of the system, which either singly or in combination appear to be significant in producing favourable outcomes.

Public concern about disruption appears to be widespread. It is one of the few areas in schools that can still command resources and finance. Much has been written and yet there is little reliable information about its nature, extent, or seriousness. Teachers are understandably impatient with explanations which appear to offer no solutions to problems they face daily in the classroom. A newspaper cartoon comes close to the point in depicting a school 'disruptive' complaining: 'She said I was an introverted casualty of a capitalistic society in an ineluctable crisis of capitalism'. Such a complaint may bear the seeds of truth but has little to offer teachers under stress in schools. In the relative absence of clear causes, capable of easy and immediate solution, teachers have tended to follow a number of understandable but *ad hoc* strategies where they either revert to well tried methods which worked in the past with earlier generations of school children, or leap on to whatever bandwagon was rolling at the time, curricular, organisational or pedagogic. Similarly, faced with major and seemingly unending problems of school adjustment and change, mostly not of their own but of demographic and central government's making, teachers have responded defensively by attributing blame to the inadequacies of children.

First and foremost this is a book which considers the possibility of change in both of the main protagonists in disruptive encounters — pupils and teachers, as well as the location and the activity of disruption. It is a book which originated in the professional and practical concern of the authors to improve on the advice currently available, to enable student teachers to cope more effectively with problems of control. The concerns are essentially practical; how to enable teachers to teach more effectively, how to promote creative and imaginative planning which will make schools more effective and pleasant places for people to be; how to remove unnecessary stress and frustration from the classroom.

The book is presented in four sections each of which stands alone and can be read separately. Part One is a general introduction to the problems of definition and methodology in research and includes a review of literature. Part Two comprises two school-based research projects referred to respectively as 'The Goldsmiths Project', and 'Behaviour Problem Dialogue'. Part Three describes techniques available for teachers to use in the classroom. Part Four is an appraisal of working papers and documents circulated within Local Education Authorities in England, outlining policies and provisions relating to the disruptive children in schools. The Department of Education and Science responses are included in this fourth part.

This last section has particular relevance in view of the widespread concern which has been expressed about the implications of setting up separate disruptive units (Mortimore *et al.* 1984; Topping, 1983), and of the renewed interest which has been expressed in inservice training of teachers and staff development projects.

The first part of the book attempts to examine some of the questions surrounding the concept of disruption. Its central premise is that, whilst much has been written as if the meaning of disruption was obvious and its manifestations immediately recognisable, we still remain largely ignorant of those elements in children's behaviour and the particular circumstances which prompt teachers to identify it as disruptive. It is perhaps obvious, but worth stressing, that there can be no disruption without a pre-existing sense of order against which disruptive behaviour is seen as a transgression; the one is dependent on the other but often, because of the deepseated belief in acceptance of rules which govern behaviour, their existence and tacit acceptance goes unquestioned. The scale and seriousness of disruption in schools is, we suspect, wider than the 'one per cent' suggested by the ILEA (1978), but probably less than suggested in the media; it includes violence both to teachers and between pupils but on our evidence the first of these is still rare. More importantly, rates of disruptive behaviour appear to vary between schools and between individual teachers. It is for this reason that the particular approach in the two whole school studies reported in Part Two tries to identify the features of those situations which elicit from children behaviour which is described and acted upon as disruptive.

In juxtaposing subjective accounts of disruption given by teachers and pupils with the supposedly more objective counting of pupil infringements of school rules, we have attempted to highlight some of the processes by which teachers can create different climates of behaviour. Schools can and clearly do make a difference both to achievement and behaviour.

Questions about what can be done about disruption usually carry the message that the disrupted activity is legitimate and should be allowed to continue uninterrupted. It implies there is an unspoken acceptance of existing arrangements in schools. Disruption always seems to have pejorative connotations.

But what of activities which may deserve to be disrupted? What of situations where a vote of confidence cannot be justified? No one doubts that much of disruption in schools is the fault of children — naughty, misbehaving children, who set out maliciously and with intent to stop the teacher from educating. But not all misbehaviour is of this kind.

Perhaps we can borrow from legal terminology which attempts to distinguish seriousness according to degree of intent and provocation. One such term is 'justifiable homicide'. Is it possible in the same idiom to speak of 'justifiable disruption' where the incompetence of some teachers and the inappropriateness of some forms of school organisation and curriculum, might try the patience of a saint and be considered in mitigation of the offence.

What is distinctive about the two school studies presented in Part Two, is the focus on the incident of disruption as the point at which teachers frustrated in their intention to teach, reassert their definition of the situation by defining and reacting to pupil behaviour as disruptive. By monitoring such incidents using information provided by teachers in the course of their normal teaching, we are able to chart the range of factors which impinge on the situation and which may well account for the different tolerance levels which teachers show. What is immediately revealed by such monitoring, is the intensity of emotion and feeling which such incidents generate and the consequent stress for those involved.

What is also revealed is the inventiveness of teachers in devising ways of coping and the extensive range of possibilities existing within the school system which can be utilised, either seperately or together, by imaginative teachers. Faced by mounting levels of disruption, schools are far from helpless and have a fund of largely untapped resources which they can call upon. These possible resources are set out in Part Two together with details of the extent, nature, pattern and seriousness of disruptive incidents revealed in the periods of monitoring devoted to the two schools. Information of this kind is essential, we believe, if schools are to pinpoint areas where change will be most effective.

This book is in no sense a handbook on disruption and it makes no claims to generalise from the restricted data which it describes. The research was undertaken with, and not for, schools and teachers; it relies heavily on teachers' and, to a lesser extent, on pupils' accounts of incidents. For many, this may be its strongest claim to interest; it is perhaps remarkable that among the plethora of writings on disruption, there have been few which have started from a description of the incident itself. The book attempts to fill that gap. Teachers' verbatim statements expressing their feelings about disruption will find an echo in most staffrooms. Similarly, some of the most fascinating comments are those which come from the pupils themselves, and serve to remind us that stress and frustration, arising from disruptive acts, is not the prerogative of the teachers alone.

The above would, suggest that the book may be of interest to the following:

i.   Headteachers and senior staff.
ii. Professional tutors and those with responsibility for staff development and INSET.
iii. Course organisers at Teachers Centres, especially those concerned with the inservice needs of teachers.
iv. Local Authority Advisers.
v.   Probationary and student teachers.

First, at the most general level, it may make a contribution to a better understanding of the nature and seriousness of disruption and of its symbiotic relationship with aspects of the school system. A shift of focus away from pupil differences and deficits, to school differences has long been overdue (Rutter, 1979) and serves as a timely reminder of the range of resources available within the system which remain largely untapped.

Second, it may contribute to the creation of a new climate in which discussion of teachers' problems of controlling children in the classroom can be more open, acceptable and frank. The experience of disruption should not, in the first instance, be a matter of blame or shame for teachers. The 'conspiracy of silence' which we are told surrounds the acknowledgement of control problems in the staffroom, is neither conducive to the confidence or morale or professional growth of teachers.

The third level at which this book may be found useful is in its contribution to staff morale by an acknowledgement of and acceptance that something can and should be done. The procedures for monitoring which we have described were perceived by many teachers as an opportunity for more direct involvement in and discussion on aspects of policy and organisation often seen as solely the concern of senior staff (Henderson and Perry, 1981). Such development of a more participatory form of decision-making where disruption is concerned may result either from pressure from below where there is a perceived gap between school policies and classroom reality, or from above, where initiatives from senior staff may create opportunities and resources for teachers to acquire new skills and attitudes to suit changing circumstances. School amalgamations, reductions in pupil numbers, changes in curriculum and mixed ability grouping all require new understandings and expertise which a policy of staff development and training, to include a consideration of disruption, should meet.

The fourth level suggests the importance of such work being school based and the desirability of all teachers being actively engaged in ongoing research and monitoring, if change is to be seen as acceptable and not as threatening and undermining. In promoting this view, the book may be regarded as a source of suggestions and as providing a model for a procedure which has proved to be economic, simple and effective to use. Interest in the two reported researches and demand for information relating to them from schools for use with working parties and staff discussions, suggest that the procedure which we have developed may provide a useful starting point and focus for such activities.

Fifth, and most obviously, Part Three, which is concerned with ways of coping with disruption, may be of assistance to individual teachers as a 'Do It Yourself' checklist and reminder of the range of variables and permutations which can be tried before resorting to official channels of discipline for resolution of the problem.

Lastly we hope that the book may make a modest, but significant contribution to the understanding of deviance and illustrate some of the practical difficulties of devising appropriate methodological approaches in an area which in inescapably subjective and value laden.

It is often difficult to obtain research facilities for studies of disruptive behaviour. This difficulty stems from a variety of reasons: breaches of confidentiality are feared, teacher competence may be impugned and teachers working with behaviour problems may be heavily work loaded and under stress. We have been particularly fortunate in obtaining facilities for the projects described in this book. These were granted usually through personal contacts and recommendation — e.g. for the first whole school monitoring study, the head teacher spoke on the telephone to the headteacher of the 'Encouragement Project' school and on hearing that the latter project had helped the school, agreed to offer facilities for monitoring in his school. Facilities for the 'Encouragement Project' were granted because the researcher was known to the Chief Education Officer of the authority, within which a senior post had previously been held by one of the researchers.

ACKNOWLEDGEMENTS

A large debt of gratitude is owed to the teachers who gave so generously of their time; and to Annette, Leslie and Tom for their continuous support.

Part One

THE ISSUES

1 INTRODUCTION: BLACKBOARD JUNGLES?

No-one any longer thinks it strange for police to patrol the corridors of downtown Bronx schools. Reporting misbehaviour in schools has become commonplace. But what are we to make of it? Are we reaping the fruits of a generation brought up on Dr Spock, the Welfare State and 'progressive education'. Are schools no longer able or willing to cope? To what extent do schools share responsibility for the apparent increase in discipline and violence at the place of work, in the streets and on the football terraces?

Given the magnitude of problems associated with unemployment, poor housing, baby and wife battering, to an outsider it can seem almost trivial and parochial to focus on the disruptive behaviour of children in schools. Haven't children always been naughty? Are they really more so, and are incidents more numerous than they were fifty years ago, and aren't the same remedies as relevant today as they were then — a taste of discipline?

Reliable answers seem hard to come by. Teachers may be reluctant to admit to problems which may reflect on their professional competence. Heads may be unwilling to admit to running a difficult school. There seems to be conspiracy of silence among those concerned, based partly on the faith that if you don't talk about problems they will go away, or conversely that if you do, it will magnify them.

On the one hand there is the seriousness with which misbehaviour is viewed as a symptom of social malaise and an emotional response, especially by the teachers' associations and, on the other hand, our continuing ignorance of its causes and significance and of effective means to control it. If we compare these points with our relative confidence in controlling our physical environment, it is perhaps not surprising that whoever speaks loudest and most often seems assured of an attentive audience in the national press.

Nor is it surprising that we often appear to be impressed most by explanations which enable us to identify targets clearly and to apportion blame. Sit for a while in a school staffroom and you are left in no doubt from snippets of conversation as to where disruption lies: it lies in the child. The child is disruptive, unco-operative, difficult, disturbed, aggressive, disobedient, awkward and bloody-minded. Every class has at least one of them who stands out; sometimes you seem to

have a whole class full of them. If you ask a teacher what he means
by this, it is apparent that the child is all these things because he is
stopping the teacher getting on with his job. Talking out of turn stops
the teacher from holding the floor, from ensuring a period of quiet for
children to answer questions or to talk in the ways which he wants. The
child who does so thwarts the teacher's plan and stops him doing the
job as he sees it. Senior teachers, too, may react strongly to forms of
behaviour which obstruct their attempts to control the situation; disobedience, which shows loss of control in the authority situation, displays
of temper which show loss of control in the personality dimension and
a lack of concentration, which shows the child to be out of the teacher's
control as far as getting work done (Lawrence, 1980). It is when these
forms of 'difficult' behaviour combine in the same child that frustration and anger may mount in the teacher, consciously or unconsciously,
to result in depression or to a rejection of the child from the class, and
eventually from the school. Reports in the press suggest that too many
suspended children are sitting untaught at home or wandering the city
streets. It is much easier to explain misbehaviour in terms of the
wilfulness of the child than it is to do so in terms of the situation in
which he has been placed and found wanting. The pupil provides the
disliked behaviour, but the teacher may also play an important part in
triggering it off, sometimes acting on it and sometimes not (self-fulfilling
prophecies operate on behaviour as well as on academic attainment).
The teacher's role in triggering misbehaviour is often not recognised,
or ignored where it is. Presumably because it seems easier to modify
the pupils' behaviour than the teacher's.

Teachers' recourse to explanations for misbehaviour in terms of the
home background of their charges serves to attach the label of deviant
to the pupil. It is amongst other things a coping strategy designed, in
part, to justify events by an explanation which is kind to the pupil, when
the teacher may well feel guilty at harbouring unkind thoughts about
him. It is a useful strategy in that it can help bring in other parties —
the welfare and psychological services who help by sharing the burden
and who systematise matters in situations which are seen as too random
for comfort.

Hardly any attention in the literature has been paid to the teacher's
background and its impact on the definition of problem behaviour in
children. Does previous experience in secondary modern, grammar or
comprehensive school affect a teacher's view of misbehaviour when he
comes to work with children of widely ranging ability? Do problems
persist for some teachers after their first probationary year? What are

the characteristics of teachers who continue to experience problems and who find the job stressful? How is it possible to give assistance in situations where it may be difficult even to admit to a problem? These are the questions that are asked by teacher educators and LEA advisers.

As well as knowing something about the teacher, there are two other related factors which require attention; the first is the school situation itself. Its ethos, structures and processes influence the definition and treatment of deviance. The second is the 'incident' of misbehaviour, the 'event' which stands out from the myriad of classroom events, as important and significant, as an incident to be remembered, reported and acted upon.

The uncomfortable fact is that we have very little reliable knowledge about disruption in schools — that is to say 'disruption', has not until recently been sufficiently considered as an appropriate area for systematic research. One of the difficulties is to conceive what such knowledge might be, how it might be obtained and what its status might be. We know a lot, of course, about children and adults who disrupt normal expectations. Research has been prolific especially within the areas of medicine and criminology and is redolent with terms applied in classificatory systems. Here the main thrust of research has been towards either cure or control (Kennedy, 1980). The target has been the individual although in medicine there have been signs of a shift towards examining the social context of disease and looking closely at the community, the home, the workplace in which the patient lives.

There is a danger in transferring research findings to education from the context of medicine and criminology for they tend to be focused on aetiology, cure and punishment. But the difficulties and absence of educational research in this area make it a permanent temptation: especially where there is a public growing concern and a belief that the schools are failing.

Although research on school disruption is limited this is not to suggest that teachers do not already know a great deal. Faced daily by intractable children, they, both at a pragmatic and superficial psychological level, have a fund of knowledge (Schutz, 1964) about children who disrupt. To apply the terms 'recipe' knowledge to this understanding is not to trivialise it but to recognise its basis in the day to day coping in situations which require instant remedies and which utilise well tried procedures of institutional control. What are the options available for different treatment accorded to children identified as 'disruptive'? To what extent is school disruption an indication of personal maladjustment or institutional malaise?

A persistent danger, from our lack of knowledge about school disruption, is that we may fall into the trap, in our concern to help, of creating a greater problem by inappropriate responses. How we conceptualise problems has consequences. It seems important, in respect of disruption that we do not fall victim of our own concern and persuasiveness by creating a moral panic (Platt, 1969). Ignorance and fear were used to create a moral climate in the 17th century when the problem of witchcraft was seen to assume such proportions that it was deemed acceptable to persecute and exterminate witches. Fear of the Elders of Zion was fostered in the 1920s in Germany to promote anti-semitism; McCarthyism in America was used as a political weapon in the war against Communism and soon we must question whether, in the absence of a clear understanding of the scale and seriousness of disruption, the present concern does not run a similar risk of assuming the proportions of a 'moral panic' where responses are intuitive rather than rational.

The consequences are as serious for schools as they are for children. The danger is that for substantial numbers of children, particularly those whom research has identified as high risk in terms of school failure and underachievement — the multi-deprived, the poor, sections of the working class, some ethnic groups — schools will increasingly be seen as irrelevant and unrelated to their subsequent life chances. For schools the danger is more subtle: that having identified the problem within children, for whatever reason — low IQ, class, inadequate socialisation, environment, poor employment prospects — the teachers will cease to look critically at their own practices and the ways in which these may contribute to the very problems which they wish to solve.

Teachers know about disruption (Marland, 1979). They encounter it every day. They have a tacit understanding (Polyani, 1964) of how to cope and manage difficult children and classes. This is what is referred to when people talk of the need for teachers 'to learn on the job'. The ability to respond appropriately to challenge in the course of busy teaching is something perhaps which can only be acquired in this way and is not reducible to any theoretical course of professional preparation however well done. The problem is that it is tacit knowledge embedded in the on-going experience of the classroom which is not easily repeatable; it is therefore difficult to abstract or to generalise about it. At an instinctive level many teachers know what to do but not why. In practice it means that teachers have to work out their own style of coping. But we also know that some teachers never achieve this and that many do so only at the cost of unacceptable personal strain. We know, too, that the cost to the child who disrupts sucessfully is too high in terms of his own risk of failure and labelling and of the loss of effective learning by other children whose studies are disrupted. Both teachers and taught need a better understanding of disruption if they are not to fall prey to oversimplified remedies (Olweus, 1978).

We are left with uncomfortable questions which have to be faced and which recipe knowledge of the Schutz kind is unable to answer fully. On what criteria is school misbehaviour graded as serious? What is normal, healthy behaviour? How far are school control procedures conducive to healthy adjustment? Given that teachers face a multitude of potentially disruptive acts of behaviour, what influences their decision to take action? Why are similar instances and incidents differently defined by teachers? What consequences follow upon a decision to treat an incident as 'disruptive'?

Disruptive behaviour in schools is not a new problem though several lines of evidence point to a recent increase in its dimensions. Clearly the nature of disruption changes with the norms of the school and what is expected of pupils. The requirements of Mr Squeers at Dotheboys differ markedly from those of A S Neill at Summerhill. Neither approach can solve the problem of disruption in a school of a different kind.

The history of disruptive behaviour in schools is a very long one. It gives little encouragement to the notion that school days are the happiest of your life. At least one strand from biblical times suggests the opposite — that learning is inevitably linked with punishment (Boyd, 1969). In Proverbs it is noted: 'He that spared the rod hateth his son'. Children were seen as in need of correction 'Foolishness is bound up in the heart of the child but the rod of correction shall drive it from him'. Sadly, by a semantic confusion, instruction from the earliest days was regarded as requiring punishment; teaching was the giving of rules to be committed to memory, learning was the repetition of precepts to be learned by heart.

The same legalistic, narrow utilitarian approach characterised much of education from Roman times, exalted the technicalities of grammar and rhetoric, and was preoccupied with analytic methods. 'What miseries I experienced when obedience of my teachers was set before me as proper for my boyhood . . . after that, I was put to school to get learning of which I knew not what use there was; and yet, if slow to learn, I was flogged'. This was written by St Augustine in his Confessions in 354 AD and expresses a sense of alienation against the education offered at that time.

Orme (1973) summarises the typical, mediaeval situation thus: 'The tedium of long hours in school on hard benches was dispelled by liberal use of the rod. Masters faced with controlling very large classes for very long hours did not expect to keep order by any other means'. At home and at school the socially established means of preserving discipline and inculcating obedience, industry, and virtue was by beating. We still permit the use of the cane in many English schools. In Erasmus's preference for removing rather than punishing dull or worthless boys from the school, to physical punishment, we see a forerunner of our systems of suspension and exclusion from school for serious misbehaviour, and also the Oxford schoolmaster of 1500, who complained about boys wanting to go to the toilet, and making excuses for leaving the room, and going home, sounds much like his twentieth century counterpart does. Children got bored, and were lazy. Schoolboys were sometimes involved in attacks on the public, and in assaults on staff or pupils.

Matters did not appear to have improved at the end of the eighteenth century. George III's standard question to boys at Eton was 'Have you had a rebellion lately?' Jarman records that between 1775-93 Winchester experienced several mutinies in one of which the boys occupied the college building for two days and hoisted the red flag (Jarman, 1963). Later in 1779 Marlborough boys blew down a door, burned books and desks and then withdrew to an island from which they were only removed by an assault by regular troops. A school rebellion in 1818 was only suppressed by two companies of troops with fixed bayonets. Even as late as 1851, serious revolts were recorded. It is surprising then that Jarman notes, 'It was possible for a normal boy to pass unharmed through the great schools'.

That such problems were not restricted to the great public schools nor to particular times and places is well known. Lowndes (1969) wrote eloquently of the pressures faced by teachers in the elementary schools at the turn of the century. A well known headmaster in London between 1889-93 is quoted as saying: 'I never remember seeing my headmaster in school when he had not a cane hanging by a crook over his left wrist. Every assistant master had a cane and so had many of the pupil teachers . . .' A dismal picture perhaps but one engendered by the brutishness created by the social and economic conditions of the time. For teachers the experience was demanding: 'every year there were many bruised shins and even broken limbs caused by rough boys kicking young women teachers'. One pupil reproved for throwing apples at girls during a sewing lesson is said to have thrown himself on the floor with the remarks 'Damn you, I'll mark your shins if you come any nearer'. A further instance records that 'a boy drew a nine-inch knife and dashed it into the back of another. The blade ran along a rib, slipped in and barely missed the base of the lung' (Lowndes, 1969).

This similarity between the types of disruptive behaviour over time and in our own period is striking, but not surprising. Human aggression takes small or large scale forms, is turned inward towards the person or outward towards others, and is expressed verbally or physically, in direct or more covert forms. But to note the similarities through history does not mean that the dimensions of the problem within the period of mass education have not fluctuated (Armytage, 1964). There is direct and indirect evidence from many sources to indicate a growth in the quantity and seriousness of disruptive behaviour in school over the past decade at least. It would seem that the growth in disruptive behaviour is no more than a mirror of the growth of violent behaviour in our society itself, as reflected in increasing concern with vandalism, rising crime figures, particularly relating to crime among young people and, increasing figures for juvenile suicide.

Other countries are also affected. A disturbed society will obviously pass its disturbance into its institutions, although precisely how this occurs is a complex issue. Thus it is known that the inner city, together with its schools, shows comparatively high figures for psychiatric disturbance, and for deviant pupil behaviour in schools, but we do not yet understand fully the mechanisms that are at work. Some are obvious. Imitation is one of these: the boy who sees thuggery outside school conferring status on a gang member, may copy it in school. The derelict house and the sordid street may lead children to accept and develop a school environment which resembles them. The despair of families where parents are unemployed may turn children to a bitter opting out from the goals of the schools of the same community.

From a longer historical point of view, the current situation with regard to misbehaviour in schools may be viewed as a culmination of social and educational developments during the past century or more which have meshed together, providing a complex and dynamic backcloth. The growth of industrial society with the development and disintegration of inner cities, associated with demands for a longer period of compulsory education, and democratically organised secondary education for all children, brought into being a number of large comprehensive schools. Aspirations for working class children, the bulk of the population, have grown, but in spite of the government sponsoring of curriculum development, the education of these children still commonly follows the grammar school model, with traditional subjects and externally set examinations in the concluding years of schooling. The progressive raising of the school leaving age up to its present point of 16 in 1972-3 has retained in the schools many children whose goals and aspirations are at variance with those of their schools, who function as young adults outside school, and are dealt with as children in the school.

Fortunately, teachers only rarely meet the grosser forms of difficult behaviour in the classroom, but it could well be that in many urban schools there are appreciable numbers of 'problem' children sometimes unrecognised, sometimes unacknowledged, because of the unwillingness or inability of teachers to label them as disturbed, or simply because diagnosis is futile except in extreme cases, because of the shortage of places in special schools or units and the frequent long delays in transfer to them. A school's response to such children needs to be firmly located within a developed system of pastoral care and rational support rather than one of punishment. Schools do have a duty of care for all their members both pupils and teachers. It is often a matter of fine judgement whether disruptive children — either for their own sake or for the sake of others they are with, should be excluded and catered for either in special schools or small units. Schools need to consider carefully what sort of support system to establish and the relationship of this system to teaching groups, remedial assistance, pastoral care and punishment systems.

Once the focus shifts away from the pathologies of individuals it becomes possible to ask whether schools can influence levels of disruption by their institutional arrangements. Schools are gatekeepers of values; at the level of publicly accepted forms of conduct and behaviour they are expected to produce children who are well behaved, who can exercise self control with the ability to match appropriate behaviour to a variety of public contexts and with an armamentarium of personal character traits which will fit them for membership of our society — a sense of honesty, truthfulness, respect for others and for authority. At another level schools are expected to produce children who are both minimally knowledgeable and in possession of certain ways of knowing. The point at which the school exercises its gatekeeping function will vary according to which audience it is most sensitive to — the local authority, the parents, the professional groups of teachers, the HMIs, the community, etc. Such decisions are likely to be influenced by previous experience of success. The possibility of achieving a match between aims of teachers, parents and pupils was always potentially higher in the grammar school than the secondary modern. In the comprehensive school the area in which it is possible to achieve consensus may have diminished and the main burden of living with contradictions which exist and the incompatability of many of the expressed aims can fall heavily on the class teacher.

If it is the policy of the school to value creativity or honesty or sensitivity, it is the teacher who has to decide, according to his understanding and commitment to these values if the behaviour of children is acceptable. At each stage, it is the teacher who is responsible for invoking the rules, whether these are explicit, as in school rules, or understood in terms of nuances of behaviour. Where it is no longer possible to accommodate behaviour within existing definitions of the rule, it is likely, given the constant pressures under which the teacher works, that they will invoke institutional definitions and procedures for coping with the infraction of rules.

When teachers decide they can no longer make allowances for disruptive behaviour, it passes out of their control and becomes an officially recognised and sanctionable instance of disruption. The quantifiable aspect of this disruption — the number of detentions, canings, etc. may enter into the folk-lore of the staffroom. The question then becomes, whether and how, this influences the ways in which staff view and interact with boys and girls defined as disruptive and, perhaps more crucially, how the pupil begins to reassess his view of himself and his relationship with other staff and pupils, and with the school as a whole.

The difficulty partly arises because of the tendency to see all disruptive behaviour as infraction of rules requiring punishment. Thus the equation disruption = punishment stems from an assumption that the responsibility for disruption lies wholly with the child and accepts, without question, the framework established either by the teacher or the school. If one starts with the assumption that there will always be children for whom the aims of school and classroom lessons will appear irrelevant and where there is a mismatch between the values of the teacher and the pupil, the question then resolves itself into whether it is possible for the teacher to continue teaching those pupils for whom the lesson does not represent such a mismatch, or who are prepared to adopt the role of the good pupil in order not to offend teacher susceptibilities. For those who are disruptive, the range of options could be wider than automatic punishment. Exclusion from class could enable the teacher to maintain his intentions with respect to the majority of the class and to continue with his plans until he has time to reassess their adequacy. For many, exclusion need not, and should not perhaps, carry a necessary implication of punishment. Most schools make obvious exceptions in respect of children suffering from major and easily recognised traumas such as loss of a parent; it requires only an extension of this notion to acknowledge a wide range of lesser circumstances for which the appropriate first response might be understanding sympathy and acceptance. This does not imply condoning or ignoring disruption but it does suggest the need for a system of control which is more responsive to and understanding of children's needs.

3 DEFINING AND UNDERSTANDING DISRUPTION

As far as the incidence of disruptive behaviour in the schools of this country is concerned, information so far gathered and published is very incomplete and often uncertain. That the problem is extensive is indicated by the opening statement of the paper for guidance published by a mainly rural LEA, Devon County Council, in 1975. 'Expressions of disquiet from several quarters indicate that the kind of misbehaviour within schools which receives publicity in other parts of the country is not unknown in some schools in Devon'. Unfortunately, from the point of view of the collation of statistics, the criteria used to define the problem of disruption vary from study to study. Thus the largely rural county reported on by McNamara (1975) focused on 'problem children', including 'difficult children', 'children with problems', and 'primary school children who might become problem children', under this heading. Not only do the criteria used vary from study to study, but the methods used to gather data are often such that they are very incomplete. Sometimes head teachers only are asked to supply information and though they may know of most 'spectacular' incidents, others may not be reported to them by assistant staff who are anxious to conceal difficulties or do not wish the pupil to be reported onwards for punishment. In the most extensive survey, reported on by Lowenstein (1975), it was made very clear that the data, particularly those from secondary schools, were very incomplete. In secondary schools large numbers of teachers are involved, and many will be too busy to supply it, and the press of events will make the accurate recall of incidents hazardous.

We have no published statistics at all for the number of difficult schools in the country, though the D E S must know most of them, nor have we any knowledge of the number of difficult classes at any one time. There are, however, criteria which could be used to assess the difficulty of schools, such as the rates of truancy, suspension and exclusion from the school, and the various indices of social disadvantage. However, some twilight area schools are not difficult, and figures such as the number of suspensions or referrals for special educational treatment can be very misleading as some schools contain or conceal their problems. Inspection — thorough inspection — and careful review of data, are what is needed if we are to get at the truth about our difficult schools. Careful researches such as that of Rutter *et al* (1979) shed light on the dimensions and nature of the problem.

Analytical research into the factors which predispose to disruptive behaviour and trigger it off is clearly of the utmost importance. Side by side with this we need to develop simple techniques which will help schools to analyse their own particular situation and to modify it if they wish, using the tools and resources which are at their disposal. Over and above the help which these techniques can give, the very fact of the analysis, the very taking-up of a research stance, can be of benefit to a school and to its teachers. All too often disruptive behaviour is dealt with in an atmosphere of aggression, and acrimony, rather than one of rationality. Of course, anger can be useful, but all too often in incidents of disruption it becomes destructive, rather than constructive. To use an analytical approach, and to use planned techniques in coping with disruptive behaviour may also reduce the feeling of impotence which teachers sometimes have, the feeling that they have 'tried everything', have come to the end of the road, and that the end is failure or degradation, or the total rejection of the child in a form of exclusion.

There will almost inevitably be failure at times particularly in this area, where criminologists also fail. But the failure can be less frequent if we utilise our resources, and realise indeed, how extensive they are. It is this belief which underpins this book.

The difficulties involved in attempting to study disruption in schools are similar to those involved in studying deviancy in society at large. Deviancy is complex in origins, and usually defies solution. There are many perspectives from which it can be viewed.

The concepts used in the area of disruption in schools are themselves interesting. Sometimes the talk is about 'disruptive children', around whom there is already a body of literature. The distinction is made now between the 'disruptive child' and the 'maladjusted child', the latter often seen as being unwell rather than culpable, and suffering from a psychiatrically diagnosable disorder (Jones and Davies, 1977). However, it is accepted that the line is blurred between the two 'types' of child, so that, for example, a disruptive child may be temporarily prone to maladjusted behaviours, and many so-called 'disruptive' children would be categorised as maladjusted if they underwent the necessary procedures.

As a term, 'the disruptive child' has the advantage of being more specific than descriptions such as 'naughty', 'troublesome', less clinical than 'maladjusted' and less criminological than 'delinquent'. There is at least some suspicion that the term has originated in the recent concern about the increase in violence in schools coupled with the frequently expressed desire to reassert the authority of the teacher.

In recent years a distinction has been drawn between 'problem children' and 'children with problems', both of whom are likely to be 'disruptive children'. This seems more promising in that it does not attempt to prejudge the nature of the problems which children experience and does not rule out the possibility that these problems may have more to do with the nature of the experience against which the child reacts than with any inherent defect in the child itself. School for many children is a problem (Musgrave, 1964). So is learning. So is relating to some teachers, meeting their requirements, getting to grips with their 'understanding' of the pupil/teacher relationship. There is some evidence to suggest that some children find 'relating to teachers' more problematic than others and need more help in adjusting to the demands made upon them. There is also evidence to suggest that this facet of schooling is not all one-sided: teachers also have their problems; they find it easier to relate to some children than others. If one accepts that, in order to explain the difficulties people experience in interacting with others around them, one needs to take into account both sides of the interaction, then a social-psychological perspective may be useful.

As well as 'the disruptive child', who presents a severe and persistent non-conformity, there is a general category labelled 'disruptive behaviour'. This may refer to the occasional or persistent behaviour of individuals, groups, or whole classes, and very rarely, to the behaviour typical of large numbers of children in a 'difficult' school. The behaviour of the 'disruptive child' may be disruptive at certain moments, but children who are not 'disruptive children' may also exhibit 'disruptive behaviour' more or less frequently. These distinctions are obvious but important.

Recent research has served to remind us of the importance of school differences. Any school environment is a highly complex phenomenon (Reynolds, 1975; Rutter, 1979). Innumerable factors may affect pupil behaviour, including time of the day, weather conditions, children who are absent so that the nature of work groups is changed, the moods of individual teachers and pupils, the system of rules employed in the school, buildings, timetable, grouping procedures, quality of teaching skill, continuity of curriculum and so on. The list of pertinent factors is enormous. A great deal of research still needs to be done in this area. Within Local Educational Authorities and schools there is now a greater willingness to admit to having problems but this is still a sensitive area because questions of teacher competence are involved.

If disruptive behaviour prevents teachers or schools from functioning normally we have to look constantly at what is considered normal.

For example, it may well be considered desirable that children should move about the school in an orderly way: it becomes potentially disruptive when some children push and shove. This is as true of schools as of institutions or factories or underground railway systems where idiosyncracies of behaviour are seen as potentially dangerous and disruptive of smooth order and therefore a fit subject for external control. As J S Mill remarked in a different context, freedom to 'do one's own thing' stops short of shouting 'Fire'!' in a crowded theatre. This is not to argue that children should not be expected to move quietly and in an orderly way. If movement in relation to others — whether in a small or large group — is expressive of attitudes, then we need to create conditions in which desirable attitudes can be learned.

Prosaic organisational matters then assume considerable importance and simple behavioural injunctions become more than matters of preferred etiquette. Holding open a door for others is not just a middle-class example of manners — it is both an organisational and attitudinal imperative.

Unlike delinquency there is no easy way to study and measure disruption. Disruption implies a context and an activity — one always disrupts something and the use of the term implies a frustration of the intentions of one partner in the interaction. Thus unlike delinquency which is measurable in terms of infractions of the legal requirements, there is no 'it' which one can easily identify and label in disruption. Its value as a term lies precisely in that it gives access to understanding the underlying and implicit norms and values which are inherent in situations. To ask about disruption is to explore different notions of order and regularity. To use Mary Douglas' analogy, to identify dirt is also to explore the concept of orderliness; dirt is matter which is out of place (Douglas, 1966). This is a valuable notion because it reminds us that there are not necessary or intrinsic qualities which one could itemise and measure across a variety of contexts; the appropriateness of using the term is largely dependent on the context of its use. To talk about disruption in schools is then to highlight behaviours which are perceived as appropriate in this context. Given this qualification, it would still seem possible to identify types of behaviour to which the terms apply. The problem, however, is compounded because of the lack of consensus which allows scope for individual interpretive activity and because it is arguable that schools themselves are divided on what might be considered appropriate.

So to describe something as threatening is at the same time to make a statement of preference for a form of order which is threatened. In schools such labelling and identification is clearly associated with the teacher's power to assert the legitimacy of his preferred sense of order.

In an educational system which is increasingly defined in terms of cultural diversity, of cultural heterogeneity rather than cultural homogeneity, there is clearly a wide area of discretion in invoking rules. Culturally different behaviours, whether ethnic or class or religious in origin may be perceived and reacted to differently (Rampton, 1981). The question of when and why teachers invoke rules of disorder to apply to such behaviours which at other times and other places may be found acceptable and even laudable, is a major concern of our research.

Disruption in school is behaviour out of place; the conditions for identifying it are a set of ordered relations and a contravention of that order. Disruption is a by-product of systematic ordering and classification, involving rejecting inappropriate elements. Thus like the notion of 'dirt', disruption is a compendium term which includes all the rejected elements of ordered systems. Behaviour is not disruptive *per se*; there are times when we positively encourage children to be talkative or boisterous, or extrovert. Behaviour only becomes disruptive at certain times and in certain places; it is disruptive to wander about in a French lesson but not in Drama, in the corridors at certain hours but not in the Craft room; it is disruptive to keep silent in English discussion but not in Mathematics. What is seen as disruption by A may be welcomed as creativity by B and for both the same behaviour may change its significance depending on time of the day or week. In each case what is identified as disruption is a response to a situation. Nor does the existence of explicit statements of school rules give any clear indication of whether, when or by whom they will be applied. For behaviour to be defined as disruptive it first has to be identified and then acted upon. There seems to be no easy way of categorising the precipitating circumstances although in many, the element of teacher stress seems important. Descriptive studies reveal an unending series of circumstances in which the teacher's patience will be exhausted and it is difficult to move from the specific to the general. Time of day, time of the year (especially when examinations make heavy demands on teachers' time) poor health, overwork, domestic upset, previous experience, age, sex, class — all may contribute to explanations of why particular forms of behaviour in individuals are sometimes allowed, sometimes stigmatized. These factors may combine and contribute to the teacher's stress. This in turn may communicate itself to pupils and bring about further disruptive behaviour — a clear example of the Self Fulfilling Prophecy (Rosenthal and Jacobson, 1975).

For a child to become disruptive, then, it is necessary to look both at the behaviour engaged in (sometimes tolerated, sometimes punished) and at the perceptions and response of the teacher who reacts to it. Like deviance, disruption is also what people define as such. Its identification and punishment serve to highlight the moral purpose of the school and to reassert the legitimacy of its sense of order. If, as Durkheim has suggested, the scaffold serves a dramaturgical function in asserting and marking out the parameters of order by punishing those who transgress its boundaries, then the school disruptive may serve the same function in signifiying the boundaries of acceptable behaviour in the school.

A recognition of the importance of the element of labelling in school disruption, on the part of the person who reacts, serves as a reminder that disruption is normal wherever there is an underlying sense of order (Schur, 1971). Concern for the level of disruption then is an indication of the precariousness of the underlying order. The danger is that threats to order will be seen only as external and located in the pathological responses of children rather than as integral to the purposes and organisation of the institution. Children who disrupt may be immediately metamorphosed into 'disruptives' or 'maladjusted' or 'problem' children where these in fact only constitute a very small percentage of the perceived problem. Children so identified and labelled may then experience the subtle shifts in attitude and expectation of their teachers and a closing of options. In relation to identifying mental illness, Erickson (1965) describes this process as a 'betrayal funnel'. Persistent disruption and failure to respond to schools' established norms of acceptable behaviour or work may then lead to the retrospective reconstruction of individual biographies to confirm the emergent identity of the disruptive; past histories are scanned for confirmation of the present emergent identity so that it becomes apparent that the child was a disruptive all along. The danger here is of what Matza (1969) describes as a 'drift' from a primary form of deviance which in itself may have little importance or persistence, through a process of public and institutional response and labelling — what he terms 'signification' — into a stage of secondary deviance where the child subtly takes on the identity of deviant and becomes more like what he is cast as. Unless the chain is broken early so that the child is enabled to establish satisfactory links with the institutional aims of the school, the danger is that the child will then become more like his label. Then the increased salience of the peer group to compensate for the withdrawal of school approval as a source of strength and identity, may actually serve to minimise the disruptive child's opportunity to respond positively (Hargreaves, 1968).

Given a bad name a child may discover pleasure in his new identity. The vicious circle is complete and the school has inadvertently compounded the process of becoming disruptive which all its measures were initially designed to prevent.

Schools and teachers differ in how they define disruption, where they perceive it and how they respond. Lateness, for example, has as its measure an optimal level of punctuality; deference is a socially learned attribute which at one extreme, may be perceived as a form of sycophancy or 'creeping' and on the other as insolence. Whether or not pupils and teachers coincide (see reported incidents page 107f) on what is expected will often be fortuitous and uncertain and will depend on the whole range of personality factors, contingent situational variables, and, more importantly on the willingness of both sides to sustain the social definition of the situation and activity engaged in.

Some observations from the 'Goldsmiths Project' reported in Section Two will perhaps makes this point more clearly. In this school, systems of control appeared to come into operation when boys were excluded from a lesson and sent to the hall where their names were entered in a book by the deputy head. The presumption was that teachers would not exclude pupils for trivial or non-serious reasons. At this point their exclusion was treated as a serious matter and could lead to automatic punishment — in the first instance detention and being brought to the attention of the head of year.

What was also apparent, however, was that this system could have unintended consequences. Designed to control and minimise disruption, it could also serve to amplify and transfer it from a level of personal conflict in the classroom between teacher and pupil to the level of institutional conflict, in which the outstanding issue became the acceptance of the authority of the school. Thus there seemed to be a a 'fast' route which, starting at the level of exclusion from class, led by rapid stages, through failure to turn up twice for detention, to an escalation of seriousness and consequences — decision to cane, a boy's refusal to accept the cane, then suspension. To the extent that staff recognised this pattern, it was possible that such a system heightened rather than diminished the stressfulness of the classroom. Staff, who on conscientious grounds, refused to use the exclusion strategy may well have been in the position of having no alternative but to cope as best they could, on their own in the classroom. Similarly if staff excluded only for very serious disruptive behaviour, it may be that there was no way in which they could receive even temporary respite from problems which although not 'very serious' in themselves, were nevertheless serious to the teacher in that they disrupted the flow of the lesson, interfered with the pattern of work and involved considerable stress. In this category came disruption from constant talking, lateness, interruptions, failure to settle etc. In addition the system appeared to close the door on the exclusion of particular children for short periods of 'cooling off' without this leading to punishment and the risk of an escalation of consequences. If, as appears to be the case, there is in any school a sizeable minority of children who have behaviour problems, it could be argued that any school system which operates to a considerable extent within a context of punishment, is not best equipped to deal with the issue.

In this research, the number of incidents and the number of boys involved suggested a disruption that was fairly widespread, though in a pyramid reflecting the broad banding system of the school.

The 'A' band was rarely disrupted. There was some reason to question whether the system of control and staff support adopted here was functional. What was initially intended as a device for enabling teachers temporarily to exclude disruptive children risked, under the weight of institutional use, becoming rigid and fraught with dangers. Such a procedure could magnify rather than diminish the problem and feed back into the system an expectation of disruption through the impression created by large numbers of boys receiving the cane or being suspended.

The effect of disruption on teachers should not be minimised; at its lowest level, it is the peculiar occupational hazard of any teaching encounter where the participants may not share the same interests and, may operate with differing perception of their role. All teachers are aware of the difference between their intentions for learning, however well conceived, and the actual learning that takes place. Disruption of plans is a frustrating business and this is accompanied by an inevitable degree of strain and stress where the disruption takes unpredictable, less conventional and more overt forms. To understand and cope with the problems this creates for learning requires teachers who are mature, secure in their teaching skills, understanding of their subject and of its value, and capable of distancing themselves sufficiently to see beyond the immediate situation to underlying problems, which may well lie outside the classroom.

Disruption is now, as it has always been, a special problem for young and inexperienced teachers. It is also a problem for teachers of all ages coming into a new school until they 'learn the ropes' and establish themselves with the children as a person to be trusted.

It remains a problem to those who lack flexibility or who are either unwilling or unable to accept the conflicting nature of demands made upon them. It is because education is always such a risky business that it is full of conflict and stress.

Many teachers are understandably reluctant to acknowledge that the reasons for pupil misbehaviour may be found as often in their teaching as in the pupil's inability or failure to learn. Having problems of classroom control is not easy to admit to. Teachers are expected to cope. Senior staff may express irritation at the number of behavioural problems referred to them which they consider should have been dealt with in the classroom. An increase in the number of exclusions may produce pressure on staff to operate selective procedures; they may become more tolerant and settle for lower expectations by lowering their demands on children to avoid conflict. In this way it might be possible for the level of disruption in a school or classroom to increase without this being perceived as a problem within the school system. More insidiously, there is the temptation to blame pupils and to attribute disruptiveness to their personal characteristics — as a defence mechanism against the strains and stresses arising from seemingly intractable problems. Writing about the reactions of personnel in industry undergoing rapid change, Burns and Stalker (1966) noted 'the tendency of people, when faced by problems in human organisation of an intractable nature, to find relief in attributing difficulties to the wrong headedness, stupidity and delinquency of the other with whom they had to deal or more widely to the irreconcilable differences in attitude and codes of rational conduct'.

Galloway *et al* (1982) provide a useful account of exclusion and suspension in schools which lends strong corroborative support to the findings of other research on the important effects of school differences upon attainment and behaviour. He claims that a pupil's chances may be influenced at least as much and probably more by which school he happens to attend, as by any stress in his family or any constitutional factors in the pupil himself.

His detailed study of Sheffield pupils suspended from school includes a careful account of ten special groups set up to deal with them. He makes the important point that these groups seemed to concentrate on the pupil more than the context in which he had presented problems. Galloway emphasises the potential of such groups to offer a cooling off period during which staff and teachers can look at the stresses in school or home which have precipitated the child's problem, and at the means of overcoming them. He concludes that the problem of disruptive behaviour is most readily solved by prevention, that special groups cannot reasonably be seen as a solution to the problems which disruptive pupils cause in schools, that effective pastoral care must embrace

all aspects of a pupil's welfare in school if it is to make an impact on
the level of disruptive behaviour and that all pupils should feel that the
school values their achievement. Like ourselves, Galloway believes that
tackling the problem through the school's policy organisation and ethos
is by no means wishful thinking. A similar point is made by Ford *et
al.* (1982). She expresses concern at the growing popularity of disruptive units, at the disproportionate increase in the number of pupils identified as maladjusted or educationally subnormal and the concentration
of interest on certain types of violent and extravagant behaviour to the
relative neglect of behaviours which may be less threatening to teachers
but which indicate deep-seated needs. Regularities in the patterning of
problem behaviour in schools — it is experienced more with boys than
girls, more in county than voluntary schools, more with older than
younger pupils, more with lower-working class and ethnic than with
middle-class pupils — suggest that explanations and remedies are more
likely to be found in the system of schooling than in the psychologies
of individual children. She expresses dissatisfaction and impatience with
what she sees as a medical model attempting to explain away problems
in terms of individual pathology which are essentially either social,
economic or institutional problems. Reliance on such explanations serves
to direct us to remedial approaches when we should be more concerned
with preventative work.

A recent book on disruptive units (Tattum, 1982) incorporates a study
of pupils' expressed motives for the behaviour as a way of perceiving
and analysing secondary schools as a step towards understanding the
disruptive pupil. It critically examines the setting up of the special units
as an innovatory measure which creates problems of identification, selection and the reintegration of pupils back into schools. The pupils' study
comprises data from unstructured interviews with twenty-nine secondary school pupils in a detached disruptive unit which leads to the
categorisation of pupils' declared motives or explanation of their
behaviour into five types:

1. It was the teacher's fault
2. Being treated with disrespect
3. Inconsistency of rule application
4. We were only messing
5. It's the fault of the school system.

Acknowledgement of the increased reliance on systems theory to
explore the complicated ecologies of schools, is a feature of Gillham's

(1982) collection of essays which brings together some of the writings of the foremost researchers into school difference in this country. It is this rethinking of the problem within a 'systems' framework, rather than anything contained in the individual contributions, which makes this book something of a landmark. The title of the final chapter expresses well the dilemma, 'Institutional change or individual change?'. A 'systems' approach does not imply that all behaviour problems will disappear as a result of manipulating institutional processes but it does suggest a missing element from an adequate psychology of individuals — the investigation of other intersecting systems whether individual or institutional.

4 APPROACHES TO DISRUPTION

The media have come to dominate the out of school lives of children to an extent hardly conceived as possible before the advent of television and pop-culture. Though the relationship between, for example, televised violence and child behaviour is a complex one, the constant presentation of violent and lurid events and behaviour, while sensitizing some children, and deterring them from violence, will inevitably have a habituating effect upon some others, leading them to tolerate and regard as acceptable in themselves and others behaviours which are cruel and deplorable. It is also possible that children become neurologically so over-stimulated by the media, that, when in school, they have a strong tendency to be bored because their work itself, which is largely reading-based, and the presentation of lessons by teachers, fails to stimulate them as much as the media. It seems entirely feasible that this could account for the low levels of concentration, the distractibility and restlessness of some children.

Explanations of disruptive behaviour show close parallels with those offered for crime. It is said that the decline in the authority of the church, of parents and of teachers makes children less amenable to discipline, and this cannot be denied. However, this combines with the development of educational thinking concerning the importance of children talking, questioning and coming to decisions for themselves, so that the child is in a double-bind situation. In other words, if his teacher wishes him to conform at times, he also wishes him to argue at others; if he wishes him to be quiet at times, he also wishes him to be vocal at others. Talcott Parsons (1964) explains deviant behaviour as sometimes due to role conflict and one can see that the child may well be confused as to the precise role his teachers wish him to adopt.

A recent example of this in the staff-room of a comprehensive school is a member of staff who commented that she was finding the behaviour of first year classes increasingly difficult. As an illustration, she said she had such a class, in which she was distributing work-sheets, which were to be the basis of her lesson. As she came to the desk of one child and was about to issue the work-sheet, the girl turned round and said 'No thank you' to her. Presumably the child was so used to being offered activities in her primary school and elsewhere, that she interpreted what the teacher regarded as an imposition, and an obligation to conform, as an offer, a choice.

Other explanations for the rise in disruptive behaviour turn on the improvement in the past few decades in child health. Our children have food in their stomachs, and are no longer, in most cases, exhausted by long hours of employment outside school. Historically the view of the child as a minor adult, to be turned by a rigid and often painful regime conducive to conformity into an adult proper, has changed enormously under the impact of psychological and sociological thinking. The development of a child-centred view of education, side-by-side with that of dynamic psychology, has led teachers in general away from harsh punishments (though the cane is still retained in many schools in this country); it has also offered explanations of deviant behaviour in terms of frustration of children's needs, and in terms of learning difficulties. Admirable as we may find all these developments, it can be argued that together they have made the teacher less secure and confident in dealing with disruptive behaviour. Previously the act could be punished, in an automatic fashion. Now it is the child who is seen behind the act, a child who is an individual, different from the others, who is sensitive to pain, and whose reasons for behaving badly may be attributable to the teacher's failure to motivate, failure to satisfy needs, failure to teach effectively.

Similarly, the growth of sociology has eroded the view of the child as guilty for what he is; he is seen as the product of factors and forces in his environment, the institutions of culture, state, family and school, and this perspective meets up with the increasing concern in psychological studies with the role played by the environment, from birth or conception, in developing any inherited components in the child's make-up. Sociology and social psychology have had an important and increasing impact upon teachers' attitudes to deviant behaviour. The teacher is asked to inspect his own biases, biases of class, for example, which he is told pervade his speech, and make for difficulties of comprehension and communication between the (stereotypical) 'middle-class teacher', and 'working class child'. The teacher is told, further, that his aspirations in teaching are those of 'middle-class teacher culture', and so far removed from the world of his pupils that the latter withdraw from, or conflict with, the teaching situation which is all he knows to offer them. He wants abstruse, traditional school subjects, examinations and safe white-collar jobs; they want immediate gratification, money and fun, and status for vocational training which leads to the only jobs they can hope for.

Sociology asks the teacher to be critical of his right to support the system in which he works, in which bias, and prejudice, and the crippling and deterministic labelling effects of streaming and some other grouping procedures create, it is argued, a situation of injustice against which not only is it legitimate for pupils to rebel with disruptive behaviour, but it becomes imperative for the teacher to assist him. In this argument language becomes the equivalent of power. The teacher of the past did all the talking, told the children the God-ordained — in reality teacher-ordained — 'facts', told the children what to do, when to do it, how to do it, when to start, when to finish, what to think and how to think. The radical sociologist tells the teacher to give language, to give the power that is in the language, to the child. The child has knowledge, as valid and legitimate as that of the teacher, and he must do the talking now, in discussion with his peers; he must ask the questions and lead the discussion in the direction in which *he* wants it to go. The teacher has to cease to be controller; it is easy to see that the teacher's rights to insist on obedience, to instruct, to punish for non-conformity are called into question in the situation described above, and that the influence of these ideas could make teachers find the control of deviant behaviour more problematic. There may also be a gap between younger and older teachers on issues of whether and how children should conform to rules, and this can present a problem for a school seeking cohesion in its control practices.

For many people, teachers, educationalists, parents, the public, disruptive behaviour has emerged as a problem of some seriousness in certain schools. Not only does there appear to be more of it, in the sense that more schools are affected by it, and larger numbers of children in a school are involved, but the actual types of behaviour seem to have become more serious. As more schools have been affected, and because the types of disruptive behaviour have come to include as well as vandalism, assaults upon teachers, and serious violence against other children, teachers' unions, and some local education authorities, have been persuaded to look closely at the problem, its extent, its causes and possible solutions to it. The implications of these are examined in Part Four.

Different groups of people inevitably have different views of the issue. The parent of a child of school age may be anxious about the particular effect of the general situation upon his own child and may indeed be affected, in choosing a school, by its reputation for coping with disruption. Is the school a 'difficult' one, and will his son or daughter be troubled by gangs of boys who may bully him, or extort money from him, or set upon him on his way home from school? Will he be involved in fights which will tear his uniform, so expensive to replace? 'Why don't teachers stop *it*?' Alternatively, the parent may have a son who is actively involved in misbehaving. He may truant, without his parents' knowledge, or 'skip' lessons. He may be involved in theft, or he may be constantly so disruptive in lessons that after a series of short-term exclusions from the classroom, he is suspended from the school pending an inquiry and will be readmitted only under threat of exclusion, for any continuation of the disruptive behaviour. For the parent of this boy the questions may change, and be accompanied by tones of anger and despair. 'Why can't the teachers control him? It's their job. Why don't they cane him? — it would be better than sending him home. It's not him, it's his friends that drag him into trouble. Are they punished? And why can't the school split him from his friends?'

A teacher's view of disruptive behaviour will, of course, depend upon his personality, but also, most importantly, upon the role that he sees himself as having, as a teacher.

Teachers set themselves, and have set for them, certain instructional goals. In the primary school these will be mainly to teach basic skills such as reading and number, and in the secondary school the goals will become more specialised, involving the learning of subjects such as physics, or geography, or French. For teachers in both age-ranges of school there will also be goals relating to the socialisation of children, teaching them to live harmoniously with others, to 'behave decently'. Whether the teacher is concerned with his goal to instruct or to socialise the child, it is clear that serious or protracted misbehaviour often interferes with one or both of these goals. The child who constantly talks instead of working in a lesson, does not learn as much as he should, so the teacher is frustrated in his efforts to instruct him, and he may also be disturbing other children who wish to concentrate on their work, so that he is being anti-social, and the teacher feels he is failing in his attempt to socialize him.

It is because there is such a close relationship between teachers' goals, and their definition of certain acts as 'misbehaviour' that we need to look for an understanding of misbehaviour in schools at the sort of life which is lived by teachers and children in British schools today, at the sort of aspirations which teachers have and the children who populate the schools. We need also to compare this with the past. Perhaps the first fact that strikes one is the enormous number of children now being educated well into their teens. Secondary education has since 1945 been provided for all children and the school leaving age raised to 15 in 1947 and to 16 in 1972/3. Formerly, state secondary education was available only to a select few, the rest attended elementary schools. We now keep thousands of boys and girls until the age of 16 in our secondary schools who some years ago would have left school. Among these are many disadvantaged children, children of low academic attainment and some children from criminal families.

Before the reorganisation of secondary education in most Local Education Authorities, along comprehensive lines, more under-privileged and less able children were to be found in the secondary modern schools established after the Education Act 1944, than in grammar schools, entrance to which was obtained through the competitive examination at eleven years of age. Thus the selective schools were insulated from certain types of children, among whom the potential for uncouth behaviour might be considerable. Thus today far more secondary school teachers than in the past, are teaching children with abilities, backgrounds and propensities which may lead them into misbehaviour. In the past they would have been sheltered from such children. Not only this, but when aspirations have been sought by educators for these children, they have usually been the same or similar aspirations as those previously held for the select few, in other words teaching of formal subjects, the passing of public examinations and this has meant that high academic goals continue to be pursued, for children who may often either not accept these goals as desirable, or may find them extremely difficult to reach. It also means that teachers today frequently have goals which are more difficult to attain than their predecessors. In addition to this, the past twenty years have seen a burgeoning of developments in teaching methods and approaches which have made demand upon demand upon the teacher. It is small wonder that teacher stress is now a fashionable topic to study.

As far as the forms which misbehaviour takes are concerned, it is easier to talk about forms of disruption such as violence and vandalism, than about the common disruptive activities that we have all engaged in at some time, talking when we shouldn't, not attending because something has caught our eye or because we were day-dreaming or flicking a pellet at an unsuspecting friend.

Similarly, it is easier to talk about the more spectacular, overt ways which schools incorporate in their systems for dealing with the more serious forms of misbehaviour, such as sending a child out of a class, putting him in detention, and suspending or excluding him, than it is to talk about the enormously wide range of techniques and styles of teaching and controlling children, which teachers deploy in the classroom (see Part Three). It is easier to talk of the more serious forms of disruption and noticeable parts of pupil-control systems than of the rest, which is in practice the bulk of what passes for misbehaviour in schools, because the behaviours of children who misbehave and of teachers who are handling misbehaviour cover almost the whole gamut of human behaviour. If we think of all that can happen when two people meet in a situation where one of them wishes to inform, instruct or control the other, and the other reacts in a way that goes against the wishes and expectations of the former, then we are thinking of all the ingredients that go to make up situations of disruptive behaviour in schools. The factors at work are many and complex, factors of personality, of styles of communication, of the number of interpersonal skills the individual has developed, and the ease with which he can switch from one to another. There are factors of intention, of reactions to frustration, as well as all the more immediate factors: the precise details of the situation, the more immediate stresses on the people concerned, and the extent to which they are prepared at that time to obey and conform to the rules of the 'games' which operate in classrooms, and the stated and more explicit rules of the school in which they are living.

Coupled with the fact that so many kinds of factor are involved in misbehaviour, is the fact that an item of misbehaviour is itself often very complicated. If you talk to a teacher about why, for example, he put a boy out of his class, he will more often than not describe a whole series of types of misbehaviour which the boy engaged in, which culminated in an incident which triggered off the teacher's reaction, which prompted the teacher to exclude him. Why the particular actions of the boy at that particular moment caused the teacher finally to lose patience with him is interesting; what may account for this, in a number of cases (see Part Two) is that the boy may have in the past already misbehaved in the same or in a similar way, but now the teacher has come to believe that he is behaving in a more deliberate way, intending to taunt and upset him. Together with the teacher's belief that the boy is acting maliciously towards him, there may be at this point in time a particular stress, or stresses upon the teacher — he may feel less well, less content than usual; it may be an off day for him, or something has gone wrong, or he may be apprehensive that something might go wrong. He may very much want to get through the work in this particular lesson without interruption. Whatever the stress on him may be, it combines with his perception of the boy as deliberately making life too difficult for him at that moment, and so he reacts by sending the boy out of the room. Some teachers will have a higher level of tolerance than others because they are more easy going than others, or they know of other strategies to cope with the boy at an earlier stage in the events, which help to control the behaviour. Some teachers will regard sending him out of the room as a failure and will do all they can to avoid it. So that as we look at misbehaviour we realise its enormous complexity. This makes efforts to study and control it as difficult as are studies in delinquency and crime.

It is particularly difficult to enquire into misbehaviour in schools because teachers and officers of education authorities are reluctant to talk about it for fear that fingers will be pointed at them personally and at the schools in which they work or for which they carry responsibilities.

This reluctance is general and stems from fear — fear of being less highly thought of, fear in teachers who believe, often rightly, that they may be labelled as teachers who 'can't cope' and who will have their prospects of promotion harmed. Headteachers, until recently, have sometimes been ashamed that their schools should be known as 'difficult', and from a practical point of view have worried lest this reputation might chase away prospective teachers who are good at their job, and could help the school, and who would otherwise have applied for vacant posts. The situation is changing somewhat. There is an acceptance by those in senior positions in local authorities that disruptive behaviour in schools has increased. It is typified by the fact that the authors Jones-Davies and Cave of a recent (1976) book *The Disruptive Pupil in the Secondary School,* are LEA officers. Their book opens with the statement: 'That there has been a significant deterioration in the behaviour of children in secondary schools appears to be beyond dispute'. It is, however, significant that as schools in this country recognise the problem of disruptive behaviour, the emphasis is upon the child who misbehaves — the disruptive child. There is a reluctance to acknowledge that the child is disruptive within a social situation, and that the definition of his behaviour as disruptive depends upon the teacher and the school. An enormous amount of work has focused upon the maladjusted child, the disturbed child, the disruptive child, and hardly any upon the disruptive incident, in which children who are not necessarily often disruptive take part, and which is the point at which some children enter the systems for dealing with disruption which all schools have. This point is developed in the section which follows.

It is gradually being acknowledged that there may be factors inside schools, such as high pupil turnover, which are related to the number of disruptive children in a school, and that other aspects of the climate of schools, such as the ways in which children are grouped, may also play a part (Rutter, 1979).

5 RESEARCHING DISRUPTION

Research into disruptive behaviour has burgeoned over the past few years, and some of these researches resemble our own in that their approach attempts to be empirical; it commonly uses lists and simple statistics, and it focuses upon the detailed analysis of pupil and teacher behaviour. An illustration of this approach is the Teacher Education Project in the Universities of Nottingham and Leicester (1978), where the teacher or student uses a classroom management observation schedule covering a wide range of items, from types of deviant act, to types of teacher response and the reactions of deviant pupils. Other unpublished and more sophisticated research has been initiated (Parry-Jones and Gay, 1980) which uses 'sequence analysis' to identify common patterns which occur in sequence when an individual teacher tries to control disruption in the classroom. As in the Teacher Education Project, the data are computer analysed. Observation of behaviour is often, as in the two examples just quoted, an integral part of the study, and an important aim is the development of training methods for teachers, so that they can cope better with deviant pupil behaviour.

The work on sequence analysis puts teacher and pupil behaviour under a microscope which is very strong and as such stands as 'purer' research than the Teacher Education Project and indeed our own work. If, however, it is possible ultimately to discover types of behaviour which, given a certain situation, successfully control classroom situations, the returns from the work will be extremely important for teachers at all stages, and indeed others such as social workers who work in conflict situations. At the present time the group of techniques subsumed under the heading of 'behaviour modification' or 'behavioural techniques' are one set of such techniques which can be used in classroom situations, and which have a body of research and experimentation behind them. If sequence analysis work can bring to light other sets of techniques, this will be of immense value to work with disruptive behaviour.

The number of books publicising behaviour modification techniques, for the use of teachers, has also grown steadily over the last few years, though the techniques are continuing to be very slowly adopted in this country (Hastings and Schweiso, 1979) and there is still only very limited use of them in the ordinary secondary school (Lawrence, 1980) and special units.

Parallel to current interest in how teachers deal with disruptive behaviour when it actually occurs, runs an acknowledgement that the disruptive incident develops from a previous 'history' of teacher-pupil, pupil-pupil interaction. This leads to a concern with the prevention of incidents, and hence to a concern with the wide range of teachers' instructional and personal skills which can avert the development of difficult control situations (Kounin, 1970). The need emerges for teachers who are able to be sensitive to their own and their pupils' behaviour in the classroom, and analytic in their approach to it. Hence the importance of real classroom experiences, as an integral part of teacher training, and the need to analyse these sensitively and fully, as part of the college course of teacher education.

The relationship between reading and learning difficulties and disruptive behaviour has for many years been a subject of concern and important moves have been taken at various levels to publicise this relationship and to deal with it. Work instigated by the publication of the Bullock Report (1975) and in the area of multi-cultural education have supported this notion that the frustration and boredom of the child who cannot cope with the written material or the level of work in his classroom programme will frequently lead him towards difficult behaviour. The precise relationships between educational problems and school behaviour are not always obvious, but some research (Varlaam, 1974) has suggested that, for example, in the reading-behaviour disorder relationship the reading problem is often the primary factor. Consideration of the relationship between language skills and behaviour, for children of ethnic minorities will be found in Part Two.

The rise in reported crime gives a perspective on disruptiveness in schools. It is realistic to expect a substantial quantity of potential disorder in schools, where the society is coping with a large and increasing quantity of crime. As Michael Zander (1979) puts it:

It is well known that a rise in reported crime may reflect changes in ways of recording rather than an increase in the level of crime itself. But no amount of fancy footwork can explain away the fact that the annual number of indictable offences recorded by the police went from 1,283 to 5,014 for 100,000 of the population in the two decades from 1957 to 1977. Offences of violence against the person, for instance, rose by about 6 per cent a year from the mid-1930s to the mid-1950s. Since then they have gone up at an average of about 11 per cent a year.

Zander goes on to point out that although the majority of those who are prosecuted are convicted, crime continues to escalate, because for most criminal acts no one is ever prosecuted. Either the crime does not come to the attention of the police, or, if it does, they do not discover the culprit. One is led from this to conclude that for schools, coping with disruptive behaviour can be seen as an extremely important social and educational function. The way a school deals with its problems of disruptiveness, pre-delinquency and delinquent behaviour may be a message to its pupils concerning such behaviour outside the school, but in particular, Zander's statement suggests that schools with high levels of disruptive behaviour will need considerable help from their LEA in controlling a situation which can easily escalate. It is also possible to suggest, from Wilson's (1980) research into the crucial effect of parental supervision on whether a child is at risk of becoming delinquent in high crime areas, that within a school with a high level of disruption, the involvement of given children in disruptive activities, such as playground violence, may depend very much on the closeness of teacher supervision during lesson breaks and other non-lesson periods.

A keen interest is currently being shown in various kinds of Intermediate Treatment (IT) as an alternative to an institutionalising approach for delinquents and children. The schemes of treatment vary, depending on local situations and needs, but basically IT looks at the need of the child for good relationships with caring, firm adults, for security, and for building up of social skills. At the present time there have been no long-term studies to prove the effectiveness of IT but statements emerging in relation to it are sufficiently positive for teachers to take serious note of the development, and to draw from it suggestions for their own approach to children who they regard as misbehaving within the school.

What this development could mean in practice, is that instead of setting up a special unit to deal with difficult pupils either on-site or off-site, a school could work out a programme of Intermediate Treatment-type activities for its most difficult pupils, under the general supervision of a teacher prepared to work after school hours in conjunction with a local youth group, perhaps, but offering basically an out-of-school approach, to a problem arising specifically within school hours. What is being advocated here is an extension of the IT approach, for the advantage of pupils whose behaviour would not necessarily bring them within the ambit of official IT, or who are in areas where IT is not yet available.

It is gradually coming to be accepted that schools have themselves an influence upon the number of their children who become disruptive and those who become officially delinquent (Reynolds, 1976; Rutter, 1979). What now provokes interest is the relative importance of the school's influence against that of the home, for example, and the nature of that influence. In other words, what is it that makes the difference in the number of delinquents in schools which otherwise appear to be similar? Sociological and psychological studies have already pointed to some likely factors — labelling and teacher expectation, for example, but there is now a search for other factors which may be exerting an influence: such as teacher's ability to operate a 'truce' with their pupils, in relation to their conformity to rules (Reynolds, 1976) or more global factors such as 'ethos' (Rutter, 1979), within which other factors can be subsumed. All this leads to questions of how educational change can be brought about — a major interest at the present time.

Given that we may know something of how schools can improve, how can schools be helped to change? At what periods in the history of a school (for example, when certain changes in staff occur) is it most receptive to change and what are the conditions in which the changes are introduced, which may determine whether the change will be substantial and far-reaching, rather than slight and ephemeral, and long-lasting rather than merely transitory?

At this stage, there is little certainty concerning the school factors which seem to affect delinquency. Suggestions that school size is a factor are difficult to support (Galloway, 1982), when the size of the schools studied varies from study to study, so that a large school in one research, becomes a small school in relation to another project. Staff turnover has been suggested as a factor, but this has in any case declined over the past few years, and even if staff turnover is a factor, it may be either the result or the cause of difficult behaviour in a school. Size of class as a possible factor is also far from being a simple explanation, since class size is arrived at for many, different reasons, relating to staffing turnover, intake, needs of pupil groups of varying abilities etc. There is some work on ritualistic externals such as prefect systems and the wearing of school uniform, which may be more important than is apparent, in that they act as part of a form of social control. Reynolds (1976), is interesting in his focus upon the relatively high degree of autonomy given to pupils:

> It is worth saying quite simply that the evidence from these schools suggests that the more a school seeks high control over its more senior pupils by increasing organisational compulsion and decreasing pupil autonomy, the

more these pupils may regard their schools as maladjusted to their needs. Rebellion within and delinquency without will be the result of the failure of the pupils and their teachers to declare a truce.

There have been a number of studies of the attitudes of delinquents and non-delinquents towards school, and their teachers, and of pupils' perceptions in high and low delinquency schools (Finlayson and Loughran, 1975; O'Hagan, 1977). The findings of these studies are interesting, in that although the differences between the groups of children are often in the expected direction, the degree of difference is often less than might be expected. Thus in O'Hagan's study sixty per cent of the offenders (and ninety per cent of the non-offenders) thought that the school had done a great deal for them. Again, both groups agreed the school would help them prepare for future employment and twenty per cent of the offenders agreed strongly with this (as against sixty per cent of the non-offenders). Such studies are not easy to utilise in relation to school practice, but they can be interpreted as encouraging. As the unpublished NFER Constructive Education Project showed, many difficult and offending children have a positive view of their teachers and their schools, and are thus not closed to help from them.

In this country the establishment of the Dicey Trust (1975) was a move towards intervening in the school curriculum, through educating in the rule of law, in an attempt to reduce disruptiveness in school. It is interesting that moves towards such instruction, as part of a programme to reduce criminal behaviour or disruptive school behaviour are apparent in other countries too. Thus in the Soviet Union, a course in Soviet Law is now a compulsory subject in the general school timetable, for pupils of 14-plus. Such courses have for some time been available as options; they are now obligatory. In the United States, after a series of school riots and disturbances, the board of education in Syracuse, New York, sponsored a research into adolescent knowledge of, and attitudes towards, the law. The research, by Rafky and Sealey (1975) comes, however, to the conclusion that legal knowledge is independent of respect for the law and disruptive behaviour. This means that merely introducing courses on the law is unlikely to reduce disruptive behaviour; clearly, if teachers are aiming at such a reduction, they must face up to the fact that they are involving themselves in an attempt to inculcate and modify attitudes. This being so, they need to learn from attitude research that, for example, they will need to work at an emotional rather than a purely cognitive level, with their pupils, encouraging them for example, to empathise with those who suffer from misdemeanors. In this area, they will be entering the complex field of moral education.

The student of disruptive behaviour can also draw upon studies of delinquency, from the vast quantity of research into maladjustment (Rutter, 1975). There is also the growing interest of some clinicians in anti-social behaviour, for teachers this type of behaviour constitutes their main problem. Thus the work of people such as Robins (1966), is proving of great assistance to teachers. Robins' longitudinal study has shown that serious anti-social behaviour is a particularly ominous childhood pattern, and that the anti-social child deserves the most serious efforts at treatment if he is not to be a psychiatrically ill adult. Particularly interesting to teachers must be Robins' finding that people who as children had anti-social behaviour and anti-social fathers have a high probability of either descending the socio-economic ladder or failing to rise above the low level at which their family lived when they were children. People of similar intellectual capacity who as children came from equally impoverished families living in equally depressed areas, but who were not anti-social and did not have anti-social fathers, are very likely to rise out of the lowest social stratum and to be indistinguishable in adult achievement from people of more advantaged backgrounds. If teachers are concerned with the social mobility of their pupils, then this statement of its relationship to pupil behaviour, at least to seriously anti-social behaviour, is extremely important to them.

It is not only research into maladjustment in general which is of relevance to schools' work with disruptive behaviour, but also, work with the most seriously disturbed child. At some time or other almost all very seriously disturbed children will spend some time in an ordinary school which has therefore to be cognizant of matters referring to these children. But in addition, developments and approaches to such children, initiated often by those working with them in residential settings, can have an important bearing upon work in ordinary schools. Thus the inspirational value of Donahue and Nichtern's (1965) work on the Elmont Project in the USA is great, but in addition it lays out quite clearly the way in which the integration of handicapped pupils requires considerable resources of staff time and skill, if the integration is to be successful. The severely maladjusted children in this project were taught in a special unit within the ordinary school system, and a number of them were successfully returned to ordinary schooling. There are pointers, for example, in this work, to the need for strong support for child and teacher where a child leaves a special unit for the ordinary classroom, if the return is to be successful. This support is sometimes lacking, when children attempt to return from special units for disruptive children to the ordinary class, in this country, and leads to further rejection of the child, and other negative consequences such as a reduction in the value of the special unit for the child.

Other work with severely disturbed pupils valuable for the assessment of those pupils in ordinary schools who may be selected for entry to special units of various kinds, is that of Hoghughi (1978, 1980).

The Schools Council project (Wilson and Evans, 1980) into the education of disturbed pupils and Dawson's (1980) study of provision for disturbed pupils are further valuable sources of information for teachers, as is the work of Kolvin (1976) while Bender's book (1976) on community psychology points to fascinating possible developments in the role of the teacher in relation to disturbed children. The thread running through this literature is the need for the teacher to accept a role with those who try to understand difficult behaviour and to control or modify it. Given the number of children involved, the dimensions of the task, and the shortage of resources, the teacher becomes very much a para-psychologist and para-therapist.

An area of concern in which teacher alertness and training are clearly involved is that of the identification of children who need special help. This can be viewed as an extension of the teacher's general and vital task in recognising children's difficulties. The issues, however, are more complex than at first sight they appear to be, ranging from questions of the validity of the concepts involved, such as 'at risk', to teachers' anxieties over the hasty labelling of children (CIAED 1977). In general teachers have been ill-prepared for their identification of needs role; this is an area in which far more work needs to be done.

Another field of importance to those working with disruptive behaviour is that of the teacher's emotional response to this work. For this reason, current studies of stress arising in the context of coping with disruption are interesting. Both Dunham (1977) and Kyriacou (1978) are working in this area, and are offering useful insights. The latter's work is starting to pinpoint the characteristics of those teachers who report the most stress.

Over the past few years it has been recognized that truancy from school has been under-researched, in spite of its well-known associations with delinquency. This recognition has led to a number of researches by LEAs and others. These have brought improvements in the collection of statistics and closer definition of the concepts involved, with more careful distinction between unjustified absence with and without knowledge of or collaboration by parents for example. They have also led to improved insights into the situation in which, as Galloway (1978) has found, a child who does not want to go to school may be persuaded to go by a parent in good health, and not dissuaded from truanting by a parent in ill-health. It may of course not be easy, with better knowledge of the origins of truancy, to act upon the situation and improve it, where the factors involved are family and community problems but Galloway's work is potentially an improvement upon the very general statements which otherwise tend to be made, more from 'hunch' than hard evidence, about truancy and reducing it (HMI, 1978). One ought also to be alert to the fact that recent high levels of adult and youth unemployment will have an impact on matters of truancy (Cope and Gray, 1978). The notion that schools themselves have an impact on their truancy problems is also gaining ground (Carroll, 1977), together with an interest in the appointment of school social workers, to reduce the problem (Rose and Marshall, 1974).

Although vandalism figures, like truancy, are an easily classified form of deviant pupil behaviour, there seems to be less interest, than with truancy, in research into pupil attitudes to the vandalism, and at possibly relating vandalism to school factors which may encourage it. This is not to say that schools are not often advised as to what to do about vandalism (Stone and Taylor, 1977; CPRS 1978), but there is a lack of specific research into pupil involvement and vandal-proof materials, perhaps because much vandalism caused by school pupils takes place outside the school itself and this vandalism is rarely brought to the attention of school staffs.

The last few years have seen a dramatic increase in the number and type of units established to deal with pupils with behavioural difficulties of various kinds, and the growth of a large literature on the units themselves (HMI, 1978; Young, 1980). It is sometimes, however, not appreciated by teachers and others that questions relating to units need to be seen in the context of broader issues concerning the integration or separation of children with special needs (Galloway and Goodwin, 1980). Furthermore, there is a lack of research into transfer of school, and its effect on disruptive behaviour, in spite of the fact that it is sometimes a key issue where a child is being considered for admission to a special unit.

By virtue of its scale and its breadth of implications, *15,000 Hours* (Rutter, 1979), is a key book for anyone interested in disruptive behaviour in schools. Much debated, it remains so far the most extensive and carefully carried out study of the relationships between deviant behaviour (difficult school behaviour and delinquency) and school factors. The authors have pointed out to their critics that they do not claim to have proved that certain school factors lead to high levels of disruptive behaviour, and that these levels could themselves lead, at least in part, to the development of the school processes they describe. The findings are both suggestive and important. In twelve secondary schools twenty-five items of pupil behaviour were studied, including late arrival at lessons, off-task behaviour, damage to school property, overtly disruptive behaviour, self-reported truancy, absconding and skipping lessons etc. When the proportion of difficult pupils (as defined by a behaviour scale) at intake was used to control for intake, it became clear that the schools with the worst intake did not necessarily have the worst classroom behaviour outcome.

The research may not have explored sufficiently the role of sex of teacher and child in the primary and secondary schools, in its findings, nor the question of parental support, but it remains an excellent description of some schools which are 'easy' and some which are rather 'difficult'. It points to the complexity of misbehaviour, which is seen as both a stimulus and a response to teacher behaviour. It supports the notion that behaviour in schools is linked to both examination success and delinquency, and that mixing with delinquents leads to delinquency.

The *15,000 Hours* study is part of an on-going debate, concerning the school's role in disruptive behaviour. Other pieces of evidence are accumulating. Thus Heal's (1978) work lends a note of caution to over-estimating the school's role, in primary schools, while Galloway (1980/82), shows that there are substantial and consistent differences between schools unrelated to catchment area in their use of exclusion and suspension, very often the last stages in the development of a child's career as a disruptive pupil.

Research Note

Perceptive and critical readers concerned to identify the conceptual framework within which we have operated and to identify our indebtedness to different traditions of thought, in order to evaluate the 'status' of our findings, should have little difficulty in locating our work broadly within the area of what has been described pejoratively as 'soft' scientific research. We have used extensively methods of participant observation — not of teachers at work in the classroom but of teachers and children talking about their experience of disruption which they regard as significant and important in their work. It is argued that access to the immediacy of feeling and emotion involved in disruption, is only possible using such subjective methods and that the method is both methodologically defensible and indeed, the only procedure which is appropriate.

In collecting, structuring and interpreting materials, we have liberally borrowed from approaches which seemed most appropriate and rewarding. In part these reflect the diversity of backgrounds and interests of the researchers. Our research (Part Two) is methodologically impure and unashamedly eclectic; for this we make no apology. Where appropriate, we followed research injunctions to triangulate and we have consistently attempted to improve on commonsense understandings by taking our findings to the subjects of our research and attempting co-operatively to formulate them in ways which were acceptable to them. At no time did we aim to do a tight piece of statistical research although we have utilised data gathered from incident sheets and submitted them to normal procedures and where appropriate, to tests of statistical significance. We believe there is value in this in posing questions about the patterning and persistence of disruption in the two schools we have studied and would see value in schools attempting to collect such data as a regular form of self monitoring. Similarly we have felt no qualms or inconsistency in incorporating a series of questions suggested by the staff of one of the two schools relating directly to specific incidents of disruptive behaviour, in a research procedure which is basically premised on the notion of teachers responding subjectively to a previously agreed broad definition of disruption.

In interpreting our findings we have similarly drawn widely from diverse traditions — Symbolic Interactionism, Action Theory, Phenomenology, Role Theory and Systems Analysis. Implicitly in looking at specific behaviours we have attempted to widen the focus of attention from the specific to the general, from the child to the teacher, to the school, to the neighbourhood, to the wider society, as these affect the procedures, styles of teaching, attitudes and expectations of teachers.

Where schools draw pupils from widely different and distinct cultural economic, social and cultural backgrounds, it becomes all the more important that these are understood, acknowledged and reflected in the curriculum and social organisation. Whilst there is a continuing need for the development of better home-school links and communication through accepted and more formal arrangements there is also a greater need for pupils and parents to feel more at home in school. Such a shift, whether prompted by the concern to avoid alienation, to increase motivation, or to avoid disruption, involves change in schools.

In the two school studies which we report in Part Two, we have attempted empirically to gain some measure of the number of incidents of disruption as defined by the teachers. Our starting point has throughout been with the subjective understanding of what constitutes disruption. In arguing that this is the only valid starting point, we have not, however, felt it necessary to deprive ourselves of the use of other measures using agreed categories in the form of questionnaire response as a supposedly more objective measure. The difficulty is rather that such instruments serve to distract attention and oversimplify a phenomenon which, as we attempt to show, is far from simple or monocausal.

For us, the critical argument against any attempt to measure disruption solely by using questionnaires is that it provides a measure only at the point where the decision is taken to define as disruptive an infringement of a rule. To do so tends, mistakenly:

(i)   To concentrate attention on certain forms of behaviour which are readily identifiable under agreed rubrics and which are widely accepted commonsensically as 'disruptive'.

(ii)   To lend these categories an importance out of proportion to their number and seriousness.

(iii)   To conceal and trivialise the submerged disruption and the sequence of events which preceded the final event which triggered the response 'disruptive'.

(iv)   To lend fuel unwittingly to a public debate already alert to the notion of 'trouble'.

(v)   To add to levels of teacher stress by not acknowledging aspects of organisation outside the classroom which affect pressure to conformity and control.

The two school studies reveal disruption as a widespread phenomenon and suggest that more and more resources are being channelled into coping strategies. Senior staff, heads, deputies, year heads, pastoral and remedial and counselling staff all devote more and more time to the disruptive child.

Methodologically, the incident of disruptive behaviour is a 'natural' focus for research, for several reasons:

1. Teachers remember incidents, even after long intervals, and so do children.

2. Teachers, senior staff, and head teachers all deal with incidents. They are crisis points in 'disruptive behaviour', leading often to reporting onwards, and to entry for the child and the teacher into the official system of dealing with disruptive behaviour. They are often quoted in relation to official sanctions such as suspension and exclusion.

3. They are noted events in the life of a school. Thus if graffiti and the wearing of uniform are included in a misbehaviour scale (Rutter, 1979), it is clear that they are not necessarily 'registered' events at all, in that both *may* go unnoticed.

4. Incidents are useful in that where they are frequent, patterns may emerge which place the incident in the context of the whole life of the school: its timetable, administration, curriculum, staffing strength, pupil intake, etc. They offer therefore an opportunity for taking a global perspective on the school, and on disruptive behaviour itself.

5. Above all, an incident occurs only when the behaviour or occurrence involved is seen as significant by a spectator or participant, so that it has an intrinsic meaning. The seriousness of the reported incident is not imputed, as in so-called 'objective' research, but is experienced.

Part Two
WHOLE SCHOOLS AND DISRUPTION

6 TWO WHOLE SCHOOL STUDIES

This section brings together two 'whole school' studies of disruptive behaviour, previously reported on separately (Lawrence *et al.,* 1977; 1978a, b; 1981). In both studies the schools were multi-racial, urban and comprehensive, but the first was a boys' senior high school, and the second an all-through 11-18 co-educational school. The first, smaller-scale study, known in the school as the 'Goldsmiths' Project' will be referred to as the 'Project' in the following pages, and the second, more developed study, known as the 'Behaviour Problem Dialogue' will be called the 'Dialogue'.

Both studies were initiated as part of a programme of research into disruptive behaviour in secondary schools, which aimed also to help the schools concerned to analyse their problems and to formulate ways of alleviating or solving them. The analysis took the form of monitoring incidents of disruptive behaviour over short periods (two separate weeks in the Project and one week in the Dialogue), using a definition of disruptive behaviour which was proposed by the researchers and accepted by the staff. This definition was 'Behaviour which interferes seriously with the teaching process and/or seriously upsets the normal running of the school. It is more than ordinary misbehaviour in the classroom, playground, corridors, etc. It includes physical attacks and malicious destruction of property'. This definition was derived and adapted from NAS survey researches (Lowenstein, 1975).

As well as the monitoring of incidents, many of the staff were interviewed and other necessary information obtained. When data had been gathered, reports were issued to the staff, and subsequently discussed with them both informally and at meetings. Both the school studies were unique, although some procedures and findings were similar in both, thus a brief account of each study follows. The section then proceeds to an examination of the findings relating to the incidents of disruption, the children, the teachers and finally to multi-ethnic considerations.

(a) The 'Goldsmiths' Project' Study

The Research was conducted in an urban, multi-racial boys' comprehensive, senior high school, located in an outer city borough, on the same site as a girls' school, with whom a sixth form and library block was shared. There were 800 pupils on the roll, with approximately 300 pupils in the 14 to 16 year old age range found in each of the fourth and fifth years (the subjects of the research), and 200 pupils in the sixth (16+) year. There were fifty-six staff including the head teacher. The school had been reorganised five years previously along comprehensive lines, from a former grammar school. Pupils were grouped into three broad bands when they entered the school, on the basis of some testing and of reports from their three junior high schools. The pastoral care and discipline of the boys was organised on a year basis.

Discussions with senior staff, followed by informal meetings with staff, in particular those with reservations about the research, were held during the Summer term. Following a suggestion from the school, it was agreed that the research should be carried out during a week in November, immediately after half-term, and a week in February immediately before half term. It was thought that the two weeks might present different pictures, owing to the possible effect of a preceding and an impending half-term holiday.

Staff described each incident of disruption on a standard form, gave details of the class, room, size of class, time of day, nature, length and seriousness of the incident, the number and names of the boys involved, and a description of the incident and they stated whether they would be willing to discuss the incident or wished to do so. The report form (including nil returns) was completed for each lesson, and after the last lesson of the day.

In general, staff who reported incidents were younger, less experienced in terms of length of teaching and range of experience in other schools (i.e. without previous experience in comprehensive or secondary modern schools) and were more likely to be in their first or second year's teaching at this school, than those who did not. Of incidents reported onwards to senior staff (69) 43% were referred to deputy heads, with 13% to heads of departments who apparently played an insignificant role in the official disciplinary system.

Comparison of the number of incidents during November and February showed a substantial increase (av. 178%) for all fourth year classes during February, which could, perhaps, be explained by the 'warming up' of boys new to the school in September or possibly a greater inclination on the part of the staff to report incidents to researchers with whom they had become more familiar, four months after the initiation of the project.

The findings suggest that the extent to which teachers report and experience disruptive behaviour expresses their frustration at the difficulty of engaging children in worthwhile learning experiences. This aspect of disruption may have been understressed. For the teachers, the perception of disruption was closely associated with the work ethos of the school; disruption amounted to anything which prevented the teacher from achieving worthwhile results with the pupils. Teachers therefore stressed disruptive behaviour as 'a general refusal to be taught', 'general disruption', 'doing no work', 'tardiness in settling', 'refusal to obey' and 'insolence'.

The system of control operated in the school made extensive use of some senior staff in dealing with the disruption reported and the bulk was dealt with by the deputy heads and heads of year. There appeared to be little scope for manoeuvre between containing disruption within the classroom and referring it for punitive measures to the official system. A danger in using the official system, except for very serious disruption, is clearly that entry into the official disciplinary system could lead by stages through detention to caning, to the refusal to be caned, thence to suspension. Owing to the potentiality for such a progression and subsequent categorisation, it may be that a stress is imposed upon teachers such that they feel an increased pressure to contain defiance within the classroom and not refer it onwards. The possibility of temporary exclusion from the class teaching situation and a 'cooling-off' period does not seem here to have been adequately allowed for. It would, however, have been possible to develop interlinking systems of control where the emphasis shifted from punishment within an official school sanction system for serious disruptions where there are no mitigating factors, to exclusion, with no punitive element beyond the act of exclusion, also embodying the possibility of counselling and the development of pastoral care. Such a system might have operated at the level of heads of department with the advantage that the curricular implications of involving disinterested pupils could immediately be pursued. This revised system was recommended to the school.

Staff accepted the paper presented to them by the researchers, and its statistics. There was little comment on the latter; if anything, the figures were regarded as low. It was accepted that factors pointed to as significant in disruptive incidents, e.g. time of day, and the imputation by the teacher of malicious intent in the boy, were indeed significant. Boys could be malicious towards the teacher, as a teacher, and as a person. Details of timetable, it was thought, could be an important area to explore, e.g. the movement heard in the middle of a double period, of other classes changing lesson, could break into pupils' concentration. Physical danger was seen as a factor, in science and craft lessons. There was some discussion of the problem of white staff correctly identifying as deviant or non-deviant the behaviour of children from other cultures. It was also pointed out that communication about disruptive behaviour was important and a problem which was often very time-consuming to deal with.

There was considerable discussion about the relationship between banding and disruptive behaviour. Could the third-band (i.e. lowest ability-range) curriculum be changed? One difficulty in the way of this is the frequent unrealistic wish of non-indigenous parents for their children to pass examinations of a high standard. Could a social worker liaison-officer help to explain the need for a realistic curriculum to parents?

The project also yielded useful insights into the relationship between resource allocation and misbehaviour. The literature relating to misbehaviour and resources has tended to reflect an interest in vandalism (Paul, 1973) — the treatment meted out to school premises and to their contents primarily by their occupants — and how this might be overcome by varying the use of materials in construction to diminish the vulnerability of schools.

The aspect of our research into misbehaviour concerned with resources, did not reflect this approach; rather interest was focused upon the ways in which existing resources were allocated and whether they were contributing factors in the quantity and quality of misbehaviour incidents recorded. Resources were interpreted to mean the building, its layout and usage, its equipment, the allocation of time and human resources — both teachers and pupils. An appraisal of financial allocation was excluded as not being feasible in such a short period of time, though this no doubt would be of interest.

The school building was perhaps the obvious starting point, the visible expression of a school's way of life. The school in question was built as a grammar school in 1906, reflecting in its design a public school element (influential not only in building but in school organisation and administration in the schools of England and Wales), with the wood-panelled hall located at the centre of the building, close to the visitors' entrance. Also reflected in the building is the assumption made when Board Schools were built at the end of the last century, that a building should withstand all the pressures put upon it over an indefinite life. Apart from its solid constructiion, a feature noticeable on a preliminary visit, and reinforced during the course of the research, was the cleanliness and tidiness of the school and its environs — the absence of litter, grafitti (other than in the toilets), broken furniture and windows — all seemed to indicate a vigilant, co-operative caretaker and his staff, an effective school discipline and an absence of misbehaviour involving school premises, of the kind met with elsewhere in the literature. These initial observations were substantiated during the course of the two weeks: only one incident out of the 101 recorded, referred to the building. One member of staff did comment that on one or two occasions, displayed work had been wilfully damaged but for the most part, pupils expressed interest and not hostility to such displays. It must be added, however, that staff in informal discussion did indicate that this situation did not always pertain. It was observed by the researchers that apart from a limited display of artwork in an area easily supervised, there were virtually no visual displays elsewhere in the school of pupils' work; the remedial department was an exception. This was an outcome, it is tentatively suggested, of the academically orientated ethos of the school and not any active attempt to restrict display in case of vandalism. There were, perhaps, some shared assumptions about the functions of the building and that even if some pupils viewed school as having a predominantly custodial role, they did not vent their hostility in misbehaviour involving the building.

There were some indications that the layout of the building did encourage incidents of misbehaviour — the placement of demountable classrooms on the playing field, some one hundred metres from the main building, the location of a separate dining hall with insufficient chairs, and a temptingly accessible pile of boiler fuel, all posing problems of effective supervision unless a large number of staff are used, thus reducing the rest periods for some teachers already under stress in the classroom. One teacher commented in the final questionnaire, 'most of my discipline problems are not in the classroom but dealing with boys in and around the school, coke throwing, litter, jostling and noisy behaviour between buildings, one has to have a confrontation which in the main leaves both parties devoid of a friendly relationship.'

Movement about the main building and to and from the huts was a source of misbehaviour. The boy who arrives 10-15 minutes late for a lesson, perhaps creating the first of a series of minor incidents leading to the recorded incident of misbehaviour; the teacher who himself arrives late to a lesson because of the distance between the rooms in which he has to teach, to find a boisterous class to be settled before effective teaching can take place. Cumulatively, the loss of this teaching time may be potentially greater than realised when planning a timetable and allocating rooms to areas of the curriculum not requiring specialised resources. It may also prove less disruptive to classroom harmony to ensure the minimum of movement for some classes or for them to use areas of the building where supervision of the pupils and support for classroom teachers is at hand.

The proportion of incidents recorded in the two weeks rose during the course of the day. This could be attributed to a variety of factors, all of which involve resource allocation. The absence of a break in the afternoon; the length of a teaching session for pupils; or perhaps the shortness of the lunch-break for both teachers and pupils. Many of the teachers encountered in the research spent much of the lunch-break engaged in extra-curricular activities for the pupils. Superficial observation in the staff room at this time of day indicated an ebb and flow of teachers, with rarely more than approximately ten out of a staff of fifty-six present at one time. There are alternative explanations, but a random sample of staff when questioned indicated this extra-curricular involvement.

The recorded incidents not only reflected time of day but also length of a teaching period. Several recorded incidents suggested an escalation towards a disruptive incident during the course of a double period. Time-tabling is a difficult exercise at the best of times; responding to the competing demands of a school is final school term preoccupation in many secondary schools. But where there is what a school sees as a problem of disruption, it may be feasible to accommodate it if such factors could be shown to be of significance.

In thinking about misbehaviour and resource allocation, three ways could be considered that might increase the productivity of the existing resources of a school; firstly, changing its technology — the timetable, the length of school day, utilisation of rooms and movement about the building; secondly, one could consider allocating financial resources more effectively among the various physical resources and labour, the equipping and maintenance of some curricular areas like a science room, the location of some classes; and finally, resources of all kinds could be allocated more effectively among pupils with different levels of intellect. Thus the concentration of finance, subject specialist teachers and other resources on the most able child should be reappraised and alternative allocations be considered.

(b) The Behaviour Problem Dialogue

An important difference between the Goldsmiths' Project and the Behaviour Problem Dialogue, was that in the former the researchers asked to carry out the study, whereas in the Dialogue they were invited to do so by an adviser in an outer London borough, who had become interested in their published work on the Project. The LEA funded the

Dialogue, and it was therefore possible to do an improved version of the research. For example, the LEA arranged for a copy of each of the two length reports to the school, to be given to every member of staff, and at the end of the research made it possible for the dialogue to continue between the staff and the researchers.

The Dialogue school was a multi-racial, co-educational, comprehensive school with 1,200 pupils and 101 staff at the beginning of the research. All years from first to sixth were studied, and unlike the Project, permission was given for a pupil study, involving interviews with some children involved in incidents. Originally planned to be a monitoring study similar to the Project, lack of staff response to a preliminary questionnaire led the researchers to postpone monitoring until the week before the Spring half-term, and to spend the Autumn term interviewing staff on the topic of disruptive behaviour, in an attempt to win their co-operation. This was achieved, and every teacher except one agreed to participate. In the event, even this teacher helped by offering interviews.

Most of the information derived from the interviews and the one-week monitoring period, is to be found in the following pages, on incidents, teachers, children and ethnic considerations, and was given to staff in the two reports mentioned above. The second report ended with a brief summary of the findings, and with the researchers' recommendations to the school. These are now quoted in full, as they show how a monitoring study, with interviews, can lead to a suggested programme for alleviating a problem of disruptive behaviour:

Summary of the Two Reports as Presented to the Staff

1. In the first report there was the suggestion that some solutions are broadly related to the curriculum. Findings from the monitoring do not strongly confirm this. Nevertheless, the fact that it is mentioned by several staff indicates a concern on their part. Therefore, a number of recommendations are made in the section headed Recommendations.

2. Seventy-seven incidents were reported by assistant staff in the week of monitoring. Of the seventy-one incidents for which this question was answered, thirty-seven were reported to senior staff. These figures confirm staff comments in interview, that disruption remains a problem.

3. The range of solutions were thought to lie by those interviewed, with the individual class teacher e.g. 'a better understanding of

cultural differences'(first report) or pedagogy. Recommendations are made relating to this point.

4. The nature of the problem of misbehaviour identified by staff in interviews can be set against the pattern thrown up by the monitoring, i.e. corridors, individual problems. No close relationship was established by the monitoring of intellectual ability, emotional maladjustment, or particular children, to misbehaviour. There was no confirmation in the monitoring of the comments (and others in similar vein) recorded in the first report 'discipline matters are related to the ability range'. It might be speculated that some pupils are underperforming beause they are 'turned-off' education rather than for lack of intellectual ability. Staff comments recorded in the first report indicate clusters of types of behaviour that are confirmed in the second report.

5. Experience of stress as reported in interviews varied widely among staff. Monitoring in February suggests that minor, continuous disruption creates tension and stress in individuals. Corridors were mentioned as a disproportionate source of stress. Children referred to corridors as a source of disruption in their writings. Monitoring revealed fourteen per cent of incidents in corridors — a smaller proportion than indicated in the interviews. Classroom misbehaviour featured more frequently in the monitoring. An associated source of stress was the time-consuming nature of attempts to resolve misbehaviour problems.

6. The list of behaviours seen by teachers as problematic '. . . noise, running, talking back . . .' was borne out by the monitored incidents. The incidence of verbal abuse mentioned by teachers in interview as a source of misbehaviour and stress featured in the monitoring. Underlying many of the interview comments and the findings was the lack of respect for persons.

7. Time of day featured in the second report but was not mentioned in the interview report. Recommendations were made:

Recommendations

In making recommendations to the teachers, the researchers were very much aware of how heavily committed teachers already were to their work in the classroom and elsewhere in the school. It was inevitable that such advice would make additional demands on their time. With this in mind the suggestions made were of a practical kind requiring, it was hoped, a minimum of extra effort from teachers.

The Curriculum and its Organisation

The curriculum was seen as a significant focus for our counselling particularly that of the last two years of compulsory education. There was already a flourishing option scheme in operation for the fourth and fifth years, but there were constraints that existed, of the kind commonly found in other secondary schools; limited breadth of professional expertise, some inflexible accommodation, and space on the time-table. It was recognised that such obstacles pose limits to what can be included in a school curriculum and inevitably compromises are made. Nevertheless, despite these restrictions on flexibility, it appeared that greater consideration might be given to that part of a fourth and fifth curricular programme commonly known as the 'option' subjects as opposed to 'core' or compulsory subjects (which included mathematics, English, social studies and general science). The optional subjects were so arranged that a number of option 'blocks' were timetabled thus all the subjects in any one 'block' were taught simultaneously. This effectively limited pupil choice particularly for those at the lower end of the ability range, where incidentally low achievement and low motivation appear to go hand in hand. It was suggested that the number and nature of the optional subjects might reflect the local environment more closely as well as offering a wider range of subject combinations.

Two reports were recommended to the teachers. One was the HMI Report *Aspects of Secondary Education in England* (1979), the other, another HMI publication, *The School Curriculum 11-16* (1980). Both have much of interest for teachers, together with practical suggestions about the extremely complex organisation required to achieve balance and coherence in the curriculum for the fourth and fifth year.

Work experience for the fifth former in the school was a reality, but not extensively used. Few pupils had more than secondhand ideas culled from friends and family. This was combined with often hazy expectations about what they could do on leaving school. Of these pupils, only a limited number of those who might be thought to be low-achievers had the chance to spend time in a work place, which was a great pity. The school's geographical location did not help matters. Although there were a number of shopping centres within reach, the opportunity to experience other service industries, light industrial or commercial work was more limited. Without some experience, however restricted, many young school leavers find it difficult to relate the curriculum they receive in school to life outside, thus disaffection and cries of 'irrelevant to my life' can be appreciated. Work experience is thought to be one of the ways in which the connections can be made, particularly by the poorly motivated, between school and work.

In various parts of the country, links are being forged between non-advanced further education and the schools where the 16-19 age group is concerned. The freer atmosphere and responsibility for oneself in further education is appealing to the young school leaver. Many links so far have been established for the vocationally orientated young person who is likely to attain the academic qualifications necessary for entering in some cases. The school in question had explored the possibilities but had not considered it for the pupil who appeared to have 'failed' or been failed by the school's programme. A second chance for such pupils as well as the intellectually able was recommended, and that as many pupils as is feasible are alerted to the vocational possibilities of further education either through a link scheme or, less desirably, through careers advice. One source of information for such links is to be found in the 1978 ILEA Pilot Project which involved four secondary schools and their connections with further education institutions.

Incidents of misbehaviour were also noted in the first year age group with a rise in the second and third years of the school. Pupils came from a large number of primary schools, but the experience they all had in common was a one teacher, one class school day. To come into a large secondary school with its complex curricular organisation and to meet a large number of teachers some of whom do not get to know all their pupils well, can be a problem for some children. We recommended that the school consider switching more of its staffing resources to deal with the issue of socialising children into the norms desired by the school. It was thought that a more intensive investment of this kind might circumvent later difficulties with behaviour. One suggestion was that the class tutor spend part of each day with his class in a mode akin to top junior school practice and possibly teaching two or more curricular areas. The problem with such a suggestion is that many teachers are specialists and not desirous of teaching other aspects of the curriculum. This would seem to us something that might be discussed in terms of the school's INSET programme where some retraining had already been considered as part of the school's response to falling rolls and maintaining a balanced curriculum.

Many a secondary school presents a strong visual contrast to the primary school with its firm emphasis on the attractive and stimulating display of pupils' work. The school in the study was no exception, there was very little evidence of young people's work on the school premises, outside a small number of classrooms. In an effort to further motivate children it was advised, for example, that a board be placed outside certain rooms illustrating the success of individuals, classes and years, jobs obtained (entry to further education and so on); the list could be a long one. Another facet of pupil motivation was considered to be parental involvement. Parents, it was thought, would welcome a family newsletter giving similar kinds of information. The legal requirement (1982) that all schools shall acquaint parents with the schools their children attend, would provide an excellent opportunity to present such knowledge in addition to that already legally required. Already a number of secondary and primary schools have produced brochures which effectively combine the two objectives.

School organisation was thought to be a factor in the number of incidents which occurred. There were clusters of incidents around the start of the morning, at morning break, during the late afternoon and at mid-week. These periods were the focus of the recommendations about school organisation.

The school in the study was a purpose-built comprehensive school but it appeared that the designers had only a limited idea of what a thousand plus pupils looked, felt and sounded like, surging round the building, at break and lunch times. It was during the morning break period that a number of the incidents were recorded when the width of corridors and the number of fire doors to be passed through impeded the traffic flow. Almost inevitably there were confrontations, particularly between pupils, that could, and on occasion did, escalate into a disruptive incident. It was recommended that staff examine the rate of flow and volume of pupils in the corridors at those times with a view to reducing the number in circulation at any one period, by staggering the timing of the morning break for upper and lower schools. A trial period was suggested to test the worth of the recommendation.

Another period for disruptive incidents was early morning before the first break. Both staff and children in some cases travelled some distance to school. Some pupils were also responsible for domestic chores in the home and delivering younger children to nursery and infant schools. Consequently they started their school day under some stress and perhaps without having sufficient time to eat before work. It was therefore possible that a lack of food coupled with stress might be a factor in early morning incidents. A school tuck shop before school and at morning break was advocated.

In common with many secondary schools there was no break in the afternoon. The school day ended ten minutes earlier as a consequence. However, not all children can sustain a high level of concentration on work for such a long period. Evidence for this statement came from a number of teachers who gave examples of disruptive behaviour towards the end of the afternoon. An afternoon break was advised for a trial period and a record to be kept of disruptive incidents to determine whether the number had fallen as a consequence.

Sixth form pupils in the school had an attractive range of social and recreational amenities that were viewed with some envy by fourth and fifth formers. The school was asked to consider whether similar provision could be made for pupils below sixth year but on a reduced scale. For example, a disco dancing session at a Wednesday lunch time when the monitoring indicated a peak in the incident rate, might reduce the level despite the fact that such recreational activities are costly of staff time.

A less costly recommendation was made with regard to former pupils. A goodly number of pupils had gone on to further and higher education, others were successfully employed. It was suggested that some be asked at intervals to come and talk to fifth and sixth formers about their experiences in the world beyond school that could further extend the horizons of those still in school. Such a programme of talks could be allied to the suggested further education links and to the careers programme already on offer.

It was also suggested that greater use might be made of workshops on the school premises where in-service training could take place, e.g. a counsellor to talk and induct teachers into ways of dealing with emotionally disturbed pupils; a workshop, possibly organised by the English Department, on children's language to assist teachers to define verbal abuse in the context of this school, and to assist with the writing of work sheets used in teaching situations etc; a workshop to explore with teachers in other disciplines what 'maths across the curriculum' might mean. Such INSET might serve two purposes — a link with individual staff development; and, as a source of additional training in skills and techniques which could form part of an in-service course in learning difficulties. Finally, the researchers recommended that the school consider a one or two day staff conference (a residential weekend?) to discuss misbehaviour and other matters of concern to staff.

Conclusion to the Recommendations

There was no shortage of data, arising from the project:

(a)   Information prior to and since the project.

(b)   Our First Report, and staff comment on this.

(c)   Our Second Report.

The school has the choice of several courses:

(a)   To disregard the Project.

(b)   To act on Project findings.

Such action can vary in scale, for example, teachers could select one or two findings and pursue them, or approach the findings along a broad front. On the question of scale, it was suggested that the school might wish to consider:

1. The dimensions of the problem.
2. The school's current priorities, relating to these.
3. The resources of time, staffing, etc., it was prepared to allocate to pursuing the data.
4. The value attached to the project, which involved an assessment of the validity of the findings.

This latter point raises the question of the monitoring reflecting only a sample of the information available, i.e. the school could consider further monitoring of the same type OR much simpler (e.g. if it were wished, senior staff could keep a tally of types of incident and/or number of incidents per day for a long period, e.g. one specified day per week for one term). If monitoring similar to the project were favoured, it would be possible to carry this out for example one or two weeks per year, for two-three years, in an attempt to assess the effectiveness of programmes introduced with the aim of reducing disruption. Alternatively, monitoring could be carried out on a departmental or year basis where there was a problem which might be alleviated by analysis and diagnosis. In all the above cases, outside help in the analysis could be requested, or a group of appropriate staff in the school could undertake the task of collation of data.

The immediate question the school faced was how to 'handle' the project data, if it was to be translated into strategies. Courses lending themselves to consideration include general meetings of staff at different levels, i.e. one or more general staff meetings, which could discuss various items of the research report or overall strategy and/or considera- tion of items at school committee level. Alternatively, a working party could be set up to over-see discussion of the project and its translation into operational terms. The extent to which the school favoured par- ticipation of one or more members of the project staff in the meetings involved in this exercise might also be considered. Even if it were decided not to pursue the project data, it might be thought that talking to staff about disruptive behaviour had in itself been of value, and that means whereby more frequent and general discussion of this topic could be held, with specific aims, e.g. dissemination of information, in-service training, or staff counselling.

In the event generally favourable reactions to the report, followed by a staff meeting, led to a request from the school that the dialogue between staff and the researchers should continue. Full details follow of staff reactions to the report, and the minutes of the final staff meeting.

Staff Reactions to the Second Report

The headmaster and a random sample of staff were interviewed, before the final staff meeting held to discuss the project, to gather informa- tion on how the report had been received by the staff. It was clear that a number of staff were not going to attend the staff meeting, and that one reason for this was unrelated to the research itself: it was simply that staff had recently already attended two full staff meetings.

It was also evident that not only had one or two staff not had a copy of the report, but that some had read only part of it. One explanation offered for the latter point was its length: one teacher commented that it had taken him over two hours to read.

On the whole the report seemed to have had a favourable reception, and parts of it had generated considerable interest. One teacher described it as 'mostly factual'. However, it had been circulated at a point in time when the future of the school — its possible amalgamation with two others — lay in the balance, and there can be no doubt that these con- cerns had reduced its impact. Among the favourable comments were some relating to the section of the report which described the children's perceptions of life in the corridors. The headmaster described the notion of asking the children to imagine they were flies on the walls as 'brilliant', and there were other similar comments.

Various recommendations in the report received some support, in particular the blocking of the first year timetable, a focus on study skills early in the school, an afternoon break, and more work experience and Further Education links.

Some staff appeared to see the recommendations in the report very much from their own personal standpoint. Thus a teacher who felt he might be asked to supervise the parents' newsletter which had been recommended, was concerned at the extra burden which this might make upon him. Another who supported the idea of blocking the first year timetable said that she had made this suggestion — to no effect — two years previously.

Some staff were seeing the report in relation to a fresh set of problems, the difficulties which were emerging in the new, first year intake. This intake appeared to some staff to contain more difficult and less able children than the previous first year which had been studied in the report, and one or two staff were suggesting that it might be useful to monitor incidents occurring with this new intake. This is important, as it offers some evidence of the project having helped staff to take a research stance towards future problems of disruptive behaviour.

The headmaster was concerned about the report, on a score which he said had nothing to do with the research itself or the researchers. It was that one or two adverse comments about the school had reached him indirectly from outside the school. He felt that the report would be helpful to him for example in his request for better lighting. He liked the section on the children. He agreed in principle that it would be good to block the first years, but pointed out that set against this, some staff liked to see themselves as subject specialists. He stated his intention to look at the paper in detail and said, 'We (he and the researchers) agree totally on our view on life in the school.' He thought perhaps there should be a working party to look again at the possibility of staggering the lunch hour. (It had been looked at but turned down two years previously.) He pointed out that the school was different this year, for example, everybody was now a tutor, with two tutors allocated to years two to five, and this would help bring about a greater involvement in corridor supervision, for example.

The Staff Meeting held to discuss the Behaviour Problem

Dialogue Project
Those present were the headmaster and some forty per cent of the staff, the senior adviser of the Local Education Authority, the adviser in charge of the project and the project staff.

Unfortunately at the last moment the secretary who was to have taken down the proceedings in shorthand had to miss the meeting; her place was taken by someone who had difficulties in taking everything down. Consequently the account of the meeting has had to be edited and even with editing, it is clear that some points have been lost. It did, however, seem useful to present the reader with all that has been retrieved, even though it reads in places rather jerkily.

Headmaster: Discipline control has been a worry to me for some time. The recent doubling up of tutors has, however, made an improvement in the situation. I am delighted with the general atmosphere in classrooms, as I walk round the school. During lesson changes there is still an amount of noise causing disruption. Research into disruption is necessary and we should be grateful for advice from the senior group of researchers who have been working in the school. I thought the first report was honest but very depressing. I am not very happy about the second report, mainly because of comments about the school from people who have read it who do not know the school and therefore do not understand the background to the report.

Researcher: I should like to thank the Headmaster for inviting us into the school and allowing us to meet with you this afternoon. Mrs Young presents her apologies for absence. The school has been offered two reports on the project and we are here now to answer questions on these reports. You will know that the project involved firstly the interviewing of about seventy staff and secondly a one-week period during which disruptive incidents were monitored, in the Spring term, and a study was made of the problems involved. From all this a number of suggestions were made to the school. I have been talking to staff, and it is clear that a number of these recommendations appear to be of interest to some. These include the promotion of clubs and societies, a focus on study skills in the first years, the home base blocking of the first year timetable, more work experience, a break in the afternoon, a curricular review and further monitoring.

The two reports should be looked at as a whole. An impression I have gained from one or two discussions with staff, is that the second report is seen as being critical of senior staff. This is not so — no such criticism is implied in any way. Indeed, we commented at the end of the section on monitoring, in the second report, on our admiration for the work of senior staff. Many staff seem interested in the pupil perspectives in the second report — in what the children have been saying about incidents, and in what they wrote when asked to imagine they were a fly on the wall in the school. It is clear that many staff do listen to the children and do try and see the thing their way.

Ours is a very difficult area for research because it exposes those people concerned in it, whether Head Teacher or Assistant Teacher, to the hazards of misinterpretation, especially by those who do not know inner city schools.

Head of Dept. A: I feel that architecture and the design of the school has a bearing on our problems. All the lighting should be improved, not only at ground floor level; the recommendation would improve the visual appearance of the corridors. It is very important that money is spent on stimulating material on those walls. We should have the look of the buildings improved, then it will be treated with more respect.

Headmaster: I have been trying for the last four years to get extra lighting!

Researcher: We can't do much about actual architecture but we accept that noise levels are high because of the layout of the building. Our study, however, suggests that there are also other factors at work — perhaps teacher tolerance in the middle of the week? The statistics show patterns in the number of disruptive incidents. We may have to accept the architecture for the time being and concentrate on the other problems, which may be more amenable to change.

Deputy Headmaster: I feel the project has not proved anything statistically. It is not a scientific document, but it's quite a nice story. I would like to see the document referred to as a series of observations. After all, the pattern of the number of incidents on each day of the week could simply reflect a pattern of reporting rather than a pattern of incidents.

Researcher: I agree, but I still think some interesting ideas have come out of the project. You need to describe and summarize the data somehow. Our analysis is what is known as a descriptive analysis. It is not intended to be analytical, by which I mean hypothesis testing, as we are still at the stage of simply determining what actually happens in a disruptive incident. All we set out to do was to represent the data in a more digestible form. By obtaining frequencies we can get an insight into the patterns of the responses which form a basis for possible hypotheses which can later be investigated in a more rigorous fashion.

There are a number of interpretations of the patterns some of which we have put forward but with which you may disagree. But we are not saying that our 'statistics' support these, merely that they highlight the patterns which we in turn have attempted to explain.

Researcher: We have never intended to do a tight, scientific survey but the general picture obtained has been important.

Researcher: Patterns can be seen, especially when added to the data from similar projects in other schools. One project finding is that small groups do not, as we might have thought, mean lack of disruption. And if a year, such as this year's first year, were showing signs of being difficult, the school could now go ahead and do its own monitoring of incidents in that year.

Head of Dept. B: What I wanted to know is why and not how disruption occurs. Is it the difference between home attitudes and the more relaxed attitude at school?

Researcher: Home background has been taken into account in the reports. There are of course dozens of causes for disruption. One recent study of social workers' and teachers' views on the causes of violent behaviour listed sixty-six causes! The trouble is, home background is not easily open to change, if one wants to change it.

Head of Dept. A: What can we as teachers do, to prevent disruption?

Researcher: Not all disruptions are caused by problem children. Our reports show that the staff themselves have suggested many ways in which disruption could be reduced.

Researcher: I think you may like to know, that as one reads through the children's accounts, they show great affection for certain members of staff. There are many positive things one would wish to say about the school. For example, one would want to mentioned the number of places at university won this year — nineteen I think the Headmaster said.

Assistant Teacher A: Different personalities will find different ways of controlling children.

Researcher: Perhaps I should mention that we found that the minor physical handling of children was quite common. In some cases it seemed to cause no problem but in others it did.

Deputy Head of Dept. A: I agree; it can be in a sense a form of communication. One can handle a child and get away with it.

Researcher: Some children do not like it.

Deputy Head of Dept. A: As face workers we wanted more than a third of a page suggesting ways by which we could reduce disruption. Some staff are very involved in their work with after-school activities etc. — which is vitally important in this school. I wonder why Dr. Lawrence and her colleagues had not attended these after-school activities.

Researcher: This report can be followed up in any way you wish.

Deputy Head of Dept. B: I'm interested in the non-reported incidents; for example, when the teacher should be in a classroom and is not there, when the lesson is about to start and the class down the corridor has no teacher, when teachers are not in their place at the right time — disruption at these times.

Researcher: This would need observation over a long period, and it is difficult to find enough resources for this. Only a third of the senior staff reported their incidents — they were probably just too busy to report. This senior staff information is also very difficult to gather.

Deputy Head of Dept. B: When I was a Year Head, I realised that often disruption was caused by bad teaching. How can one obtain information of this nature and use it in a positive way rather than a negative way, to improve teaching?

Assistant Teacher B: On page twenty-nine of the second report 'accepted norms' are mentioned. Sometimes disruption is desirable and it may be that the 'norms' are not always the 'norms', that is to say, sometimes disruption tells you that the learning situation is breaking down. There is a fair amount of agreement on this.

Researcher: I agree; for example, it may on occasion be good — good for the child — for a very inhibited child — to 'let go'.

Headmaster: It is not possible to allow a child with a problem to disrupt a lesson.

Assistant Teacher B: I would like to see an analysis of our norms.

Assistant Teacher C: I am worried about what one colleague has said — that the quality of the teaching was the main cause of disruptive behaviour. It makes teachers hesitant to ask for help. I agree that both the curriculum and the quality of teaching has improved. However, our children do have a lot of problems.

Head of Dept. B: A teacher who is under stress and consequently feels a failure is frequently absent, which causes more disruption. It is something we are very much concerned with, and staff are very reluctant to admit to it.

Researcher: That is why more in-service training is suggested.

Researcher: I am glad that the subject of disruptive behaviour has now been aired in conversation among staff — there has been a good deal of useful discussion.

Head of Dept. C: Courses have been arranged to assist teachers who are not managing very well in their teaching. These courses have been very helpful. In-service training should be extended. I don't think we all agree on norms and there should be more discussion about what is, or is not, acceptable behaviour.

Researcher: I think this is a significant point; that there was an absence of agreed norms affecting the children is important and worth discussing in a staff meeting.

Assistant Teacher D: We mean a breach of the peace rather than an interruption of the learning situation when we mention disruption. I am surprised that we can get children to do some of the things we ask them to do so willingly and cheerfully.

Headmaster: I once had a colleague in another school who seemed to have excellent control. Then I discovered how he did it. He would set some handwriting. The first child who started to fidget was beaten and the first child to finish was beaten!

Comment on the Staff Meeting

As one reflects on the staff-meeting, it is clear that as in any other such meeting, roles are being played out, some of them obvious, others less evident. Thus the Head Teacher wishes to appear to lead, both to his staff and to the Advisers present. The latter say nothing in the discussion, but their presence necessarily affects the behaviour of all the participants — head, staff and researchers. For the Head the need is to appear to run a school which is moving forward. He early on refers to the improvement in the situation brought about by the recent doubling up of tutors which he has initiated. He refers to his walking round the school, showing he is very much an inspector and controller. While admitting that he is grateful for advice, and accepting the need for the research, he criticises its reports, calling the first one depressing and pointing to the fact that some people had read the report who will misunderstand it, because they do not know the school.

Most of the staff who speak during the meeting are heads of departments or assistant heads of departments. The weight of the authority present (advisers, headmaster, etc.) is likely to account for assistant staff feeling diffident about presenting their views, at such a meeting. Among those who speak, there is, however, little fear of being critical about the project. The deputy headmaster voices a serious reservation concerning the research findings as a whole, calling it 'not a scientific document, but . . . quite a nice story', while Deputy Head of Department A criticises the researchers for not attending after-school activities.

Staff raise a number of questions during the meeting, questions which they are left with at the conclusion of the project. Clearly these could become the focus of further work at the school and by the local authority. They include questions of architecture relating to disruptive behaviour, clash of parental attitudes with school attitudes, measures to prevent disruption from occurring, the impact of teacher personality and bad teaching, the need for an analysis of the schools norms, and the need for further in-service training. What this staff meeting seems to have distilled from the project is a set of details for a further phase of discussion and action, by this school, relating to disruptive behaviour.

7   INCIDENTS OF DISRUPTIVE BEHAVIOUR

Gathering 'incidents': How many?

The first question which the two school studies attempted to answer was whether it is feasible to look at disruptive behaviour through a close examination of incidents. It should be remembered that most work on misbehaviour has been focused upon children, rather than events, so that this was an important question. In addition we needed to know whether a focus upon incidents was useful to the school, as well as to us as researchers. As the studies proceeded it was clear that the answer to these questions was very positive. Teachers were able and willing to describe incidents, and they described a sufficient number of them to make analysis of them feasible. The success of the technique of monitoring incidents was seen very clearly in the Project.

From the researcher's point of view it ran very smoothly. It was helpful to be located in the staff-room, in which staff were very ready to discuss matters relevant to the Project, as they occurred. The return of forms went well; clearly, if no incident had occurred in a day, there was little incentive to return the incident forms, yet in spite of this, the returns of these averaged 90% for the two weeks. 86% of the final questionnaire forms were returned, and 90% of the staff questionnaires.

Inspection of the final questionnaires showed that half of the staff who returned forms (28 out of 50) did not think the Project lasted too long, and most (42) did not have difficulty in completing the incident forms. Many (28) found it helpful to discuss misbehaviour with an outsider, and found it (35) an interesting experience. Almost all (44) thought the topic an important one to investigate. Furthermore they did not feel (41) that it made them less confident in coping with misbehaviour, nor that talking about misbehaviour simply increased the problem (42). The Project did not interfere with their work (44), nor was it embarrassing (45). There was little indication that the reactions of senior staff to the Project differed from those of the staff as a whole. It is obvious that in a large school there will be some staff who are not committed to almost any research which may be carried out in the school, and who will not take an active part in it, if it involves form-filling, often a much disliked activity. In the Dialogue a handful of staff did not remove their incident sheets from their pigeonholes. It also became clear in the project that when the quantity of disruption is large, accurate monitoring becomes difficult; staff forget to record incidents. Time of year also affects completion of forms. There was more urgent work, i.e. report completion, to do in February than in November, and more stress in that a half-term's work had been done without a break, whereas the November week was one immediately after a half-term holiday. In the Dialogue a few staff left the school between the interviewing in the Autumn Term and the monitoring in the Spring Term; and one or two were absent for the whole of the monitoring week. Notwithstanding these difficulties, participation in both of the studies came from almost the whole staff and was willingly given throughout. The Project yielded data on 101 incidents over two separate weeks, the Dialogue on 144 incidents over one week. A total of 245 incidents were reported on by seventy members of staff. In the Dialogue, about half of the incidents were reported on by staff who had direct experience of them, and the rest by senior pastoral and faculty staff to whom the incident had been reported. In the Project a comparison between staff who reported incidents and those who did not, showed that the former tended to be younger, were more frequently in their first year of teaching, had fewer years of teaching experience, less experience in teaching in secondary modern or comprehensive schools, and had been at the school for a shorter period.

It is of course difficult, to obtain a perspective on the number of incidents reported in the two schools. Are the numbers involved 'high'? Even without comparative studies, two things are clear. Firstly, each school was 'difficult' in the sense that it had a problem of disruptive behaviour which it wanted eased. Secondly, the numbers are underestimates: they represent a part only of the total picture. In the paper presented to the Project school, the researchers wrote:

In all 101 incidents were recorded, 47 in November and 54 in February. These figures need to be regarded as underestimates, e.g. in a number of cases staff failed to submit forms which they said they would do. Nine incidents were described as 'very serious', five in November and four in February. Fourteen subject departments (half those in the school) reported at least one incident. If these figures appear high, it should be remembered that teachers do not always report onwards incidents which are serious, for various reasons such as personality, anxiety lest they be categorised as 'weak' teachers, and wish to avoid boys being sent into a referral system which could lead to serious official consequences, e.g. suspension. The research thus taps information about incidents which under normal circumstances may remain unknown in the sense that they are not officially reported, but which may filter through and become known to senior staff because, for example, the noise of a commotion reaches them, or they spot the incident as they move informally round the school. There is an indication of the extent to which serious incidents in this school are reported onwards, or not, in the research forms which show that of 94 incidents for which the question concerning reporting onwards was answered, 62 (66%) were described as being reported onwards and 32 (34%) as not being so reported. In one or two cases it was clear that a teacher intended to report, but forgot to do so.

Seriousness of Incident

A similar illustration that the monitoring tapped only some of the incidents which were occurring is found in the Dialogue, where the option to report to the researchers incidents reported to them by staff, was taken only by nine of the twenty-seven senior pastoral and faculty staff. Finally, it may help to provide a perspective on the number of incidents if it is pointed out that the Dialogue school appeared from observation to be considerably more difficult than the Project School, and this is borne out by the number of incidents described as 'very serious' in each school. In the Project, of the 9 incidents designated as very serious (i.e. 11%), 4 in week one and 5 in week two, only 2 were reported by the same member of staff, i.e. eight different teachers were involved, including both young and older, junior and more senior staff. In all but one case, these incidents were reported onward, to more senior staff. There were several different reasons for which an incident was regarded as very serious. In one case a whole group of boys, during mid-morning break, became excited and abusive, in another a whole class of boys would not settle down, a group supporting one particularly disruptive boy. These two incidents came from one inexperienced teacher. In a third incident an older member of staff reported blank disobedience as very serious. In a fourth the use of threatening language after several refusals to obey instructions was reported on by a Head of Department.

Other 'very serious' incidents were a fight which greatly disturbed the lesson for an inexperienced teacher, the finding of stolen property, which required police intervention, and an incident involving incompatibility of personality of boy and teacher. In the Dialogue, the picture was different. Of the 70 directly reported incidents whose degree of seriousness was noted, 21% were described as very serious, 54% as serious, and 16% as not serious.

If it is accepted that very serious incidents will be reported to senior staff, it would seem to be clear that the number of very serious incidents in number is an underestimate.

Examination of the incidents described as very serious shows that this designation often accompanies a cluster of two or three of the following descriptions of the behaviour: abuse or bad language, refusing authority, dumb insolence, rowdy behaviour.

Almost all of the 'very serious' incidents were reported to very senior members of staff; one involved suspension. Two were 'dramatic incidents', i.e. one involved a boy jumping from a first floor window, and another involved a disturbed pupil losing control and becoming violent. Three involved large numbers of pupils.

The fact that a teacher may view relatively minor incidents as seriously disruptive, that is, worth reporting to a researcher, poses the question of why this should be so. Clearly this may be for reasons of personality (a teacher has his own level of tolerance), and of goals. But the research suggests that three other factors may be operating, within a given situation. The Project showed that these might be firstly, stresses upon the teacher, (e.g. where the teacher has the same class for several periods in the same day, and worries about this). There were twenty-nine cases in which some special stress appeared to be operating. An interesting point is that the feature was one of a series of incidents, i.e. the boy has done the same thing before. In forty-five cases, the repetitive nature of the incident was pointed to. Thirdly, it can happen that the teacher imputes intentionally malice in the boy and thinks 'he's done it deliberately', 'he's getting at me', 'he *knows* I won't stand for it', i.e. the teacher becomes personally involved in the incident, rather than remaining detached. In forty-one cases the boy's behaviour appeared to be regarded as intentional.

We believe it may be helpful if teachers understand the dynamics of their reactions to misbehaviour. Additionally, the above factors point to other aids, such as the averting of disruptive behaviour in its first, minor form.

Staff Characteristics

A look at the characteristics of staff who reported incidents compared with those who did not, showed in the Project that they differed somewhat, in their views on their areas of personal success in the school. Staff who reported incidents tended to mention examination/academic work, and getting on well with fourth and fifth year boys as areas of personal success, more frequently than staff who did not report incidents. The latter tended to mention helping boys towards a good future, pastoral care activities, relationships with other staff and success associated with a specific departmental or administrative role, more frequently than others, as areas of personal success. In considering areas of particular success for the school, staff who reported incidents tended to place more emphasis than others on success in examination/academic work and extra-curricular activities than the others, who tended to emphasise success in non-examination courses and fulfilling comprehensive school aims. Although it might be thought that assistant staff would report far more incidents than senior staff, it is clear that in the more difficult Dialogue School, this was not so: assistant staff were only slightly more likely to submit incident sheets than senior staff. In the same school only three incident sheets were completed by probationers and supply teachers. There were five probationers and three supply teachers in the school. This may be because beginners' difficulties and supply teachers' difficulties are such as to make reporting too onerous. It may equally show the effectiveness of teacher tutor support to probationer teachers. (At least one interview suggested this).

Day of the Week

The numbers of incidents reported on each day of the week in the Project showed a tendency to rise towards Wednesday, the middle of the week, and to then fall off towards Friday, and in the Dialogue this trend appeared with increasing clarity (see Table One).

TABLE ONE: Incidents Reported on Days of Week (Dialogue)						
The number of incidents reported directly and indirectly was as follows:						
	MON	**TUE**	**WED**	**THU**	**FRI**	**TOTAL**
DIRECTLY	18	15	24	13	7	77
INDIRECTLY	7	18	20	12	10	67
COMBINED DIRECTLY AND INDIRECTLY	25	33	44	25	17	144

There appeared to be an increasing number of indirectly reported incidents from Monday to Wednesday, followed by a fall in numbers towards Friday, and this pattern is the same for the directly and indirectly reported incidents combined.

The low number of incidents reported on Friday may reflect the anticipation of a half-term holiday, leading to increased tolerance and relaxation among staff, coupled with a reluctance to undertake the chore of form-filling on that day. Similarly reporting incidents to senior staff may also be fatiguing. Senior staff reports show that for staff to report onwards to them may be as stressful as relieving it!

The peak in the number of incidents reported on Wednesday may indicate a reduction in teacher tolerance towards the middle of the week, when strain has built up, but is not yet dispersed by the prospect of the weekend. The weather was fine throughout the weeks when the monitoring took place and so is unlikely to be a factor.

It should be noted finally that one senior teacher in the Dialogue, who reported less heavily on Monday and Tuesday pointed out that this was because his heavy teaching programme on these days meant he was not available to support colleagues, and so he did not receive so many reports. If this teacher's incidents are excluded from the analysis the curve for the week, however, remains the same (Monday: 22, Tuesday: 28, Wednesday: 36, Thursday: 21, Friday: 10 incidents) for direct and indirect incidents combined.

Time of Day

A study of the time of day at which incidents were said to occur also yielded interesting findings. In the Project approximately half the incidents (42 out of 88 for which information was available) occurred during the three periods in the afternoon. Several explanations of this are possible. Staff may become tired as the day proceeds so that they become less tolerant of behaviour, and boys may become tired and less in control of themselves. It may also be that the lunch hour period is less satisfactory than it could be, in that boys are not able to find a release for their energies, and staff do not rest sufficiently, but are busy working, seeing boys and engaging in activities with them. This latter point, the task of a restful lunch hour for staff, was borne out by observation of the staff-room. In the Dialogue the afternoon was again found to bear a heavy burden of incidents, but other interesting points emerged, too, in relation to the pattern of incidents in the morning.

By the beginning of break, 36% of directly reported incidents had already taken place. This may suggest that home stresses were impinging on the child early in the day (e.g. minding younger children) and that the journey to school presented difficulties for both staff and pupils. Lunch and dinner break incidents seemed to be reported onwards to the senior pastoral staff, rather than on direct report forms.

The rate of incidents per hour of teaching time ranges from one to twelve minutes for modules 6-8, i.e. the period after break in the morning, to one per five minutes for the first part of the morning (modules 1-5) and the afternoon (modules 9-14). This could reflect a relative lack of tension among both staff and pupils after the morning break and one wonders whether fewer incidents might occur in the afternoon if it, too, were punctuated by a break.

Fourteen percent of directly reported incidents occurred during the morning break or the lunch hour. This number may appear small in relation to staff statements, in the report on the interviews, about the corridors presenting a problem. It may be that corridor incidents are frequent to the degree where they are not thought worth reporting.

Incidents occurring outside school hours are not reported on directly, but would appear to be reported on by senior staff, on senior staff report forms.

Banding, Class and Set

The Project School was a senior high school, where incidents among fourth and fifth year pupils only were monitored and where these pupils were banded for teaching purposes. When the classes and years involved in incidents were examined, very clear patterns emerged (see Table Two).

TABLE TWO: (Project) The Classes and Years Involved in Incidents			
	NOVEMBER	**FEBRUARY**	**TOTAL**
4_1	1	4	5
4_2	4	7	11
4_3	13	21	34
			50
5_1	5	1	6
5_2	8	11	19
5_3	12	13	25
TOTAL	43	57	50

While there is no difference in the number of incidents in which fourth and fifth-year were involved, over the two weeks there was a noteworthy increase in the number of incidents in all three fourth-year classes from the November week to the February week. The increase is particularly large in terms of the overall number of incidents for class 4_3 (November: 13, February: 21), an increase which occurred in spite of a 2% drop in 4_3 attendance, between the two weeks.

Reasons for these results are perhaps some combination of the following factors:

(a)   Frustration may have increased for less able boys particularly because exams and reports have underlined their academic inadequacies.

(b)   The fourth year has 'warmed up by February; the school was relatively new to them in November. By February, pupil-staff dynamics have developed, and stereotypes have crystallised.

(c) 4_3 appear to spend a lot of time together as a group; their class identity may therefore be stronger than that of other groups.

The classes involved in most incidents are 4_3 (34), 5_3 (25) and 5_2 (19). Clearly life in a third band class, and life in a first band, is very different, with regard to the disruption of lessons. In seeking to understand why the number of incidents (59) in which third band classes were involved was so high, a curricular explanation suggests itself from many areas of the research, e.g. the staff questionnaire, and some interviews. It is possible that an integrated, rather than a fragmented programme, taught by members of staff who within their department (as for Maths and English already) have special interest in teaching less able pupils, might help. Indeed, this suggestion was put to the school. A year later, an integrated third band curriculum had been implemented by the Headmaster.

In the Dialogue, incidents for first to sixth year were monitored. The school favoured mixed ability classes, with some setting, especially in the senior part of the school. Information concerning class or set was available for 58 incidents. The heading was left general, in accordance with staff anxieties lest too definite a description on this point might lead to a breach of confidentiality. Partly as a consequence of the generality of the heading, but also owing to an apparent scattering of difficulties among many classes and groups, no fewer than forty-six differently named classes and sets were referred to. As far as year of school was concerned, of the 63 directly reported, 38.1% occurred in the lower (years 1-3) school, and 61.9% in the upper school, with the fifth-year being involved in 39.7% of the incidents (see Table Three). The figures for first and second year were extremely low (3.2% in the first year, 7.9% in second year).

TABLE THREE: Incidents Per Year of Pupils	
YEAR	**ADJUSTED FREQUENCY (PER CENT)**
1	3.2
2	7.9
3	27.0
4	19.0
5	39.7
6	3.2

A study of Dialogue length of incidents showed that most incidents were brief (almost half of the sixty-six cases for which this information was available, lasted five minutes or less), but a substantial number lasted a long time (see Table Four). There was no indication that length of incident was related to seriousness of incident.

TABLE FOUR: (Dialogue) How Long Did the Incident Last? (66 Incidents)	
LENGTH OF INCIDENT	**NUMBER OF INCIDENTS**
Less than two minutes	11
3-5 minutes	20
6-10 minutes	11
11-20 minutes	7
1-2 modules (20 to 40 minutes)	11
more than 2 modules (40 minutes plus)	6

Sex of Pupil

The Project school was a single-sex school, but in the mixed Dialogue school it was possible to see whether boys and girls were involved in a similar number of incidents, or whether one sex was more frequently implicated. The findings proved interesting. Most (57%) of the 49 directly reported incidents involving boys involved only one boy, while six (12%) involved groups of more than five. In all at least 120 boys were involved. Girls were less likely than boys to be involved in directly reported incidents. There were 24 directly reported incidents in which a total of sixty-five girls were involved. As for boys, most (58%) of the 'girl' incidents involved only one girl.

Senior staff reports (31 incidents) refer to thirty-seven boys and over forty girls. These proportions are similar to those for the two sexes in the school as a whole. This suggests that girls, while producing fewer behaviour problems overall, (i.e. fewer directly reported incidents) tend to produce more serious ones (i.e. those that are reported onwards). It may be of interest in supporting the notion that the 'difficult' girl may be exceptionally difficult. It may also be that staff tend to be more anxious about difficult girls than boys. Male staff were slightly more likely to fill in incident reports than women.

Number of Pupils

As might have been expected, most directly reported incidents appeared to involve first one pupil, but a large number involved two or three, and a number involved most or all of the class. In the Dialogue the percentage for these three kinds of directly reported incidents were: 48 involving one pupil, 36 involved two or three, and 12 involving most or all of the class.

Of 66 indirectly reported incidents, i.e. those dealt with by senior staff, 74% concerned only a single pupil and a further 12% only two pupils. This may reflect that groups of pupils tend not to be sent to senior staff, and that dealing with very difficult individual children is seen by assistant staff to be a main function of senior pastoral staff.

It is frequently said that disruptive incidents are related to class size, that large classes will be conducive to misbehaviour. In the Dialogue information relating to class size was available for 54 incidents (see Table Five).

TABLE FIVE: Class Size (Dialogue)	
NO OF PUPILS IN GROUP	**NO OF INCIDENTS**
1 — 5	4
6 — 15	7
16 — 26	34
26 plus	9

Information was not available on the number of teaching groups of each size in the school. It was also not available in relation to ability alas. It is of interest that contrary to the impression given by some staff working with very small groups (fewer than six pupils) a few incidents (4) did occur with these groups. There is some evidence from the study to suggest that where a pupil is disruptive in a very small group this may be because the pupil is exhibiting emotional disturbance.

Other studies, particularly large scale studies, may wish to explore the relationship between disruption and class size, and also between disruption and the different subjects in the curriculum. All that can be said on the latter point, in the relation to the two studies, is that incidents were well scattered; thus, in the Dialogue, in the 51 incidents for which subject information was available, sixteen different subjects were mentioned as being taught at the time, i.e. half of the subjects taught in the school. Incidents were reported directly by staff of five out of the six faculties in the school.

Roughly half of the incidents appear to have taken place while whole class teaching was taking place (see Table Six).

TABLE SIX: Type of Teaching (Dialogue) (56 Incidents)	
TYPE OF TEACHING	**NUMBER OF INCIDENTS**
Whole class	30
Group Work	3
Individual Work	17
Other	4
Whole class and individual work	2

Location of Incident
In the Dialogue, a study of location of incidents yielded a finding which was in contrast to teachers' impressions, gathered from interviewing them. Teacher interviews had suggested that classrooms did not present a problem. Yet of the 70 incidents whose location was named, no fewer than 60% occurred in classrooms. It should, however, be mentioned that of this 60%, 11% centred about the child 'bursting in' to a classroom, which means that the disturbance occurred within the room but seemed to originate elsewhere.

Types of Behaviour
A great deal of information was obtained, about the incident itself, and the pupil behaviour involved. In the Project, a free description of the incident was asked for.

The picture which emerged was of general disruption and difficulty, rather than aggressive, dangerous behaviour. There were ten cases of fighting and three of dangerous behaviour. There were seven cases of incidents involving food; items which were termed disruptive in ten or more incidents were throwing things around the room (14), bad language (18), insolence (22), lateness (12), with the largest number of instances of particular forms of disruption being those for doing no work (35), talking (41), general disruptive/general refusal to be taught (50), tardiness in settling (29) and a refusal to obey (36). This pattern seems to relate to the general ethos of the school which is a study ethos. (This is confirmed by information given on the staff questionnaire.) General disruption comes to mean defeating the aim of teaching, which is cardinal to the staff.

In the Dialogue, more extensive data was obtained. In this study, (see Table Seven) the incident sheet contained both a closed and an open question relating to a description of the incident. The closed question listed thirteen behaviours, to be ticked in answer to the question, 'Which of the following best describe the incident?' The open question asked for 'Full details of the incident'. The two questions were analysed separately. The total for the closed question is larger than the number of incidents, because staff ticked several behaviours for each incident. This shows that a disruptive incident usually centres around a cluster of behaviours rather than a single behaviour, a finding borne out by the Project.

The open and closed question data for directly reported incidents shows the frequency of rowdy behaviour, and an absence of theft. It may of course be that most thefts are minor and too frequent to be reported. Abuse or bad language, talking/chatting, refusing authority,

TABLE SEVEN: Description of the Incident (Dialogue)					
BEHAVIOUR	**DIRECTLY REPORTED**				**INDIRECTLY REPORTED**
	Open question 71 incidents		Closed question 68 incidents		67 incidents
	Frequency	Rank Order	Frequency	Rank Order	Frequency	Rank Order
1. Abuse or bad Language	8	4	20	4 =	8	4
2. Vandalism	2	9	3	10 =	6	6
3. Stealing	0	11 =	0	13	0	11 =
4. Dumb Insolence	3	6 =	20	4 =	1	9 =
5. Extreme lateness to lessons	4	5	14	6	2	8
6. Talking/Chatting	10	3	28	2 =	0	11 =
7. Refusing Authority	15	2	39	1	17	1
8. Sudden temper	3	6 =	10	7	1	9 =
9. Bullying or violence to peers	3	6 =	8	8	9	3
10. Rowdy behaviour	22	1	28	2 =	7	5
11. Threatening behaviour to staff	0	11 =	3	10 =	0	11 =
12. Violence to staff	0	11 =	1	12	3	7
13. Truancy (internal or external)	1	10	4	9	10	2

NB: 'Open' refers to a free response. 'Closed' refers to specific questions.

and rowdy behaviour are frequent, figuring high in rank order, for both open and closed questions. The 'violence to staff' incident occurred accidentally rather than deliberately but caused physical injury, as a result of a pupil running and banging into the teacher.

For senior staff reporting 'indirect' incidents, no closed question was available. Senior staff reports yield 'open' information, however, which was also categorised. The ranking of senior staff reports is similar in some respects to that of the directly reported incidents, e.g. refusing authority is extremely important, and abuse or bad language is important. Differences show the character of senior staff's work, e.g. they deal with truancy, and with bullying or violence to peers, and, where it occurs, to staff.

In 38% of directly reported incidents, it was clear that the behaviour was a repetition of previous bad behaviour. This finding had already emerged from the project. Clearly repetition may sensitize the teacher, or may open the way to escalation of the difficult behaviour. (As one would expect, senior staff reports showed that repetition of behaviour was a very common cause of referral of an incident to senior staff).

'Bursting in' figured in 13% of cases, and 'sudden outburst' in 18%, showing that teachers saw many incidents as flaring up, developing very quickly. Talking/chatting is not serious enough to be mentioned by senior staff — even if staff reporting to them mention it — in their reports. Refusing authority has 'first rank', as for the direct report closed question. Bullying or violence to peers ranks higher in senior staff reports, and absence from scheduled class attendance much higher.

Further details for 106 incidents direct and indirect showed that incidents occurred in eight cases where the teacher was on duty, and in seven cases where the teacher was covering for another teacher.

The Role of Senior Staff

An important question concerns the role of senior staff in dealing with incidents reported to them: how large a role is it, which staff do most and what sort of work are they involved in. These questions themselves lead to questions relating to their resources, support services, and training for the job. In the Project some incidents (9) were reported to heads of departments, more to year staff (16) and ultimately to deputy heads (30) while seven were ultimately reported to the head. These figures are based on a questionnaire item and are thus likely to be underestimates. The cases reaching the deputy heads were also usually passed on for necessary action to year staff, so that both year staff and deputy heads had numerically a very large disciplinary role. Having pointed this out, the following suggestion was put to the staff in the paper presented to the school, at the conclusion of the research:

> If it were wished to reduce this role, and indeed to reduce the number of boys who pass into the official disciplinary system which can lead to detention, caning, refusal to be caned, and suspension, it might be possible to extend and develop the role of departments for this purpose. Where a teacher in a department wished to exclude a boy from a lesson, he could do so by placing him with a member of his department, where the nature of the boy's disruption did not warrant his being sent to the Hall. This would have the additional advantage, that departmentally curricular and teaching-technique factors could be investigated, as possible contributory factors in the situation. Heads of departments might be guided in these functions by a deputy head. Assistant heads of year could liaise with heads of departments and undertake preventive pastoral care work with the boys involved in these 'minor' incidents.

> Alternatively, boys could continue to be sent to the Hall as at present, but a distinction could be made between those whose offence is:

(a)   serious, so that the boy should be passed along the system, to the head of the year, etc.

(b)   not serious, so that no further action than housing him in the Hall should be taken.

In the Dialogue, staff were again asked to say if and to whom they had reported, or would report the incident. Of the 71 incidents for which this question was answered, 52% (37) incidents were reported to senior staff either immediately or by the end of the day. Nine of the twenty-seven senior staff, using forms for 'indirect' reporting, reported on 74 incidents which included seven which had already been reported onwards that were notified to the researchers. No explanation was forthcoming when others did not report. It may be that assistant staff who reported incidents to senior staff assumed that senior staff would report the incident, and that they had no need to report it themselves.

Senior staff's accounts of the incidents reported to them showed that the incidents were frequently complex and very difficult to resolve, requiring speed of action, patience and ingenuity. Certain senior staff carried very large disciplinary 'loads' which they fitted into a teaching programme. The incidents illustrated well that these staff have the 'problem-solving' role that Hoghughi (1978) believes characterises work with exceptionally difficult children. (Few of these pupils were exceptionally difficult, but the situations which arose certainly called for problem-solving skills).

The reports show the degree of team-work needed in dealing with disruptive incidents. This can be difficult where for example senior staff — and this is inevitable at times — do not have the same view of a case. Senior staff need to 'carry' a great deal of detailed information about different children, and any mistake may have serious consequences. Their role is demanding in that they try to help staff and pupils in difficult situations, so that they have to cope with others' anger, feelings of frustration and unhappiness, as well as with their own. A sense of humour proves a boon. They have to carry out delicate negotiations between the various parties involved, e.g. staff and pupils. A lot is at stake in these negotiations — teacher self-esteem, and for the pupil, possible suspension, or being 'advised' to leave the school. Cases are often long-term, needing a lot of follow-up. Occasionally there is potential danger, e.g. in dealing with an intruder, or a seriously disturbed child.

Some Incidents

The following section presents largely verbatim accounts from the Project of thirteen incidents, as they were reported on in writing, or described in interviews, by the staff and, taken together, illustrate many of the points made elsewhere in the book. The accounts range widely in length and complexity, and range from incidents which appear and remained relatively minor (though all were classified by the teacher as serious), to those with serious consequences for the boy concerned. All names are fictitious, and only minor alterations have been made in the verbatim accounts, where these were necessary to maintain confidentiality or facilitate comprehension.

It is helpful to know that the periods of the school day were as follows:
● Periods 1, 2. ● Morning break. ● Periods 3, 4, 5. ● Lunch hour.
● Periods 6, 7, 8.

Incident 1

The incident took place on Friday, 11th February, period 5. The class was a second band class in fifth-year. There were sixteen boys in the class. The incident lasted three minutes, and two boys were involved, Paul Skreel and Peter Mitchell. The teacher was highly experienced.

Written Report

'Mitchell claims he was hit twice by Skreel. Mitchell was sitting by the radiator in a seat Skreel claimed — wrongly — to be his own. Immediately Mitchell got up — on the verge of tears — and left the room. I followed him out on to the balcony whereupon he told me Skreel had hit him once in the stomach and once "in the mouth". I called Skreel to come out of the room to apologise to Mitchell. He reluctantly did so; he quietly but politely asked if Mitchell would come to him. I had, therefore, to tell Skreel twice to come out of the classroom. He apologised to Mitchell immediately after he had come out onto the balcony. (Three or four minutes prior to the incident, I had to have severe words with Skreel to stop him from verbally intimidating Mitchell re their seating arrangement. I had sent Skreel away from Mitchell to the back of the class.) The class were not excited in any way by the incidents — being scared of Skreel's reputation as a bully, in my opinion.'

The teacher mentioned this incident to his head of department who came out of the adjacent room onto the balcony to see him 'interviewing' both boys. He had not had a chance to see the head of fifth-year by the time he completed the form at the end of the day. By the time he was interviewed (on the following Monday) he had still not seen him, but felt he should have done. He had also forgotten to fill-in details of another incident outside a classroom at the beginning of a lesson. There had been a fight between two boys who were being slow at getting to lessons.

Incident 2

The incident took place on Wednesday, 3rd November, period 6. The class was a third band class in fifth-year. There were sixteen boys in the class. Two boys were involved, Christopher Praha, and Alan Thorn. The teacher was highly experienced.

Written Report
'Two boys mentioned arrived at class, then wanted to wander off (until the rest of the group arrived) to fool about in corridors. Pretexts: to fetch a book, to go to the toilet. I said if they left the room they would stay out. I felt that immediate confrontation was appropriate here as these two are particularly wilful (especially Thorn). When they returned I sent them, despite protests and threats from them, to the Hall — as per procedure.'

The teacher mentioned this incident to the deputy head, at the end of the day.

Interview
'This has happened before, but this is the first time I've put my foot down. The whole class is delinquescent. Thorn is very aggressive. A couple of weeks ago he attacked a teacher. One says: "Let's save confrontation for an important time." They were more boorish and arrogant than usual. Knowing I had fifth-year all afternoon, I might have unconsciously stiffened the sinews, and summoned up the blood. You have to allow yourself the opportunity to back down. You learn this early on in teaching. *They* have to be given a chance to back down. Sometimes they are disruptive as an offshoot of a non-disruptive, undeliberate disruption. So few of them come into the room (except boys like Thorn), determined to cause trouble, to "mess him about". Things build up so quickly. They might come into the room shouting to friends. You say "You were shouting!" "No, I'm not!" "Yes you are!" (Lesson changes create difficulties.) It doesn't help to have them charging around the room every thirty minutes. Every lesson change is another break for them. Every couple of yards along the corridor they have a rough and tumble.
    However long you teach, you can't divorce yourself from your own grammar school education, where you sat in rows, in a formal situation, where the teacher was in charge of the class and it was very womb-like. One tries not to set-up false standards, expect them to behave like grammar school boys. I can't help wishing that they would be. It seems much easier to teach that way. The teacher's task, role, was so much easier.'

Incident 3

The incident took place on Wednesday, 3rd November, during period 8. The Class was a third band, fifth-year set, in which there were eighteen boys. One boy was involved, Richard Link. The incident lasted two to three minutes. The teacher was inexperienced.

Written Report
'Link was sent out because he was talking during a reading lesson and interrupting the progress of the play.'

Interview
'The boys had roles; four were reading. This is a very rowdy class with me. I try to vary my tactics. I try to browbeat them for a couple of weeks, then I change to another tactic, such as sending them out. This is the second sending out in the last two weeks.'

Incidents 4 and 5: Both incidents were reported by the same teacher, on the same day, Thursday, 4th November. The teacher was inexperienced and the class was the same in both incidents.

Incident 4

The incident took place during period 4. The class was a top band, fifth-year class, in which there were twenty-eight boys. A group of three was involved: Pritchard, Dohni and Ranu.

Written Report
'I sent Pritchard to the Hall for telling me where I could go. This was after I spent a long time trying to keep him, and the rest of the form, working rather than larking about (kicking over chairs, annoying one another, chattering, etc.) My argument with him revolved round whether he should stop playing with his scarf or not. This was a double lesson when the class should have been writing an essay.'

The teacher talked about the incident, and the class generally, with a head of year.

Incident 5

The incident took place during period 8. Class and teacher were the same as for incident four. Two boys were involved, Sketchley and Plant.

Written Report

'Sketchley was sent to the Hall for being surly, at the beginning of the lesson. Plant was given detention for scrapping with another boy just after the lesson ended.'

Incidents 6 and 7 were reported by the same teacher, on the same day.

Incident 6

The incident took place first period on Monday morning, 7th February. The class was a third band class in fifth-year. There were eight boys in the class for a double lesson. The incident was 'drawn out' and involved one boy: O'Riorder. The teacher was inexperienced.

Written Report

'O'Riorder seems to go out of his way to be thrown out of my lessons — he will make a noise, disturb other people, refuse to work, start a squabble, anything in fact. This happens nearly every Monday (I only have O'Riorder then, but have the others for five periods) and this week was no exception. As usual, others got involved — mainly because he annoyed them too much and the general atmosphere was not one of work. I sent O'Riorder out at 10:05 for cheek to me — the immediate result was an improvement as the rest settled down.

Minor problems also included Docker and Fillimore ariving late, and what I regard as 'start of week boisterous behaviour' by Orr, Gold and Lomas. Not really a problem.'

Incident 7

This incident was reported by the same teacher as was involved in incident 6, on the same day. The class was a third band, fourth-year class and again it was a double lesson, periods 6 and 7. There were twelve boys in the class, and five of these were involved in the incident, which lasted through the double lesson.

Written Report
'Five boys sat as a group at the back, something I have objected to
before, and decided to stop. They refused to move point blank after
being asked, then told, several times. They then spent the whole double
lesson making a noise, being rude, obscene, etc and did no work. I
reported the incident to the head of year, and as an exception to my
usual views, asked for them to be caned which shows how annoyed I
was. The matter was taken to the deputy head on Tuesday morning and
he caned them.'

Incident 8
The incident took place on Monday, 7th February, period 6. The class
was a second and, fourth-year class, with twenty-four boys in it, for
a double lesson. One boy was involved, John Pridie. The teacher was
experienced.

Written Report
'There was persistent refusal to settle to work — moving around the
room, shouting to others, etc.'

Interview
'By persistent refusal I mean persistent in previous lessons and in this.
He was suspended from his previous school. He has been in trouble with
the police. He's a very difficult boy with some. We've taken an instant
dislike to each other. I used to have him for ten periods a week. If he
is suspended again, he will go before the courts. If it's a personality
clash . . . It's a voluble group as a whole. If I ignored it, it would continue. The incident was minor *but* it had happened before.'

The boy was sent to the Hall, and the incident mentioned to the deputy
head. The incident was dealt with in conjunction with three further com-
plaints from other members of staff, within two days. One of these was
reported to the researchers. It involved a very experienced teacher who
complained of Pridie's 'Refusal to work or to be quiet; general insolence
and insubordination'.
    The senior staff report on these incidents stated 'Awkwardness in
class. Sent out of class. Unruly behaviour/attention seeking/disruption

coming after light punishment in court last week for taking and driving away a car. Deputy Head was told by boy that he would not accept cane. Taken to Headmaster 10th February. Cane again refused. Boy suspended.'

Incident 9

The incident occurred on Monday, 7th February, period 7. The class was a third band, fourth-year class, with ten pupils in it. It lasted three minutes and involved one boy, Spencer Mitcham. The teacher was inexperienced.

Written Report

'He would not shut up during an aural comprehension. Whistled, hummed, etc., deliberately. Seems to have a Pavlovian response to lessons at times, where he creates a barrage of noise to drown out my voice. Eventually, after repeated warnings, pleas, etc, I sent him into the Hall to sign the deputy head's book.' (A head of year saw the boy in the corridor and sent him to sign the book).

Interview

'There was a confrontation (a potential fight) early in the lesson between Spencer Mitcham and Paul Simon. I wanted to avoid a fight, especially as there had been one some weeks ago. (Paul Simon was attacked by fifth-year in a snowball fight.)

This incident is typical. Some days he's like this. That group are usually fighting.'

Incident 10

The incident occurred on Monday, 7th February, period 6. The class was a fifth-year, second band class with ten pupils in it. The incident built-up over the double lesson, into a two-minute episode. It involved one boy, Jack Broggs. The teacher, who was experienced, informed the head of the year of the boy's rudeness, etc. She expressed a wish to discuss the incident with the researchers.

Written Report

'The boy refused to work for the first twenty minutes. After repeatedly urging him to do so, I decided to ignore him. He decided after a few minutes to talk to some of the others, throw paper, whistle, move desk noisily, etc. When reprimanded he was very rude in his manner. (He is skilled at being very offensive without saying anything that can be defined!) Three minutes before the end of class I told him to leave, which blew up into a worse episode.'

Interview

'He was late arriving. When (after the first twenty minutes) I decided to ignore him, he said he had stomach ache. I was rude about it. When I told him to leave the class he went past my desk. I told him to go the other way. I pulled him. He was very rude. This was really a minor incident.' (N.B. The teacher also called it serious, on her form.) 'One boy in the class who is leaving at Easter is also a problem. I intervened when Broggs interfered with the others. He has only just returned after absence. He was very rude to me. He joined the school late — transferred. I haven't asked for a detention.'

Incident 11

The incident occurred on Monday, 7th February, period 3, in a second band, fourth-year class, with twenty-six boys in it. The teacher was inexperienced. He mentioned the incident to his head of department. It involved all of the class.

Written Report

'On collecting the equipment, I found some items missing. No-one would admit to having them and therefore the whole class was put on a late detention and told they would have to pay a small sum of money each to cover the cost of replacements. This meant a delay in dismissing the class and allowing the next class into the room, and lack of equipment for the next class.'

Incident 12

The incident occurred on Monday, 7th February, period 2, in a second band, fifth-year class, with twenty-six boys in it. The teacher was highly experienced. It lasted ten to fifteen minutes and two boys were involved: Kraft and Kelley, Kraft was sent to the Deputy Head.

Written Report

'Constant talking — no work done. Kraft discovered eating packed lunch sandwiches.'

Incident 13

The following incident occurred on 7th February and was reported by head of year only. There was no report from the teacher concerned. He was inexperienced. The teacher asked the boy to leave the class.

Written Report

'Third instance of this, this term. Detention 10th February after contact with home on "phone". Boy is in care and I heard comments on changeover of houseparents, its effect on boy and details of his current behaviour, which is improving, but has a long way to go yet.'

Comments on incidents/interviews with children
Some reflections on the thirteen incidents

From these incidents, it seems legitimate to distil the following 'do's and don'ts' for teachers, and school administrators:

1. Try to nip the incident in the bud. It won't always work but it might help. In incident one the teacher sensed a problem was brewing up, and had spoken to Skreel about verbally intimading Mitchell. Could he have done more? (Moved his place? Warned him off?)

2. Be alert as to how you are feeling. Try not to over-react because you are in a mood. (Incident 2).

3. Those preparing the school time-table should space out periods with the same class. Seeing the same group several times in the same day can cause problems, particularly with potentially difficult classes (Incident 2).

4. If you decide to have a confrontation, do it on your own grounds rather than being precipitated into it by events. And know exactly what you are going to do about it (Incident 2).

5. The school needs to develop carefully its policy with regard to lesson changes (Incident 2). It has an important implication for behaviour both during lessons and during the changeover itself.

6. Where a child is becoming a persistent nuisance over a period of several lessons, the teacher should try to speak with him outside lesson-time about the situation, its roots and ways of averting further trouble (Incident 6).

7. Where a group of pupils present as a problem, tactics should be sought which take account of group dynamics, e.g. that the group will 'close-up' if reprimanded as a group (Incident 7). Did the group have a leader or leaders whose co-operation could have been won? Could a classroom activity have led to the formation of an alternative grouping? Could the teacher have moved his position so that these boys were no longer 'at the back'? Could the group have been involved in a useful task? These were some of the questions the teacher should have been asking of himself. He had had time in which to do so, since he says it is not the first time the same problem had arisen.

8. The teacher should try to avoid becoming personally involved to the point where he says of a child, 'We've taken an instant dislike to each other', and must avoid stigmatising a pupil by reference to his past school history, and delinquency record (Incident 8).

9. Schools should wherever possible avoid telling staff of pupils' previous suspension from a school. In Incident 8 it sounds as though the school had good intentions, in warning staff that a further suspension could be critical for the boy in question, but that the information may have fuelled the teacher's dislike of the boy and may actually have contributed to his ultimate suspension.

10. Schools must avoid over-rigid sanction structures (Incident 8). This school operated a series of structures which inevitably led to a large number of suspensions. One sees the need for clarity and firmness

of a system, but the possibility of the exercise of discretion must be there.

11. It is sometimes possible to defuse situations by using humour — cracking a joke, which has an underlying control message. In Incident 9, the teacher had warned and pleaded with Spencer. This had not worked. One wonders what effect the teacher might have had, if he had said to the class, 'I hold whistling and humming lessons at 4:15 pm. . .!' Admittedly the teacher's anxiety about avoiding a fight may have made him unlikely to use a humour-based tactic.

12. It is difficult to know how truthful a pupil is being, when he gives an excuse such as 'stomach-ache' for his behaviour. He could be given the benefit of the doubt; in any case a rude response from the teacher, is unlikely to improve the situation, if it is becoming tricky (Incident 10). Pushing or pulling a pupil, as in the same incident, is equally provocative and together the rudeness and physical handling could account for it '(blowing up) into a worse episode'.

13. Missing equipment can constitute a taxing problem. It is wisest if possible to delay the imputation of theft (Incident 11), to allow pupils time to return the items. Once theft is implied, resistances arise, and admission of guilt is hardly possible in front of the whole class. Opportunity for individuals to 'find' the items, while the teacher is out of the room, is sometimes helpful, as group pressure can be exerted in his absence.

14. Food often figures in disruptive incidents! Some teachers get very angry at the consumption of food during lessons, etc. One wonders why what some would regard as harmless and slightly humorous behaviour should be regarded so seriously. That it 'makes a mess' may be so. That it infringes a school rule is generally true. But as we are a nation of nibblers, one wonders whether quite so much fuss needs to be made . . .

15. Incident 13, about the behaviour of a boy in care, going through a change in houseparents points to the context of the child's life outside school — and indeed the teacher's life outside school as the background against which disruptive incidents in school need to be seen.

8 CHILDREN AND DISRUPTION

The research reported here takes the school as its focus, rather than the disruptive child. The reason for this — that disruptive behaviour in a school is more than just its highly disruptive pupils — is well illustrated by Table Eight which shows that only four boys in the project were involved in as many as four incidents in the two weeks, whereas as many as fifty-eight figured in just one incident.

TABLE EIGHT: (Project)	
NO OF INCIDENTS	NO OF BOYS
1	58
2	18
3	7
4	4

The transitory nature of much minor disruptiveness is again illustrated by the fact that the number of boys involved in at least one incident in both weeks was only seven. This is interesting in showing that with a gap of three months between the two weeks under study, with the exception of only seven boys, the second week threw up a different group of boys involved in disruption from the first.

A large number of boys was involved: eighty-seven boys, i.e. 15% of the boys on roll (taking 585 as the average number on roll over the two weeks) were mentioned by name in connection with one or more incidents. There was a wide range of variation in the number of boys in each band who were mentioned (Table Nine), which again suggests a relationship between school factors such as grouping and curriculum and misbehaviour.

There was plenty of evidence that among the children taking part in incidents were many with adverse background factors. Thus in the Project indications of poverty and other stresses upon the boys were plentiful. Sometimes staff suspected these, rather than being certain of them. In all some form of background stress was mentioned in thirty-three cases, i.e. 38% and this figure is almost certainly an underestimate.

Stresses include the recent death of a father, after a long illness, father's unemployment, chronic parental or sibling's illness, being in care and being thrown out of home.

TABLE NINE: (Project)		
	Year and Band	No of Incidents
(4 = 14-15 year olds)	4_1	9
	4_2	5
	4_3	25
(5 = 15-16 year olds)	5_1	7
	5_2	20
	5_3	21

Only three fifth-year boys were mentioned as having been recommended for special educational treatment. This small number is probably attributable to the school being a senior high school, catering for boys at an age by which time such referrals, if they are going to be made, have usually already taken place.

In the Dialogue, of the sixty-eight pupils who were named a number (9) were said to have appeared in court, charged with an offence. This number may be an underestimate as one member of staff preferred not to divulge this information. Seven of the children had been referred for Child Guidance, and two for special educational treatment outside that offered by the school in terms of remedial teaching or sanctuary place provision. Eleven were thought to be under stress at home. The stress varied from particularly strict parents, being kept at home by a sister to look after her child, to lack of a father-figure, or mother receiving psychiatric help in a family where divorce was imminent.

In the same school staff were asked for their impression as to how the intelligence of the child involved in an incident compared with that of other children at the school, on a five-point scale ranging from Very High to Well Below Average. During the Autumn Term a senior member of staff had suggested that information on this point should be gathered, to examine his impression that many 'disrupters' were children slightly below average in intelligence for the school. The results, although skewed as it was not possible to rate whole classes, are given in Table Ten.

TABLE TEN: Dialogue	
Intelligence Relative to the School	**No of Pupils**
Very High Intelligence	—
High	12
Average	32
Below Average	13
Well Below Average	8

Staff were also asked, if they could, to offer an explanation or reason for the incident pupils' disruptive behaviour and a large number of very interesting suggestions were made, as follows:

(a)   *Personality reasons*
Dislikes authority
Strongwilled
Emotional — uncontrollable
Moodiness
Temper, needing little provocation
Argumentative
Likes to feel big, 'gets kicks from being one of the wild characters'
Maladjustment
Cultural arrogance? He feels too aloof

(b)   *Reasons relating to work in the school*
Needs to feel a person of worth
Inability to cope with lessons
Frustration at not being able to read
Limited in concentration
Not liking the work
The system
The failure of the Primary School to deal early with truancy
Bored with lessons. Bored with school
Not entered for exams
Recent arrival in School

(c)   **Developmental reasons**
Childishness
Immaturity and laziness
Obesity
Low intelligence
At the awkward, adolescent stage
She is tiny, so won't be put upon
Just physical; enjoys pushing and shoving

(d)   **Random reasons**
Just naughty
Likes to stir it a bit
He thinks he's better than he is; he's very proud
Wants an exciting life. Has a sense of adventure
One-parent family
Gets very firm handling at home, so when people reason at school
    he thinks them weak

(e)   **Friends**
Friends lead him/her into trouble

Of all these explanations, the most frequently mentioned were temper, inability to cope with lessons, frustration at not being able to read, limited in concentration, low intelligence and friends lead him/her into trouble.

The above list was compiled from statements by senior staff relating to the children actually named in incidents, but in addition, in the course of the seventy staff interviews a good deal of reference was made to causes of disruptive behaviour relating to children thus:

(a)   *Lack of intelligence/reasoning ability* was seen as explaining some disruptive behaviour:

> 'A lot of the weakest children can be totally unreasonable. Some of our younger children a few years ago would have been in a special school.'

The teacher here is suggesting, quite correctly, that the current trend is for the integration of the handicapped child into the normal school, and that handicapped children by virtue of very low intelligence can be 'difficult' — in his term 'unreasonable'.

(b)   Home problems — Where home problems were seen as being conducive to disruptive behaviour, there was often something of a sigh, suggesting that these were not readily amenable to change, or a recommendation that contact be made with the home. On suggestions for strategies:

> I just don't know at this stage — I really don't. It seems to be a problem not just of schools. One has all sorts of thoughts — about parents, about parents working (I'm one) but one can't change this way of things now.
>
> So many of them come from difficult homes. The school is S.P.A. There are lots of one-parent families.
>
> Exhibitionist behaviour I find *very* annoying. We get that here quite a lot, because they come from deprived homes.
>
> The child who is tired and dispirited after too many home chores.
>
> Lack of backing from parents . . . who have washed their hands of their children.

In considering the effect of parental deprivation and the disadvantaged home, on the behaviour and performance of their pupils, teachers have a real dilemma. Clearly in some cases the former may be critical and will account for the child's behaviour, but in other cases, they may be far less important and overestimation of their effect will lead the teacher to have low, detrimental, expectations of the child in the classroom, etc.

(c)   Unsatisfied needs — Occasionally one explanation of disruptive behaviour offered was in terms of unsatisfied needs, e.g. cases where the child is lonely and therefore tries to attract attention through bad behaviour:

> What I find hardest is making children conform to rules when they are being disruptive — anti-social that is — when I know the disruptive behaviour would not occur if needs were being met. I'm put in a wasteful, authoritarian position — that I find very hard, frustrating.
>
> One boy has special English and he comes in to the others . . . he's aware he's lonely and he tries to attract attention.
>
> Disruption is the kids' survival mechanism.
>
> Fifty-three applied to Firm X; only three passed and one was offered a job.

The above teacher comments show clearly the compassion of these teachers for their pupils and how far they have gone towards viewing disruption from the perspective of the child — the child who is lonely, the child who is suffering, only just 'surviving', and the youth who faces unemployment when he leaves school.

(d)   Boisterousness as a reaction to being controlled — There were occasional references to disruptive behaviour such as boisterousness being the result of an over-controlling regime, whether at home or at school.

> Others tend to be very boisterous; the school is terribly bureaucratic, controlling, controlling, controlling.

> For West Indians it's a response to being held on a tight lead in the family. They're not given enough freedom at home . . . when they come here they erupt. Parents feel it's the teacher's fault. The child senses the teacher is a different animal — a response to freedom.

> Asians are now getting boisterous.

The use of the term 'boisterousness' here is interesting. Though it is regarded as a form of disruptive behaviour, it is seen to have a 'natural' quality being a response to a restriction of freedom. Again, these teachers are trying to take a pupil perspective on the behaviour.

(e)   Not knowing who the teacher is — This was mentioned by many staff in different contexts, as giving rise to some disruptive behaviour. It was offered as an explanation of children's hostile reactions to supply staff, and to teachers new to the school, and also of strongly aggressive reactions, e.g. in corridors, where a pupil is questioned or reprimanded by a teacher who has not taught him.

On solutions:

> The only thing is time — when they get to know you it's O.K.

Comment on an intervention into a fight:

> Within seconds about sixty or eighty had gathered round. Because I was known I was able to get (here) into a room. If I hadn't been here for X years, the situation would have got out of hand.

> The class needs to know *who* the teacher is, where he comes from.

There is clear relevance in these comments to the much-debated issue of size of school, in relation to disruptive behaviour. At its baldest, the issue takes the form of the question, 'Has the growth of large comprehensive schools led to a deterioration of behaviour'. These teachers' comments suggest that within such schools, efforts must be made to combat the problem of teachers and children not *knowing* each other, and that staff stability can help.

(f)   Problems of identity — The relationship between identity problems for some ethnic minority and mixed race children is dealt with later (pp.105-6). In addition, the relationship was pointed out between some disruptiveness in senior school pupils and the absence of acceptable adult figures with whom they could identify.

One teacher thought that it would help, in connection with this, to invite successful former pupils in to talk to groups, as these young adults could provide suitable such figures.

(g)   The chemistry of the classroom — was mentioned by one or two staff as giving rise to behaviour problems, i.e. the coming together of children and staff with incompatible personalities:

> Certain kids in some rooms and with some teachers provide a volatile mix.

It is interesting that although the teacher-pupil personality clash referred to in this comment is very common, and teachers accept the possibility as a fact of school life, there is little open reference in school to the related phenomenon of certain teachers being better teachers with certain children. Certainly Thelen's (1967) thesis of 'Teachability' as being a possible basis for the organisation of teaching groups has evoked even less interest and take-up in England than in the USA, as far as one can gather.

From the dialogue interviews with staff, there emerged a fascinating picture of the types of child behaviour, and the types of children which some of the teachers were finding the most difficult to cope with. Once again the teachers statements are quoted verbatim, for the sake of vividness and explicitness.

● **Types of behaviour**

> What I find most disruptive is talking — continual talking . . . giggling, joking, getting up and walking round, other children barging in . . .

. . . noise, running, shouting, fighting . . .

. . . noise, loud talking, talking back, tendency to argue.

Inability to concentrate, joking, laughing.

Unco-operativeness which wears you down; apathy, aggressive churlishness.

(a)   *Blank defiance* — Blunt refusal by a child to do as told or asked constituted a problem for a good many staff:

What I find the hardest to deal with is silent insolence.

I find hardest to deal with the open way in which they defy you . . . ignoring you. If you tell someone to do something, they'll just go on with what they're doing. You can't physically make someone do it. They treat you with utter contempt.

What I find the hardest to deal with is when I ask them to do something and the child says NO! Then I spring into action and I pursue him.

Outright defiance makes me the maddest.

Of dumb insolence: 'There is a West Indian attitude involved in this behaviour' . . . this is sheer hunch.

People who are blatantly rude; usually they are the non-participants who I can't send anywhere else.

No real sense of fear and certainly no respect for teachers in general — or the headmaster.

Sheer bloody-mindedness at times.

In these comments two threads are discernible: firstly, the child is seen as bringing the situation to the point of confrontation; there is an 'absolute' quality in his behaviour, and secondly, the child is seen as bruising and wounding the teacher as a person.

(b)   *Rejection of reasoning* — Often staff referred to the failure of their attempt to reason with particular children as being particularly frustrating:

What I find most disruptive is when you get a torrent of abuse then the child just wanders off — you can't reason with him or pacify him.

Here the teacher sees the child as beyond all normal means of control. The child himself is not within his own control thus this abuse has broken its bounds, it is a 'torrent', and the hopelessness of the situation is expressed by the random nature of the child's exit: he 'just wanders off'.

(c)   Noise — Unacceptable noise levels constitute a problem to a number of staff.

> What I find most disruptive is the general level of noise, especially at lesson change. When I chastise, pupils can be surly; this forces confrontation.

> Noise in corridors and round school disrupts and offends me as a person.

> It's a problem across the board — so many of the children are noisy, so that it's difficult to deal with . . . once noise is a problem with some children, it spreads.

Noise as a phenomenon in schools has not been studied, yet it is integral to school life, and figures importantly in disruptive behaviour. It is teacher tolerance, and teacher and pupil perception of noise levels and noise differences, in different contexts, which would be particularly interesting to consider.

(d)   Physical violence — There were a number of references to acts of physical violence between pupils, and occasionally by pupil against teacher; in the latter cases including one or two senior teachers, and incidents in which a teacher intervened to prevent fighting between pupils.

> What I define as disruptive behaviour here is when certain individual children go out to attack others in an unpremeditated attack.

> They wait for you to put your hands on them . . .

> Four to five months ago assaults on staff . . . were often retaliatory . . . almost all were reactions to teachers' initial approach.

> Fight outside school . . . immediately 50-60 children gathered round . . .

> Giving the birthday bumps so that they hurt is common.

Very often the layman interprets 'disruptive behaviour' as simply synonymous with 'physical violence', partly of course because of its presentation by the media. The reality in school may be different. As this chapter makes clear, physical violence is one type of disruptive behaviour, regarded as very serious, but not necessarily or always causing the greatest 'difficulty' to all teachers, though sometimes it did. See under bully-boys (and girls) pages 107-7.

(e) **Threat** — There were one or two quoted instances of a pupil issuing a threat to a teacher, or to another pupil.

> The children have threatened me twice . . . to 'do me' outside school. A well-known disruptive said I'd soon regret coming into teaching — and proceeded to disrupt the class.

> Children are intimidated by threats in the corridor.

> Has arisen with expelled boys and those who have left . . . boy under influence of drugs threatened staff — was abducting a white girl under duress.

(f) **Theft** — The need to protect money and property against theft was mentioned by some staff, as commonly accepted.

> I was warned on coming here that I must lock doors. Things are stolen.

> It flows over into classrooms — the boy who steals comes with a guilty conscience, the boy who loses bears a resentment.

> You can't leave your bag unattended. You have to look to the safety of your personal possessions.

There is now solid research evidence (Belson, 1975) pointing to the common nature of theft among — for example — inner-city schoolboys. As Chapter Eleven makes clear, the empty classrooms found in many schools testify to its prevalence. In Cohen's terms (1979) schools have learnt to adjust to this form of deviance.

(g) **'Taxing'** — There was some mention of this, as a practice in which the property 'stolen' from a child can be redeemed on payment of a 'tax'.

> Taxing is generally acknowledged in the school — that is, stealing and offering back articles for sale.

> . . . a boy . . . had an expensive watch removed by another boy — he was told he could buy it back — 'the going rate is £10'. The boy who took the watch passed it off as 'a joke'. But within two minutes of restoring the watch to its owner, it was again removed in the corridor.

Here the teacher is faced with dealing with a sophisticated form of blackmail.

(h) **Graffiti and vandalism** — it was unusual for graffiti to constitute a significant problem. There was only one instance of this, where an incident involving graffiti 'washed over' into a lesson:

> I've had my day today disrupted by graffiti outside my room.
>
> Every morning we wipe it off (graffiti). Sometimes there are spates. Outside we can't cope.
>
> Toilets get blocked up with tin cans and coats . . . spate of breaking ceiling panels. Wash basins. We replace windows quickly.

It is interesting to compare the great importance attached to vandalism by the media, and by some researchers into disruptive behaviour with its relative lack of importance to teachers, compared with other phenomena. Clearly, for education authorities the cost of vandalism makes it prominent, and for researchers its visibility leads to ease of data collection.

(i)   Verbal abuse — This type of behaviour, from pupil to staff was found to be particularly shocking to a large number of teachers.

> What I define as disruptive behaviour at this school is noise — the way they shout and swear in corridors and at teachers. When you say: 'Quieten down' they look at you as though you'd just crawled out from under a stone.
>
> They'll turn round and swear at you. They can be very abusive.
>
> What I find most disruptive is verbal or physical aggression whether for 'sociological' or emotional reasons.
>
> The child who comes into the class looking for a battle. It starts in this way, angling for a confrontation.

In view of the current and progressive dilution of the strength of four-lettered words among large sections of the population, it may be that in some cases teachers overestimate the abusiveness of the language they are hearing.

(j)   Lack of concentration — This was very worrying to some teachers.

> They have the intelligence but just don't concentrate.

Lack of concentration in a difficult pupil can be a critical factor for some teachers, in their response to the pupil as a whole. It is as though the child is out of the teacher's control, in relation to the work situation, and this rouses the anxiety in the teacher.

(k) **Boisterousness** — General boisterousness was acknowledged as a problem by a number of staff.

> Shouting and bouncing around are the greatest problems.

> . . . it could be inability to sit down — for more than five minutes — physical incapacity to sit down.

> Corridor behaviour is noisy, playful — it's their way of life. The second years are the worst.

(l) **The child who won't answer** — Refusal to answer could present a problem. Clearly this would sometimes be akin to 'blank defiance' (a) and 'rejection of reason' (b).

(m) **No respect for persons** — This was seen as underlying behaviours such as a child not holding back a swing door, for someone going through it after him.

> The manners are atrocious. Rarely does a child notice you are going through a door. It's quite frightening to go down stairs between lessons . . . a tornado.

> What I find the hardest to deal with is the answering back. They just take no notice of you, they don't want to know.

> Personally, in teaching, and mentally, what upsets me is the way the pupils can't accept that the teacher has more experience of life, and knows what is best for them. At twelve or thirteen they think the teacher can't tell them anything — won't take advice.

> Outside the classroom is the most disturbing. The running, jostling, noisy behaviour as if they are unaware of one another.

> The child swears at me when I speak about behaviour in the corridor, and runs away, knowing I am unsure of his identity.

> I try to use basic politeness, but it doesn't work. There is no respect for a person, most of all for each other.

In these comments we see poignantly the regrets of teachers that they should be disregarded by children, thought to be of no account, not worthy of respect. Clearly the teacher will by virtue of his profession and his reasons for joining it, view himself as deserving of esteem and respect, so that the absence of these in given situations will be particularly painful to him.

● Types of children

> It's not a type of behaviour, but the personality behind the behaviour which is hard to deal with.

(a)   The emotionally maladjusted child — The concept of emotional maladjustment or disturbance was one commonly used to describe certain children.

> What I find the hardest to deal with is seriously disturbed children who can't see that their behaviour is unreasonable.

> For me, the most disruptive and the hardest to deal with in the classroom is the emotionally disturbed child, requiring constant attention (I've got one) . . . her disruption affects the others and it affects me. She can't be excluded, for special education, as she hasn't been through the psychological channels.

It is accepted that there are a significant numbers (twenty percent according to Warnock, 1981) of children with special educational needs including children diagnosed or diagnosable as maladjusted who are and can be educated in ordinary schools. Important questions of the psychological and practical support available to the teachers in those schools need, however, to be answered. Can the staffs of special schools in the neighbourhood act as a training resource, for example?

(b)   Underachievers — Regret was expressed for children not achieving to the limit of their potential so that this led to their disruptive behaviour.

> Many of the children here underachieve, can't gain attention through their work, and seek it through standing out in class, being noisy and so on. This covers most pupils.

> The underachievers are the most disruptive . . . the low-intelligence disruptive may get the stick at home, but withdrawal of the stick at school and lack of success in the classroom leads to big problems.

> Discipline matters are related to the ability range. So many cannot seem to grasp basic rudiments, even at fifteen.

> Too many domestic responsibilities. They are tired, dispirited before they come to school in the morning.

> Low achievers are made to feel bad . . . they're devalued.

> . . . a fault of mixed ability; the hardest part is those who get left behind. All a matter of the three R's. They can't read.

> In the first year I can identify the disrupters . . . thirty-nine have reading ages of eight (twenty under seven) and they can't cope with my subject.

Clearly the relationship between disruptive behaviour and under-achievement and learning difficulties is of the greatest importance to teachers, even though in some cases the disruptive behaviour may precede the learning difficulties, since it points, for example, to a relatively straightforward way of reducing the behavioural problem. If the school helps the child to learn successfully and to progress, improved self-esteem and security in the learning situation may lead to improved conduct. It is in this context that cut-backs in staffing which lead to cut-backs in remedial teaching (many remedial teachers work part-time and are among the first to go) need to be seen.

(c) *Some fifth-year pupils* who were presenting behaviour problems were seen as threatening the examination success of their peers.

> I'm worried about the fifth-formers whose work is being disturbed by a small group.

> The disillusioned fifth-former, disenchanted with school and much else. Apathy can be catching so I work at it. Successful sometimes.

> The fifth-year has 266 kids, of these perhaps two or three are real problems.

> They get the 'X school feel' worst in the fourth-year. In the fifth they feel a pang of conscience.

> . . . biggest problem is fifth-year boys running riot in the school. Some of these feel rejected across the board.

In both this study and the Project study it was clear that disruptive behaviour in senior classes was affected by pupils who knew either that they had not been entered for external examinations (CSE etc) or would not be entered because they were not deemed to be good enough. It remains to be seen whether the introduction of a bigger component of vocational orientation into the work of senior classes will improve this situation.

(d) *Mixed-race children* — An interesting suggestion was made, that some children of mixed race were engaged in disruptive behaviour par-ticularly with certain teachers (of similar/dissimilar, sex, type and racial

origin) because of identity problems (e.g. tall, heavily built West Indian boy with tall, heavily built West Indian father and petite Irish mother).

> Some of our kids are mixed-up — half-caste kids identify with blacks in lower school, then change friends in upper school.

> Teachers need to talk to these children about their mixed race, individually — to tell them how well they can do, and so on . . . these children have to accept themselves as people of worth.

On a related point there is a little research evidence suggesting that mixed-race Asian youths show delinquency rates which are higher than the commonly low rates among Asian youths. Given that we can look forward to an increase in the numbers of children of mixed race, the counselling needs of such children will require consideration.

(e)   West Indian children's problems — The general problem of whether to identify with black or white heroes/culture was seen as predisposing some black children, especially West Indians, to engage in disruptive behaviour. Employment prospects and racial prejudice affect them too:

> What goes on outside school at home etc; black kids who go off; their willingness to learn dissipates. Motivation goes when they see what happens to their brothers and sisters; for West Indians learning becomes redundant. Asian kids keep their willingness to learn.

> West Indians are different in temperament; aggressive and loud . . . express a different life style; we have to know more about their cultures. Are we trying to turn them into our ideal?

> West Indians are sensitive to touch.

> West Indians are a problem; volatile, lackadaisical, casual. 'Is it inborn?' . . . a lot were lively and noisy; reacts differently when disciplined, 'confronts you back', a definite skill required for handling.

In the light of the Rampton (Swann, 1981) Report, one wonders to what extent it is fair to regard some of these statements as 'implicitly racist'. Further consideration of these issues is given in the section: 'Disruptive Behaviour and Some Multi-Ethnic Considerations'.

(f)   Bully-boys (and girls) — These were seen as presenting something of an 'ultimate' problem, because they were physically frightening to even very senior staff.

There are some very big boys . . . I would land in hospital if I antagonis-
ed them. So I leave them and they do nothing . . . no work at all . . .
I have felt like an animal in a cage, with other animals about to attack me.

The real disrupters menace teachers, they're the bully boys — or girls!
They shout teachers down; you cannot say a word to them.

Special problem of boys suspended and those who have left coming back
into school.

A recent study of bullies is that of Olweus (1978) in Norway. It found
five percent of the twelve-sixteen year-old sample designated as bullies
by teachers. Olweus offers a personality explanation of bullying, finding it mainly but not exclusively a boys' problem and little affected
by situational variables. He deplores physical and mental maladjustment of children in and out of schools and seeks to achieve better peer
relations in school. He favours teaching parents to use behaviour
modification reward techniques, the repudiation of bullying by school
authorities, and the use of school psychologists as consultants to teachers
with problems of bully pupils. Ultimately he sees improved child-rearing
as the 'solution'. A different American research, which teachers may
find more pertinent, is Lefkowitz's longitudinal study, *Growing up to
be Violent* (1977), which points to the effect of a preference for television violence on the development of aggression in boys and some girls.

Interviews with children

Introduction

Where an incident of disruptive behaviour occurs, in which one or more
pupils and staff figure, feelings sometimes run high, and at most any
negotiation following the incident has to be sensitively handled. It is
for this reason that a school, such as that in the Project, may not wish
for children to be interviewed, in relation to disruptive incidents, even
where these are the subject of study. In the Dialogue school, however,
permission was given for a limited number of children to be interviewed.
By interviewing a modest number only, it was hoped that 'fuss' among
pupils, in relation to the inquiry, could be avoided. Care was taken to
approach the staff involved in the incidents concerned, to explain what
was happening, and to obtain their agreement to the interview taking
place. In all cases this agreement was obtained without difficulty. Some
heads of year, who were also contacted to explain about the incident

interviews, said they considered it a valuable exercise, as an attempt to gain a pupil perspective.

The choice of pupils interviews followed the following principles:

- Only incidents involving one or two pupils would be selected, as those involving whole groups would be difficult to handle in an interview situation.

- Incidents had to occur suitably early in the week to allow for contact with the staff concerned, to obtain their agreement to the interview.

- It was hoped that both boys and girls would be interviewed, and pupils in a range of year. In the event owing to various circumstances, nine 'misbehaving' boys and only one girl were interviewed, in year 2-5, as hardly any pupils in years 1 and 6 were involved in incidents. It was also decided to aim at two sorts of information: a comparison of the incident as described by pupil and staff, and general information relating to the children's view of disruptive behaviour, in the school.

In all ten interviews were given; four 'incident comparison' interviews and six general information. Details of a number of these follow. The interviewers introduced themselves as researchers, interested in the views of children and teachers on incidents of disruptive behaviour. The incidents occurred two weeks before the interviews.

Incident 1: *Leaning on a nose*

Details given by teacher:

'Whilst getting some . . . equipment, one child "leaned" on another, causing him to knock his nose, and subsequent nose bleed. The "leaner" was then very insolent when questioned about it. He continued to refuse to work and answered back repeatedly.'

The incident was categorised as dumb insolence, refusing authority and bullying or violence to peers. It was referred to both head of department and head of year.

Interview

Boy B has been at this school for a year and a half, Boys A and C for two terms only:

Researcher:	How do you like it here?
Boy B:	I don't dislike it here. It's about the best school around — a good education, not too strict on the children. Sometimes they make you play . . .
Researcher:	What do you mean — they make you play?
Boy B:	You can tell the teachers jokes . . . you can have a good talk to them, if you have problems.
Researcher to Boy A:	Do you like it here?
Boy A:	Yes.
Researcher:	Why?
Boy A:	Because the teachers are good.
Researcher:	What do you mean?
Boy A:	Help us work.
Boy B to Researcher:	He means, they try to help you solve your problems, like our head of year, Mr X, he'll do anything what he can do to help.

At this point, it is discovered that it is boy A's twin brother Boy C, with an almost identical name, who is concerned in the incident. Boy C is fetched, and Boy A returned to his class. The first paragraph of the teacher's account is read out.

Researcher:	Is that what happened? What happened?
Boy B:	I got up, went over to his desk and I went to see what he was doing and I leaned on his head accidental. And his nose wasn't bleeding. I apologised, and he accepted it.
Boy C:	I was just writing and B came. Then I felt something . . . like . . . hitting my nose. It was the desk. Then, I went to the nurse 'cause I thought it would start bleeding.
Researcher:	Did you hear B apologise?
Boy C:	Yes.
Researcher:	Did you accept the apology?
Boy C:	Yes.

Boy C the 'victim' was excused, and left.

Researcher:	It says you were insolent. How do you feel about that?
Boy B:	I feel bad.
Researcher:	What do you mean?
Boy B:	. . . upset that they said it because it's my word against theirs. But it doesn't bother me, because it's their word against mine.
Researcher:	What does insolent mean?
Boy B:	Insolent means I'd give them lip.
Researcher:	What might you have said, for the teacher to think you'd given him lip?
Boy B:	There are lots of things I might have said for the teacher to think I gave him lip. I said 'I don't care if you give it to Mr X'?.
Researcher:	What was the 'it' "in I don't care if you give 'it' to Mr X?"
Boy B:	The letter about me not doing my work and being insolent.
Researcher:	Was that lip?
Boy B:	That's not lip.
Researcher:	It says it lasted two minutes at first and then went on through the lesson.
Boy B:	It lasted more than two minutes at first. It didn't go on through the lesson.
Researcher:	How long did it go on for?
Boy B:	I don't know how long it went on for. She took me to Mr Y first. She showed him the work and said I'd been rude and insolent. She said to him as soon as I came in, for ten or fifteen minutes, I hadn't done any work. But as soon as I got in I started. Then he questioned me and then gave me a pack of cards to do and said I must bring it back the next day. I got all of them right.
	Someone else took a note to Mr X and he said he'd see me tomorrow, and he saw me and he gave me a big piece of paper and he said do a page if I can of writing, on what I'd like for the school if I can . . .
Researcher:	What do you mean?
Boy B:	What education you'd like, what you come to school to learn. But I never done it.

In this incident we see first of all how a child who is awkward in a lesson or lessons, and is reported on for this and punished, may generously disregard this feature of his school life in his general assessment of the school saying shortly after the punishment — 'I don't dislike it here'. Indeed, he praises it, 'It's about the best school around — a good education'. He praises it for being, 'not too strict on the children'.

When the boys hear the teacher's description of the incident interesting differences are pointed to, between what the teacher and the boy saw as happening. Boy B saw his leaning on Boy C as 'accidental'; the teacher saw it as deliberate. The teacher saw the result of the leaning as 'a bleeding nose', but the injured boy went to the nurse because he thought it would start bleeding. The teacher mentions no apology, but both boys agree that not only was an apology given, but it was accepted. The guilty boy comes some way, however, towards seeing the teacher's point of view over his insolence. Although he says 'it's my word against theirs', he admits to understanding why the teacher sees him as insolent. He admits he said many things which could have contributed to the teacher's perception of him — for example, 'I don't care if you give (the letter) to Mr X'. But having admitted this, he goes on to disagree with the teacher's version of the length of the incident. Then, having poured out to the researcher his account of the consequences for him of the incident he proudly announces that, having been given an imposition to write, 'I never done it'!

Incident 2: *Running out of a classroom*

Details given by teacher

'As I was walking down the bottom corridor of Block A, a boy ran out of his form room, apparently being chased by a girl. He ran straight into my open hand which I put out to stop him. He was in an excited state and immediately became aggressive. (His head of year) . . . was a few yards behind me, saw the incident clearly and was able to reinforce my remarks to the boy. I saw him back to his form room — and intend to speak privately to the form teacher concerned.'

Interview

Researcher:	How long have you been at this school?
Boy C:	Three years.
Researcher:	How do you find it here?
Boy C:	Sometimes it's alright. Sometimes you get frustrated by teachers.
Researcher:	What do you mean by that?
Boy C:	Some teachers are not all the same — it's the way they talk to you.
Researcher:	Can you describe the way they talk?
Boy C:	Some talk nice to you and some don't. It's the way they say it that I don't like. It gets you mad when they talk to you like that.
Researcher:	Do you lose your temper?
Boy C:	Sometimes.
Researcher:	Do you lose it with teachers?
Boy C:	Not all the time . . . I don't like wearing ties.
Researcher:	Why is that?
Boy C:	Most people don't like wearing ties. They don't like being forced to do things they don't want to do.
Researcher:	Like what — apart from ties?
Boy C:	I can't really think.
Researcher:	*Reads brief details of incident (from incident sheet).* Do you remember the incident?
Boy C:	Yes — with Miss Y. I was playing with a girl and she ran after me and I ran out of the class and Miss Y was there and she tried to stop me.
Researcher:	*(Reads description of incident to him).*
Boy C:	Miss Y pushed me. She pushed me here *(points to his chest)*. She sort of used her arms to push me back.
Researcher:	*(reads)* 'He was in an excited state' . . . Is that right?
Boy C:	. . . no way in an excited state!
Researcher:	. . . and became aggressive?
Boy C:	Yes . . . if she pushed me! If she didn't push me, I wouldn't be aggressive. She didn't describe the incident right. She never said that she pushed me.

Researcher:	It lasted two minutes . . . is that right?
Boy C:	Yes . . . nothing happened to the girl.
Researcher:	Do you think something should have happened?
Boy C:	No.
Researcher:	How can you avoid these incidents? What about the rule about no running? Is it a good rule?
Boy C:	Yes.
Researcher:	You were a breaking a rule, were you?
Boy C:	Yes.
Researcher:	How could you make people stick to the rule?
Boy C:	I don't know.

This incident illustrates the 'two sides' of an incident: the teacher who is hurt when she puts out an arm to stop a boy careering down a corridor, putting others at risk through the infringement of a rule, and the boy who is running away from a girl, playfully and who sees himself as struck in the chest by the teacher's arm. When the researcher spoke to the teacher later on, it became clear that one of her reasons for regarding the incident as serious enough to report was that she had had shoulder problems previously, needing medical treatment, so that she felt herself particularly vulnerable to behaviour such as the boy's. This incident may well be typical of many, included under the heading of aggression, where a teacher's gesture either is 'aggressive' or is perceived as such, and triggers off aggressive behaviour in a pupil. Thus the boy argues 'If she didn't push me, I wouldn't be aggressive.' It also points to the tremendous speed of events, in some disruptive incidents, which open an easy way for misinterpretation to take place, and for hostility to escalate. Both teacher and boy agree on the shortness of the event: Both say it lasted two minutes. Finally, the rule aspect of the incident is interesting. The fact that he knew he was breaking a rule, had no impact on the boy in stopping him from running, even though he admits it is a good rule. Nor has he any suggestions to make, as to how the school can enforce the rule.

Incident 3: *Running around the room*

Details given by teacher

'Boy D — running around the room, shouting and waving arms about. No work done during the lesson. Refusing to sit down and work.'

The incident was categorised as talking/chatting, refusing authority, rowdy behaviour, and — the teacher added this category to the list — 'loony' behaviour. It was reported to the head of year for the purpose of punishment.

Interview

Boy D has been at this school since the beginning of first year.

Researcher:	Do you like the school?
Boy D:	Yes, it's all right.
Researcher:	What's all right about it?
Boy D:	Everything.
Researcher:	Anything special that you like?
Boy D:	I like cookery and PE and woodwork.
Researcher:	What are you good at?
Boy D:	Woodwork and cookery and PE.
Researcher:	Anything you don't like?
Boy D:	X.
Researcher:	Why?
Boy D:	The teacher, I suppose.
Researcher:	What about the teacher?
Boy D:	'Cos sometimes you forget your homework and he just slaps you round the face.
Researcher:	*Reads brief details of the incident.* Do you remember the incident?
Boy D:	Yes.
Researcher:	What happened?
Boy D:	Boy E was chasing me.
Researcher:	Why?
Boy D:	I don't know . . . he just acts stupid sometimes. He just comes up to you . . . you push him away because you know he's going to do something, then he just comes back and then you just move off from him.
Researcher:	Why couldn't you move away from him?
Boy D:	I don't sit with him. He comes up to your desk, and then he just starts trouble . . . he just starts mucking about.
Researcher:	What could you do to stop him?

Boy D:	Even if you'd have pushed him back into his seat, he would've still come back and if you tell the teacher to put him back, he'll still come back again.
Researcher:	Did Boy E get into trouble?
Boy D:	No, I don't think so.
Researcher:	Should he have done?
Boy D:	Yeh.
Researcher:	You say its all Boy E . . .?
Boy D:	Yes, that happens . . . he just acts stupid sometimes.
Researcher:	*(Reads)* Waving his arms around . . .
Boy D:	I wasn't waving my arms around . . . I was just telling Boy E to move and running away from him.
Researcher:	Your running around disturbs the lesson, doesn't it?
Boy D:	Yes.
Researcher:	Why didn't you sit down?
Boy D:	Because he'd just do something stupid.
Researcher:	What happened afterwards, in the end?
Boy D:	I was sent to Miss X and she gave us . . .
Researcher:	Who?
Boy D:	Me and this other guy from another class, some work to do, and I did it and that was it.

This incident again shows clearly the divergences of the teacher and pupil perspective. For the teacher, the problem and the guilt lie with Boy D, who has acted so badly that she needs to add the word 'loony', to describe his behaviour, to the list of behaviours offered her to tick. The number of types of behaviours ticked are an indication of the degree of her frustration. For Boy D, however, the whole of the incident is blamed on Boy E, although he does admit that his running around disturbed the lesson. For Boy D, his class-mate presents a major problem, as is well illustrated by the great detail in which he can describe Boy E's behaviour, and in which he can forecast how Boy E is likely to behave, in given situations. Thus '. . . he just acts stupid sometimes. He just comes up to you . . . you push him away because you know he's going to do something, then he just comes back and then you just move off from him'. Although in this excerpt, the boy's use of the present tense has elements of a vivid past tense in it, so that he is probably in part describing the recent incident, since he has said 'he just acts stupid sometimes' it is likely that what he is saying is meant to describe a recurring situation, likely to occur in future, as it has done in the past. Boy D feels that Boy E has a problem, is beyond even the teacher's control: 'if you tell the teacher to put him back, he'd still come back again.'

The incident shows also that pupils may not know important facts, such as whether another pupil is punished for his involvement: Boy D does not know whether Boy E got into trouble. An incident is often highly complex and those involved can easily lack significant pieces of information, which would affect their reactions to it. The conclusion of the interview is also interesting, for the boy describes the imposition he was given and says 'and I did it and that was it'. The boy seems to say that the pace of life in schools is fast, incidents come and go, and when one concludes, the door opens on fresh events.

Incident 4: *Disruptive behaviour in a cover lesson*

Details given by teacher

'I was asked to cover this lesson in an emergency — (parents to see Year Head who was teaching the class). There was no time to set work but I was able to start something on the subject which I thought could be interesting and stimulating. It was a low ability group. Boy F came to the lesson late, without writing tools, immediately began talking and moving about, destroyed the concentration of the class; had to be made to stand at back of class, where he continued to disrupt.

I sent him with a note to his head of year . . . he came back without finding either head of year or deputy. I followed the incident at break . . . discovered that this boy has a history of disruption — a very low reading age — needing remedial treatment which has been applied for and is in process of being supplied.'

The incident was categorised as extreme lateness to lessons, talking/chatting, refusing authority and rowdy behaviour.

Interview

Boy F has been at this school for three years.

Researcher:	How do you find the school?
Boy F:	Not bad . . . it's all right.
Researcher:	What's all right about it?
Boy F:	Friends.

Researcher:	Anything else?
Boy F:	No.
Researcher:	*Reads brief details of incident.* Do you remember the incident?
Boy F:	Yes.
Researcher:	What happened?
Boy F:	I was talking and had to stand up at the back of the room. That's all
Researcher:	Then what happened?
Boy F:	Nothing . . .
Researcher:	*(reads)* 'Boy F came to the lesson late'. Is that right?
Boy F:	I was at Special English.
Researcher:	Was that why you were late?
Boy F:	Yes.
Researcher:	*(reads)* 'Without writing tools' — that means pen and pencil?
Boy F:	My friend had it. I lent it to him at registration but I forgot to ask him for it.
Researcher:	*(reads)* '. . . immediately began talking and moving about'.
Boy F:	I wasn't moving about. I was only talking.
Researcher:	What about?
Boy F:	Nothing much.
Researcher:	Can you remember?
Boy F:	No.
Researcher:	*(reads)* 'It destroyed the concentration of the class.' Is that right?
Boy F:	No. I wasn't talking loud.
Researcher:	*(reads)* '. . . where he continued to disrupt'. Is that right?
Boy F:	No, I wasn't talking too loud. I was talking to someone who was sitting next to me.
Researcher:	You'd been sent to the back and went on talking, so the teacher thought you were disrupting the class again. Do you see that?
Boy F:	Yes.
Researcher:	I suppose the teacher was worried because you were interfering with the learning of the class. Is that right?

Boy F:	No. I wasn't talking loudly. No-one could hear me. Anyway, the classroom was loud — nobody was doing any work.
Researcher:	Which subjects do you like?
Boy F:	Woodwork and metalwork and TD and English.
Researcher:	Which do you not like?
Boy F:	Geography and Music
Researcher:	Do you get into much trouble?
Boy F:	I used to get into trouble in first and second year, but I don't any more.
Researcher:	Can you see it from the teacher's point of view?
Boy F:	Yes.
Researcher:	If you'd been the teacher, would you have done the same thing?
Boy F:	No.
Researcher:	Why not?
Boy F:	Because everyone was talking and I wasn't talking loudly.
Researcher:	Why do you think the teacher was like that?
Boy F:	Dunno.
Researcher:	*(Explains that the teacher was covering for another teacher)* Was the teacher fed up?
Boy F:	No, it was the first or second lesson of the day, 'cos he probably didn't take any other lessons beforehand.
Researcher:	So would you expect it to happen at the end of the day?
Boy F:	Yes.
Researcher:	When do teachers get most cross?
Boy F:	At the end of the day.
Researcher:	Had it happened to you?
Boy F:	Yes.
Researcher:	Can you give an example?
Boy F:	No.

This incident occurred in a 'cover-lesson', a lesson where the teacher was called on to teach or supervise the class, at a time when he would normally have expected to be free, either to do his own work or simply to relax in a staff-room. These facts do much to explain the teacher's feelings. What is more, he had attempted to do some real teaching in the lesson, when he could have just 'baby-minded' the class, and he had no notice that he would be called on. The parents clearly arrived without notice, and he would have had to drop what he was doing, to go into the class. The total situation was therefore likely to be one of great frustration in which relatively minor disruption might be viewed as significant.

The boy explains his lateness as being because of his Special English lesson. He may have assumed that the teacher knew of this, and not mentioned it, but of course for this lesson he had a teacher who would have had no knowledge of this special arrangement. Similarly, his arriving without a pen or pencil will have irritated the 'cover' teacher, already irritated by a late arrival, in a difficult 'emergency' teaching situation. The boy's explanation appears reasonable: he had loaned his pen or pencil to a friend and had forgotten to ask for it back, but for some reason he did not tell the teacher this, or the teacher disregarded the explanation. Again, the 'cover' nature of the lesson, with an unexpected teacher taking a boy of low intelligence may explain what happened. The boy is adamant that there was lots of noise in the room, that there was little work going on, and that therefore his talking was not 'loud' or disruptive. Furthermore, he refused to accept that the 'cover' nature of the lesson entitled the teacher to feel 'fed-up'. At the end of the interview (low 'intelligence' or not!) he shows a keen understanding of how teachers function at different times of the day. He knows from personal experience that teacher tolerance varies, depending on how much they have taught during the day, and that at the end of the day it is low, so 'watch-out'!

Incident 5: *Refusing to sit down, etc.*

Details given by teacher

'Girl G came late to the lesson, refused to sit down for no apparent reason, then proceeded to tell me not to pick on her. Sent to the Head of Year.

Forty minutes later second incident. Sudden outburst correcting me when I asked who had lost the work that I had just picked up from the floor. I was informed that I had not got it from the floor at all. Mr P arrived almost immediately afterwards and informed me that Girl G had not been to see him but she was now wanted by the head of school. Purpose of the report onwards: to remove from the situation for a short while (fourteen minutes) to allow the rest of the class to get on. Girl G has been suspended twice recently for other incidents with other people. Delights in disturbing the class when they are working. A capable girl doing excellent work in this subject in spite of these outbursts.'

Interview
'I was in the sanctuary in third year. I argued with teachers and had a fight with another girl — broke her nose. It was unfair (being sent to the sanctuary) I was the only one sent although others were involved.'

The incident . . . 'I went into the classroom . . . just came from Mr R. He'd said to me "keep cool". We (me and the teacher) don't get on — she's always complaining about me; say I go in and I'm late — she only complains about me — she is always sending me out. I must have done something — answered her back — she asked for an apology. Mr R came along — I went to his office till the end of the lesson then I went back. She asked me to behave myself. She nags a lot . . . you can't hardly talk — you can't whisper . . . if you talk you mustn't say nothing; they (teachers) do things to annoy you — she starts shouting straight away. They see you as a baddie if you won't work.

'Some say if you won't work it's your bad luck. I don't like this. They should force you. With Mr X you wouldn't think of not doing what he asked you . . . for some they don't force you.'

Incident 6: *Talking non-stop*

Details given by teacher
'Boy H came late to the class from a careers interview. He talked from the moment he came in, making it impossible for any of the group to concentrate or any systematic teaching to be undertaken.'

An incident described as 'serious' lasting forty-five minutes, and categorised as talking/chatting, extreme lateness, refusing authority. (The boy was not entered in this subject for the Certificate of Secondary Education and was therefore thought to be unsuited for public examinations.

Interview
'He (the teacher) says I'm disturbing. I was late; everyone disturbs the class. We chat quietly; he thinks everyone should be perfect. Everyone

was talking. he said: "Before you came in there was no-one". I said: "If you won't want me I'll go". We can't get along.'

Incident 7: *Abusive Language*

Details given by the teacher

'He appears at the door of the class. This time I asked him what he was doing and he says he is running messages for the year head. I checked this and found it to be the case. Not a very suitable boy to do errands, however. On leaving he said, "Stick your finger up your nose". As I know him to be odd, I didn't pursue him or comment. (A "serious" incident. Categorised as abusive or bad language). The boy did not take the mock exams. He is leaving in May, and is now on three weeks' work experience.'

Interview

'I was talking to one of my friends in the corridor — she came out — I told her to piss off — she banged the door. It was at change of lesson. I was there for about fifteen minutes. I was arguing with her. She said, "Why don't you go to your class". She sent a note to Mr X — I was bursting in on them — it's a habit. I do this. I was meant to be with Mr F. I like to see my mates. I like the fun of chasing. They take the Mickey. Some (the teachers) take it into their own hands — he (Mr Q) hits you. They all know me.'

It should come as no surprise that disruption is an emotive issue about which teachers and pupils feel deeply. Both experience it as a personal afront; one is personally demeaned. It is a personal slight involving a reflection on one's adequacy as a person. It is stressful at a number of levels, firstly at the level of the disputed which may well for the teacher act as a negation of his purpose and implicitly disvalue it. It calls into question the investment of time and effort which the teacher has put in; it may well implicitly deny the usefulness of the subject; to the extent that teachers have invested time and effort in becoming subject specialists, rejection may be perceived as personal. At the second level, to the extent that they have internalised values regarding teaching and education, rejection may also be seen as a personal afront. Hence the apparently immoderate language which is sometimes used to describe disruptive children and comparison of the teacher's role with that of a 'soldier in the front line'. It is easy to see why teachers may describe their feelings after a class as 'shell shocked' or 'being in the trenches'.

Pupils are also sensitive to any imputations which they see as personally demeaning and this emerges in the interviews. They are sensitive to being ignored or slighted. In the same way that teachers scrutinise pupil's behaviour to detect indications of intent so pupils sometimes scrutinise their teachers.

Interviews and the children's writing indicate that many have a simple and clear-cut notion of the role of teachers. Teachers should teach. Educational nuances and subtleties of role differentiation do not clutter their thinking. The good teacher is someone who makes you learn. It is not strictness or authority *per se* which they appear to resent provided these are exercised with an underlying and explicit respect for and recognition of them as persons. Authority for pupils has two dimensions; one in situations where teachers are recognised as being in the estimation of the pupil, i.e. where they teach and where the pupils' learning is recognised, and the second in situations where teachers are granted authority conditionally by pupils in recognition of a personal bond for which the pupil re-affirms their own sense of personal worth and of being accepted. Differences and misunderstandings are likely to arise in respect of both of these. Teachers view their role less simply often dismissing the notion that they could force the pupils to learn as miseducation.

The interviews with the children and a comparison of what they and their teachers say about the incident show how difficult it is in the rapid course of events in school, for both to arrive at a common perspective, and how there is a great deal of room for misunderstanding and misinterpretation to occur.

Children's Writing

The basis of our work in attempting to monitor disruption in school using an agreed broad definition, attempts to explore the subjective understandings of teachers. Other approaches have attempted to use check lists of types of disruptive behaviour to arrive at a more 'objective' account. Teachers' subjective accounts invite serious consideration for whatever a person defines as disruptive is presumably experienced as such; whilst such accounts invite the criticism that no two person's tolerance of disruption is the same nor their definition, their strength lies in tapping the depth of feeling and emotion which is connected with disruption and the range of behaviour — only some of which is officially sanctioned or sanctionable, which teachers find stressful.

By the same token, if attention to subjective meaning deserves our attention, if when teachers tell us something we take it seriously, then equally children's accounts deserve the same attention. It is true that their accounts may often be based on partial misunderstanding or knowledge, often misleading, often biased but this is true also of all accounts, whether from adult or child. Edward Blishen (1969) used children's writing as a basis of his book called *The School I'd Like.*

In the dialogue we attempted to use children's writing in a small way — to explore the very different way in which the world of school appears to them. We asked the English department to invite children in the first year to write, imagining that they were a fly on the wall of the school, detailing what they saw and experienced.

In presenting some of their work we would argue that often what is revealed by such writing is not children's ability to enter imaginatively into situations alone, but their own mixed inner feelings and experience of life for a child in the first year of secondary school. The fiction of the 'bird's or fly's' eye-view may become a vehicle for autobiographical reflection and expression. Thus the child can literally move in and out of the account he is giving, at one moment using writer's licence in the pursuit of imagination, at another integrating his own perceptions and experiences.

The picture which emerges, as one might expect, is varied, diverse and often contradictory. Other features are recurrent and persistent and it is these which in general give interest to their accounts. These common features convey a world of big boys and girls, all too often seen as threatening and frightening to a 'little fly like me'; a world of noise, of fights, of fierce teachers who hit you and give you lines and 'who always talk about children'; sometimes a world of gentle teachers, 'who allow you to sit quietly in their car' or, a world of long corridors where danger threatens and where violence erupts, of deafening sounds. Children's accounts speak best for themselves.

(a)   Teachers looked very strict and very cross . . . it was very crowded; boys and girls looked like a herd of hundreds of sheep . . . I could see a long passage . . . there was a tall girl, I flew up to her and she hit me . . .

(b)   I was in A block . . . there was a big boy . . . he was fighting with a girl so I tried to help . . . a bell rang; I thought it was a fire; in the corridor big boys tried to kill me. The only school I like is . . .

(c)   I saw a fight . . . a girl was crying . . . teacher was shouting. I flew away
       from the racket . . . teachers always talking about children . . .

(d)   I am a little fly . . . B gives me a lift and I sit in the car quietly . . . Mrs C
       goes round with a smile on his face . . . you should see the state of some
       of the kids here . . . boys normally wear their ties hanging out . . . girls
       in long skirts or kilts . . . the playtime is noisy . . . to tell the truth the
       peace and quiet is what I need and like . . . it is so quiet in the classroom
       where there is a strict teacher . . . please keep this as it took me twelve
       days and nights to do as I am only a very little fly.

(d)   Children are playing cards and running round . . . someone threw a paper
       dart . . . one child poked another with a pin . . . someone hit someone
       else over the head with a handle of a chisel . . .

(f)   Next room . . . very quiet, that's good. All of a sudden I heard
       HERAAAAAA it was the bell. It went like this three times . . . outside
       it was raining or snowing or even bad weather . . . I saw some really nasty
       writing and drawing . . .

(g)   The boy stopped in front of the nurse room . . . I knock on the door
       and in the room is a teacher teaching Indian boys and girls.

(h)   I am a lady fly. I also went to visit a school called B . . . I have to do
       this to be called a brave fly. What happens is that every year six flies are
       chosen — the first back alive is the brave fly of the year . . . It is awfully
       big . . . woodwork room, noisy room, must be because of those girls
       talking . . . a little thing like me . . . what's that noise Ooooh, ah, that
       hurt, watch it. What's this . . must be the sale at Williams or something.
       Oh, it's a dinner hall, thought it was a mad house . . . a buzzer, that
       horrible sound.

(i)   I am a fly, just a little fly . . . I flied to . . . I wondered where they were
       all going so smartly dressed . . . they were going to school.

(j)   I see a fight between two boys . . . a kid chewing a sweet . . . Mr H hitting
       a kid, a teacher shouting . . . a boy trying to hit me, Mr Q calls Gary
       and give him ten sheets of paper to write lines . . . I bumped into a 5th
       former . . . he was running away from a teacher . . . Gary came out with
       a tear in his eye and a big hole in his pants.

(k)   I wanted to go inside because it was so cold outside . . . Miss came in
       and was talking to this girl because she was hitting a boy and made the
       boy cry.

(l)   Then the buzzer went and all the children came running out like lunatics
       . . . at the other end of A block some people were eating sweets and
       smoking cigarettes.

(m) A funny noise nearly made me fall down . . . I was so angry that I flew inside to beat the buzzer and smash it to pieces . . . I nearly got stamped on by a whole gang of boys and girls came rushing down the corridor . . . suddenly a boy with a comic in his hand started hitting me . . . I flew into the boy's changing room, well I had to close my eyes.

(n) In the corridor I see a girl chasing two boys . . . I see that someone's about to hit another boy with a mallet . . . the teacher came along the boy accidentally hit the teacher.

(o) I see people messing about in the corridor . . . in the corridor I see Mr L the BIG man then I get one whacker on my head.

(p) I am amazed when I saw 100 children rushing through . . . a little boy tried to hit me . . . there was a girl her name was D . . . she was an unhappy girl she had never been to school before so she could not read or write so she came to this school.

(q) I am a fly in A block . . . everything is quiet 'how peaceful' I think when I hear a big alarm 'oh dear' I think 'the Third World War'. Boys and girls came rushing up and down the corridor . . . I'm getting a headache.

Is it merely fanciful to see anything beyond these flights of imagination? Is it just coincidence that corridors, which figure so prominently in teachers' accounts, do so also for children? Notice their comments . . .

> I could see a long passage . . . it was very crowded . . . boys and girls looked like a herd of sheep . . . (a), in the corridor . . . boys tried to kill me (b), all the children came running like lunatics . . . people were eating sweets and smoking cigarettes (l), in the corridor I see a girl chasing two boys (n), I see people messing around (o), I saw a 100 children running through (p), boys and girls rushing up and down . . . I'm getting a headache (q).

Such accounts bring into focus one dimension of the child's experience at school. Size, bustle, noise, the imminence of potential threat and violence all figure prominently. There is real pathos in the repetitive phrase, 'I am only a very little fly' and the vivid imagery to describe the experienced shock indicates perhaps something more than mere literary skill. In what other institutions — surely not hospitals or libraries — would we incorporate features designed to shock and startle like the school bell? Perhaps teachers are so desensitised that they no longer perceive it as worth comment. For children, the buzzer signifies, 'the beginning of the Third World War' and the ensuing rush of children in the corridors is like the 'first day of the sale at Williams'. If children learn from aspects of the hidden curriculum, what do they learn from these features of school life? If the early years of secondary school are crucial for the development of good attitudes as Rutter's *15,000 Hours* suggests, what can school do to improve on the child's first impressions of school?

Children's Games, and Clubs and Societies

In the Dialogue study it became apparent that not only was there a need to absorb the physical energies and playfulness of the children, who used these break periods to be 'disruptive', but there were fewer clubs and societies than one might have expected in a school of this size, which could have channelled some of these pupil energies. It seemed important to draw these points to the attention of the staff, and so as part of the second report to the school, the following statement was made, which highlights the vicious circle which can arise in a school experiencing problems of disruption. Dispirited or tired staff may offer fewer absorbing free-time activities to children, who therefore disrupt more, which itself leads to increased dispiritedness and fatigue.

Note on Clubs and Societies

It may be that it is because of the pressures experienced in the school and in the area of discipline and control, that staff are left with less energy or inclination to undertake additional work during lunch-time and breaks than they would wish to have. This explanation (i.e. that teacher stress levels inhibit further involvement) is perhaps supported by the general argument that it is precisely with difficult uninvolved children, that 'out of school' activities offer an opportunity to establish links and a rapport which is not possible in the classroom where their continued failure might explain their alienation. Further, if corridor supervision and buildings control figures prominently in teachers' perception of disruption and experience of stressfulness, then one persuasive argument would be to provide a wider fare of clubs and legitimate and supervised activities during the periods when such disruption is most prone. It seems to be the case that much of the activity which staff find tiresome — clearing form rooms, supervising corridors, is difficult precisely because the children perceive it differently — i.e. in the nature of a game in which they can generate some excitement and interest with only a slight risk of danger. If there were more on offer, it is arguable that fewer children would find the need for such games.

Observations during our stay in the school, indicate the widespread nature of these 'games'. Frequently they involve groups of children using the building and the corridors and toilets in an elaborate game of 'escape'. Supervising staff are cast as the enemy and the game consists of trespassing in forbidden areas, avoiding contact wherever possible and talking yourself out of difficulty when apprehended. The number of corridors and stairs make apprehension difficult. Staff appear to cope remarkably well with what is for them a tiring, time-consuming and irritating situation. In some parts of the building, the presence of staff at all times appears to act as a deterrent and it is apparent that where there is agreement among staff on strict supervision and intervention it has been possible to eliminate the problem.

Typically what starts as a 'game' ends in a form of confrontation with staff which calls for all the skills of a teacher; usually the teacher is in a situation of 'maximum exposure' and vulnerability; i.e. he is out of the classroom, his 'usual' habitat; the situation is unstructured and the rules for the interaction of interactors are either unclear or non-existent; the likelihood is that pupil and teacher may be unknown to each other. Part of the game element for children may be the gamble that teachers will not know who they are, and that they may effect escape by giving a wrong name or by showing a clean pair of heels, on the assumption that they will not be pursued and that anonymity will ensure a 'clean escape'; it is a situation where it would seem that the teacher's authority is most in doubt and which therefore calls for qualities of charisma in imposing authority (Lefkowitz, 1977; Olweus, 1978). Typically the situation is one of argument; the teacher questions a child about what he is doing; the child gives a justification — the situation is compounded because, by and large, it is without witnesses and in the event of the teacher taking action involving reference to higher authority — year head or deputies, it is one in which what happened or what was said is in question. In view of the known and almost inevitable differences in the ways in which referred situations are subsequently treated by various senior staff, this creates yet another area of uncertainty for supervising staff. Sometimes such situations turn 'sour' — perhaps this is seen as part of the risk and the excitement for children involved. Justification becomes a shouting match; in the heat of the moment verbal abuse is seen as a legitimate form of self-defence. The danger of the creation of a serious incident is always there and escalation may have serious consequences for children, leading to suspension. However they are handled, such an incident involves severe stress for the staff concerned — more so perhaps for inexperienced and young staff, and for those new to the school, where they do not perceive the 'game element' and where they over-react and provide children with legitimate grounds for defence in subsequent inquiries. At its best the situation is one of enormous expenditure of time and effort.

A further possible explanation for the relative scarcity of lunchtime and out of school activities may lie in the priorities which staff may accord to recreational or social activities compared with academic activities. Given the commitment to useful work which will be reflected in a child's academic profile, and in his ability subsequently to get employment, it is understandable that many staff see their first task within their subject area — hence the concern for maths, law, economics, Hindi, etc.

Societies could provide a counter attraction to 'games' and hive off potential troublemakers. One could also argue that more provision would in any case be a good thing in that it would contribute to better staff-pupil relations and that this would spill over into other aspects of school life — i.e. supervision during breaks. There would be less likelihood that staff would confront pupils they did not know. It would also meet some of the pupil claims that some staff are not interested in them.

It might also be feasible to arrange 'large-scale' activities such as discos which could cater for large numbers, in the lunch-hour.

9 TEACHERS AND DISRUPTION

In the two studies, an impressive amount of assistance was given to the researchers, by busy teachers in demanding urban schools. The virtually one hundred per cent co-operation in the monitoring of incidents, although it involved irksome form-filling at busy periods of the school year, together with staff's williness to talk both in general about disruptive behaviour, and particularly about incidents were admirable in both schools. There were understandable reservations on the part of both heads and staff concerning the project's conclusions, for example, but both schools were examples of communities prepared to scrutinise their procedures, to take a research stance towards their problems and to ask for help in alleviating these.

The teachers concerned admitted that misbehaviour was an area which could cause embarrassment and frustration. As two Project staff put it: '(the research) might have been a more embarrassing experience if it had arisen when I had less confidence, e.g. in first year of teaching' and, 'almost all misbehaviour is dependent upon the personality of the offender, and insofar as this is a variable factor, one is always lacking confidence in the manner adopted for the situation, even if a mask of confidence is worn at the time. Exasperation so tries the temper that a reasoned calculated approach is temporarily lost'!

Some were aware that the Project was studying only the tip of the iceberg. For example, the Head of Department and Senior teacher who commented:

> The project did not penetrate deeply enough — just dealing with the serious disruptions. The boy who arrives ten to fifteen minutes late, and has a quick, cheeky reason for his lateness that makes the rest of the class laugh, has to be dealt with; the pupil who flicks ink on the floor has to be made to clear it up; the pupil who perpetually talks, has to be warned, and warned again, then acted upon; the pupil who opens a pot of paint with a chisel has to be reprimanded and the verbal abuse from him has to be dealt with etc., etc., etc. None of these disruptions (as far as I am concerned in the workshops) are 'serious', or 'very serious' as your brief indicated, but every one takes time and perhaps more importantly, a large drain on one's nervous energy. Most of my discipline problems are not in the classroom but dealing with pupils in and around the school — stone throwing, vandalism, litter, etc. One has to have a confrontation which in the main leaves both parties devoid of a friendly relationship. I have in the last year suffered many nights of

sleeplessness. I felt I could not relax, was tense. I could not attribute it to anything other than school. These occur usually on Sunday or Monday nights prior to a difficult day or house assembly the next day. I find it takes about two weeks to unwind in the holidays. *(Head of Department and Senior Teacher)*.

But others were grateful for the help offered by the project and were interested in the analytical approach it took. One head of department said:

I think it is encouraging to us to feel that someone outside is aware of and interested in the problem. It has also had the effect of making members of staff more ready to reveal their teaching problems — many of which are clearly common to most of us.

Two assistant staff commented: 'All schools should have some permanent records of disruption as some people will stand out as being a problem. Trends can be detected early, and action might be taken.' And 'Perhaps such analysis should be full-time process in all schools?'

One teacher spoke to the researchers in the staffroom and asked whether they had realised that what they were doing, in talking with staff, might constitute therapy. They answered that they had indeed realised this!

In the past it has been said that a conspiracy of silence operates in relation to teachers talking about disruptive behaviour, partly because teacher competence is questioned, by admission of problems. The teachers to whom we spoke, however, were frequently ready to question teachers' competence and even their own involvement in the escalation of disruptive behaviour.

In the Dialogue an explanation of some disruptive behaviour in terms of lack of skill was sometimes offered. Occasionally this was excused as due to youthfulness or inexperience. It was also suggested that teacher insecurity or tenseness communicated itself to pupils who behaved badly as a consequence. One member of staff saw the teacher's voice as critical in this relaying of anxiety:

I'm more tense if I expect these boys to be there. If a teacher is tense, it tells and seems to escalate the situation . . . when you as a teacher are tense you pitch your voice in a special way and this 'gets' them. West Indians are sound conscious . . . quiet teachers often do well.

It comes down to an individual teacher's competence.

There are some youngsters who can't sort out the problems of black kids.

There is an absence of older staff — with experience.

As an experienced teacher I feel dismayed when I don't circumvent situations.

Depends on the tolerance level of teachers, at this time of year with 'flu absences, lots of cover . . . children come in a bad mood and tension rises quickly.

While acknowledging their own role in exacerbating the situation, there was very frequently expressed regret, that dealing with disruption led the teacher to neglect other aspects of his job:

What I find hardest to deal with is when they are in a little gang of them. No-one will own up to it. You have to see them individually. It's time consuming!

In the staffroom all they talk about is disruption problems. This is bad — you're not devoting much time to teaching — only keeping law and order.

I haven't been able to do an important part of my job — being involved with pupils other than disruption. A large amount of time is spent on deviancy of some sort, so I can't spend time on progress etc.

As we talked to staff in the two schools it became clear that even in a school where large numbers of teachers appear to agree on the dimensions of their problem, and on whether it is increasing or decreasing, other teachers will hold a contrary view. In the Project school a picture emerged of a staff coming to feel that parts of the situation were becoming more difficult for them.

Two staff talked of 'violence bubbling below the surface' but a distinction emerges in the comments between serious disruption, of which one commented, 'There is no more than there was fifteen years ago', and 'boisterousness and high spirits' which appears to have increased over the years. One comment that 'there seems now to be a series of minor problems which, if unchecked by staff, become more significant', seems to indicate the greater difficulty in establishing classroom order. Many children are disruptive in the sense that they increasingly resist any notion of education and frustrate the teacher's intentions. They have discovered that school work will be of little use to them outside and it has become almost impossible for younger teachers (and some older ones) to get a completely quiet and attentive class. In the sense of upsetting normal, classroom teaching, disruption exists in almost all classes. Boys are now less likely to accept work or to behave according to the rules. There has been a decrease in respect for teachers coupled with increased rudeness and insolence — where five years ago there was no ill feeling associated with the giving of punishment — no bearing a grudge: 'today they remember the incident for weeks'.

Senior staff commented that 'there hasn't been much change over the past two years in terms of amount but violent outbursts are more frequent' and that there was some intimidation between groups of children. Other staff commented that the school had an 'average load of disruption' but that it was not a 'stress situation'.

In the Dialogue, admission that there was a problem figured side by side in some cases at least with feelings that it was within limits and controllable:

Behaviour problems here are manageable, i.e. can be researched into, and discussed and staff can think of steps which can be taken, to reduce them.

The problems are soluble — there is a body of expertise which, if practised, will allow you to cope. There is some inadequacy on my part . . . sometimes, of course, a child will 'flip', but if I'm 'together' I can handle it.

The school is fairly safe but staff are apprehensive . . . it's controllable.

It is a problem in the school . . . personal pride prevents admission; there is a lot of covering up; there is a problem here.

Many staff saw the problem as having decreased recently owing to the arrival of the present headmaster, falling rolls which increased staff stability, and improved structures for pastoral care.

Until five years ago a third of the staff were probationers. School is a haven of peace now compared with then.

Things have changed quite a lot. The school was grossly over-crowded. There was a charging mob; there wasn't room. Now there are fewer kids, so there is better behaviour.

It's much less now — the violence, heavy fights in the corridor every day. Worries about fifth year are nil in comparison with what we had . . . now people are worried about fifth year who are 'turned off' or who wander the corridor.

Even so, there were occasional dissenting voices. One senior member of staff commented:

> I wouldn't say disruptive behaviour had reduced. Young, inexperienced teachers still have problems.

The extremely personal and often conflicting views of two members of staff in the same school, the Dialogue school, are vividly illustrated by the following two remarks. The first teacher had recently come to the school, from another where there were no girls and no Asian children:

> Children here are quieter in lessons than in school X where I came from. The girls calm it down . . . I expected this to be more disruptive from what I'd heard of the area . . . here the Asian children are hardworking.

The second teacher was also new to the school:

> They go around kicking and punching each other — even fifth year they're wild animals. In most schools by that year they've started to mature.

When the report which included the above remark was circulated among the staff, a teacher protested to a researcher that she was distressed at it, saying 'surely he didn't call them animals, he said they were like animals'. In fact the metaphor used by the teacher was indeed as it stood in the report. Only one other teacher used the same metaphor in the course of the research — a supply teacher with extreme problems.

There is frequently, in teachers' comments, reference to a sort of scale of disruption, a scale with three grades, ranging from boisterousness, through minor infringement of rules, to serious disruption in relation to staff and other boys. Absenteeism constitutes a fourth grade, attached to the others, but of indeterminate value. In relation to boisterousness, staff in the project saw many boys as 'prankish . . . with little real or deep intent' '. . . naturally high spirited' '. . . to some disruption is a way of life, a bit of a game . . . prankish annoying but rarely malicious'.

Minor infringements include breaking any school rule, throwing stones and coke bottles, walking along forbidden paths, out of class vagrancy, wandering into other classrooms, being slow to get to lessons, preventing others from working, talking, playing around, being noisy, refusing to take work seriously, being an out and out nuisance.

More serious disruption would include acts of vandalism such as 'urinating in waste paper baskets', friction between groups, demanding money with menaces, violence to other boys, quick flare-ups over minor matters, occasions when a whole class just 'flips and goes beserk', 'insouciant response to threats, imprecations, and warnings'. Much of this, it was suggested, was not individual disruption but group oriented. For the teacher it presents the difficulty of getting an ordered classroom situation.

When the teachers came to consider the causes of disruption, they seemed to use four categories of cause; psychological explanations, teacher personality and behaviour, the ethos of education and physical conditions such as buildings.

Psychological explanations include reference to 'boys with severe emotional disturbances . . .' and 'aggressive personalities coming within striking distance of each other'. Teacher explanations talk of teachers appearing to contribute to the level of disruption 'by not containing children in the right way', by 'their failure to establish in each class a normal, reasonable pattern of behaviour before they teach a topic', by 'not quelling trouble-makers quickly enough . . . for fear of losing good relationships or by too much discipline which provokes the emotionally disturbed child . . .', by 'inadequate preparation' and by 'negative expectations'.

Explanations in terms of the ethos of education state that much disruption is created because of the 'type of discipline and method of enforcement', supporting a general ethos which boys are out of sympathy with. The school is seen as an 'examination factory' which offers 'literacy, numeracy and time-keeping' — qualities not directly related or relevant to the jobs boys will go into but claimed by the school to be gateways to success. Boys with learning difficulties are alienated by academic values . . . the school caters for a clientele which has disappeared and looks back to the standards of the good old days . . . it holds fast to the belief that 'if only children would dress correctly and open doors for each other and us all would be well . . . there is a refusal to face up to a vastly changed situation . . .' The result is that many children are bored — disruption takes the form of talking in lessons, constant niggling over a long period of time which it is difficult to do anything about. For many even the Certificate of Secondary Education examination is beyond them . . . there is no really suitable curriculum for the less able — for those who find a gap between the values of school and outside . . . much disruption comes from pupils who don't identify with the overriding exam emphasis and who find little else as an alternative. Many children are disillusioned . . . they find the exam emphasis beyond them.

Among physical conditions affecting disruption space was extremely important. The Project staff complained of:

lack of space and relaxing activities . . . cramped conditions and a girls' school on the same site . . . the buildings are not ideal; corridors and doors are too narrow; there is a lack of an on-site playing field . . . cramped conditions in the playground . . . too many types of problem in a cramped environment.

Teachers in a school will obviously look at its problems from the point of view of its own school type. Thus the Project was a 14-18 school, and some of its staff related its problems to the characteristics of such a school. They said:

like teaching in three separate schools . . . the problem of getting to know children . . . having them long enough to make any impact.

The nature of the 14-18 school is said to make it difficult to get to know boys and establish relationships.

Misbehaviour and Teacher Stress

Recent research confirms that disruptive pupil behaviour is an important factor in the development of stress among teachers, and has begun to consider whether the teacher's personality plays a role in the experience of stress. So far findings suggest that teachers with a general belief that things in their lives are largely outside their control are particularly prone to experiencing greater stress (Kyriacou, 1980).

There is one sense in which most of both of the school studies was concerned with teacher stress: for a teacher to report an incident as seriously disrupting the teaching process will usually imply that for that teacher it was stressful, more than his limit of toleration would permit him to accept as 'not serious'. Only where he reports an incident purely in order to fulfil a school regulation will he designate it as 'serious' yet not be personally involved and experience stress. Thus several of the sets of data gathered from the research are relevant to the question of stress. In studying the categories of disruptive behaviour we can glean the types of behaviour teachers find stressful; in looking at the teacher questionnaire we find in the comments, clues as to the types of stress to which teachers are exposed. Our findings corroborate some of those of the NAS/UWT study *Stress in Schools* (1975), e.g. that stress is not confined to probationers but may be felt by teachers of all degrees of experience, and that reorganisation to a comprehensive system of education is a common stress situation, with some teachers experiencing grief as a result of the loss of a former system. (One teacher in our study referred to the 'womb-like' nature of a grammar school). The NAS study, however, pays scant attention to stress in relation to disruptive behaviour, perhaps because it is a survey based on teachers and lecturers taking part in conferences and courses, who were either unwilling to admit — even to themselves — to difficulties in this area, or who, by virtue of seniority, were less affected than average by them. Our own studies make it clear that disruptive behaviour is an important area of potential stress for many teachers, which can combine with stress due to reorganisation (e.g. having to teach a broad ability range for the first time, perhaps not by choice), or to teaching an urban pupil population itself under environmental and home stresses, in physical conditions which are far from good (e.g. with inadequate grounds, in which boys can work off energies).

In the Project the concomitants of stress in evidence are much as would be expected: loss of patience, anger, frustration, occasionally reference to a psychosomatic disorder, anxiety, and feelings of depression. There is tiredness, associated with feelings of guilt:

> I get tired with them. I am worried that unless I exhaust myself they won't make progress . . . it's usually OK now when I have enough energy . . . I'm feeling tired, I'm moaning too much and threatening too much. I'll have to throw them out rather than tire myself out moaning. *(Young teacher)*

> This group is very stressful for me. I often go home feeling very wound up, as I am used to fairly consistent discipline in all my other classes. This makes the sense of never having controlled the situation particularly hard to cope with. *(Highly experienced teacher)*

Although the above statements refer to the Project as a whole, there were a limited number of incidents — twenty-eight in all — in which there seemed to be certain aspects of the situation which were acting as strains upon the teacher, as factors in the general stress of the incident, judging from his written description of the incident, or from his description of it during the subsequent interview. The following account of some aspects and characteristics of teacher stress associated with handling disruptive behaviour includes quotations from the twenty-eight 'stress incidents'. The picture that emerges is one that fits well with Mandler and Watson's (1966) interpretation of some anxiety as caused by the unexpected interruption of a 'plan'. In this case, it is the interference, by the disruption, with the teacher's determination to teach according to his curricular or lesson plan, which produces the emotional behaviour, the 'stress'. The clearer the plan, the greater may be the stress. This accounts well for the fact that sometimes an experienced teacher will be under stress, particularly where he cannot consider an alternative plan. Similarly, the more value the teacher attaches to the plan, the more he may be prone to stress, in Lazarus's (1966) terms. For Lazarus stress occurs partly because the most important values and goals of the people concerned are endangered or disrupted.

It is clear from our research as a whole, and from the 'stress' incidents that the repetitiveness and persistence of disruptive behaviour often causes a build-up of frustration and anxiety in the teacher, which sensitizes him, and makes apparently minor disruption stressful, and turns it into an 'incident'. The teacher may be fully aware of this process and apologise for it:

> 'A certain group of boys from this set has been continually disruptive throughout the year — appear completely disinterested in the work and talk continually. Although this may not be seen as a 'serious' disruption in itself, I find it far more disruptive than a violent outburst. The latter is a 'once-off' soon forgotten incident which perhaps disrupts your lesson for a few minutes. The continual talking I am encountering from this group is a constant source of annoyance that damages the learning chances of the more academically motivated members of the group. (A second-stream group).

This function of the repetitiveness of a form of disruption in inducing stress comes out clearly from many descriptions of incidents. Even where only brief details are given, words like 'continually', 'a recurring problem', appear frequently. Above all, the disruption thwarts the teacher's attempt to get on with the lesson, to get on with his job: 'Branksome would just not settle down and stop talking. He prevented me several times from starting the lesson.' So frustrated is he, that the teacher loses his sense of humour. As part of the same incident: 'Grundy caused a disturbance by making an exhibition of farting. He found the reaction it provoked extremely funny'. The second major theme running through the descriptions of incidents is that the teacher sees the disruptive behaviour as deliberate, malicious. The boy is seen as being intentionally difficult. He is no longer merely boisterous, having fun, but is setting out to disturb the lesson, and is spiteful:

> He goes out of his way to annoy me, succeeded for once.

> C.S. in particular holds a grudge and is making sure I know it.

It is not difficult to see that when the teacher believes he is being hurt as a person, by a boy acting rationally, he experiences stress. Timetabling can operate as a stress factor. Where a teacher commonly finds difficulty with a particular group, he may find a day when he teaches them more than once a particularly stressful one. Looking back on such a day, one teacher said:

> They have me . . . too often . . . they were intending not to do anything . . . No identifiably serious incident took place but teaching could not take place . . . the single incident is not the problem in disruptive behaviour. It is the passive refusal to work. It is the irritating things . . . sometimes one's no longer prepared to go through the rigmarole again.

Another teacher analysing his reasons for putting his foot down and creating an 'incident' over behaviour he had tolerated from the same boys in the past, reflected:

> Knowing I had fifth year all afternoon, I might have unconsciously stiffened the sinews and summoned up the blood.

Pupils' possessions can become a point of stress. Difficulties may arise where a pupil brings in a piece of his own equipment, e.g. a tape recorder, and takes it into a lesson where it is not to be used, and uses it. It is his property and a teacher who wishes to remove it may meet strong resistance, and become involved in a stressful situation:

> He played the tape recorder again. (He had played it during an earlier lesson, and turned it off when told to). He wouldn't give it to me. He swore when I insisted. I had to take him to the head.

Events occurring during break periods — such as a playground fight — can wash into subsequent lessons, which may become stressful:

> The group arived late (after a playground fight), highly excited. They would not settle, especially Swingle. He would not leave the class. Eventually he did leave, swearing at me. I had to go to the deputy head with him. Swingle's behaviour was noisy and he 'danced around' the room, giving impressions of the playground fight he had just seen. He refused to sit down and be quiet.

A break may find a teacher on duty. In this situation, levels of tolerance may be lowered so that a piece of mischievousness such as a boy chalking on the teacher's back can make a young teacher angry, though the deputy head may require only that the boy apologises.

Stress may be increased by another member of staff being directly, even though inadvertently, involved in the incident. Thus one boy in the midst of being loud and disruptive, swore at a member of staff outside the classroom.

There are incidents which may appear dramatic and likely to cause stress but which in fact are coped with by skilled routines and therefore are not particularly stressful, e.g. a boy sets off a stink bomb, but the class are quickly settled by being given a copy task. As the teacher leaves the room, he meets a senior teacher, and mentions the incident to him, making what may well be a stress-reducing communication. These chance encounters in which a teacher mentions an incident are interesting in that though the encounter may be fortuitous, the actual reporting onwards of the incident may be stress-reducing.

Fighting may present a teacher with a number of stress-provoking problems. It may be difficult to find out the cause of the fight and to deal with it, so that the fight stops. The fight may also generate disturbance in the class as a whole so that children other than those in the fight also pose a problem which requires settling. One fight involved the possession of a magazine:

> There was noise and shouting until I finally confiscated the magazine and sat them down.

In another incident:

> It had become apparent that Brown was being baited by a number of the group during the previous lessons. I moved him away from the immediate area, but when my back was turned something happened and Brown lost his temper and started fighting Smith. The disturbance so disturbed the class that all told a good ten minutes of lesson time was lost. It had cooled down by the end of the lesson.

A fight involving the use of implements can be particularly worrying:

> During the lesson I looked up to see the two pupils mentioned chasing each other round the benches. They were told to stop but continued arguing. Scobie actually went over the top of the bench on two occasions, attempting to catch Scarbrook, who had a wooden mallet in his hand and was threatening Scobie. Scobie picked up a mallet also and they were both about to strike each other when I managed to intervene and take them both to a deputy head . . . these boys flare up very quickly.

Dealing with theft can also be stressful. During a lesson, as soon as an object is reported to have disappeared, a search is initiated. If the object — an expensive biro for example — is not found, then it is difficult to know for how long the search should be continued. In one case a biro disappeared:

> twenty minutes before the end of lesson . . . there was a full-scale search and it was not found. It was only recovered ten minutes after the bell, after the Head of Department had been called in to read the riot act.

In practical classes the abuse of apparatus may be stressful to the teacher. Where practical exercises are reduced to their simplest denominator, and yet apparatus is damaged and stolen, and not recovered in spite of pro-tracted enquiries, there may be considerable frustration:

> In the second part of the double period the class had a simple practical involving a magnet, a small compass and a piece of paper. About a third could not cope and played with the apparatus. One magnet and two compasses were broken, and one magnet and one compass were stolen. Enquiry into this until 12:45 failed to bring the missing items to light.

Stress may arise around the physical containment of a pupil within the class, where he is finding an excuse for leaving it which the teacher does not accept:

> I had to stand by the door to prevent him leaving in the first place, and he repeatedly refused to sit down . . . five minutes later he used threatening language when refused permission to leave the room to go to the toilet . . . he had often claimed he was 'desperate' in previous lessons with no ill effects.

Sometimes a teacher can feel trouble escalating but the lesson ends and solves his problem.

> Five minutes before the end of the period there was a quarrel between Johnson and Gray . . . It had a disturbing influence on Jacobs who usually works quite well. The disturbance was exacerbated by the others putting their books away and then the bell ringing. I managed to cool them down but there could have been a nasty incident if it had been earlier in the period.

The whittling away of effective lesson time by what in themselves are minor forms of deviant and disruptive behaviour may be seen as stressful:

> It seems almost impossible to get them to go directly from one room or lesson to another to arrive punctually. At most, a half to two-thirds of the class are ever on time and even then are seldom ready to start work in that lesson. As always, constant interruption through talking, non-attention to instruc-tion, ejection of chewing gum, removal of outdoor garments, loss of pencils, etc., reduced the effective lesson length to as little as a quarter to a third of timetabled time.

The building up of several minor bits of disruptive behaviour may com-bine with problems of encouragement of the boy by his class-mates and friends, into a particularly stressful situation:

> Clarkford arrived wearing a brown mac and had to be told three times at intervals to remove it, which he finally did as slowly as possible, so his friends wouldn't think he was going to do as he was told. Later he dropped his pen down the sink and involved everyone round him in his efforts to fill the

sink with water to 'float it out'! He did this twice in spite of instructions to leave it till later. Finally he began tossing a coin 'heads and tails' until I lost patience and removed him, with work, to the Hall. (Clarkford is troublesome only when all his friends are at school, which is not often! If there is no one he can show off to, he's all right).

The above examples are taken from the Project, but are fully endorsed by the Dialogue.

It appears that the development of pupil behaviour into its recognition by the teacher as an incident of disruptive behaviour is a function of many possible factors, among which the repetitiousness of the behaviour and the perception of the pupil as malicious, will often figure. These factors may combine, and contribute to teacher stress, which in turn may, of course, communicate itself to the pupils and help bring about further disruptive behaviour.

In schools with problems of disruptive behaviour there appears to be a wide range of variation among staff in the experience of stress. Some do not find behaviour problems at all stressful, e.g. because they have been working with them for so long. Several refer to an initial stress, now gone, while at the other end of the continuum a few staff are under very considerable stress. Supply staff may be particularly vulnerable.

We close this section with some comments of Dialogue staff:

I am under more stress here . . . but it doesn't interfere with my private life.

I have spent X years grumbling at children, being under pressure and tension all the time.

I'm not very experienced. In the beginning I used to take it to heart — get emotionally involved, but now I relax. Otherwise I'd lose all my energy.

I find that towards end of term I fly off the handle too quckly — my fist clenches more often. When I came here first I had no violent feelings — since then I've found I feel perhaps only violence would help.

It used to affect me — I used to worry whether I was doing my job properly. Now I just go home and forget about it. There's no point worrying about what's going on, as I can't affect it.

10 DISRUPTIVE BEHAVIOUR AND SOME MULTI-ETHNIC CONSIDERATIONS

The two school studies were concerned with schools which were multi-racial, containing large numbers of coloured children, particularly Asian children and children who were second-generation Black British, of West Indian origin. The relationship between ethnic origin and school behaviour was one which was of interest to some staff in both schools and to some of those who organised the study though there was a tacit acceptance that not only was this potentially a very difficult and sensitive area for research, the researchers knew that any statements made would need to be based on the most careful definition and evidence relating to ethnic origin. It was not possible, within the limitations of the two studies, for example, to be as precise as Rutter's (1974) research into rates of perceived behavioural deviance and psychiatric disorder among children of West Indian immigrants. For this reason no systematic study was made of ethnic origin.

However, as work proceeded, particularly in the Dialogue school, questions of ethnic origin arose in interviews with the staff and generated great interest, when the report on the interviews was disseminated, so that the researchers could not ignore them, but responded to that interest, with a statement in the second report issued to staff. Thus questions of ethnic origin and behaviour became an integral part of the dialogue between researchers and teachers.

In the course of the early Dialogue interviews, racial tension was hardly ever mentioned as a factor in disruptive behaviour. Thus it was pointed out that while certain large West Indian boys might bully Asian boys, this behaviour was not racial in origin, since they would also bully small, white boys, and since the Asian boys sometimes by virtue of their personality and size 'called forth' bullying. The absence of racial tension in the school was contrasted with that in the area around it:

> Racial tension doesn't exist at school as it does in the streets. The school is sheltered. There's no racial tension here.

An interesting suggestion was made, that some children of mixed race were engaged in disruptive behaviour particularly with certain teachers (of similar/dissimilar, sex, type, and racial origin) because of identity problems, (e.g. tall, heavily built West Indian boy with tall, heavily built West Indian father and petite Irish mother).

> Some of our kids are mixed-up — half-caste kids identify with blacks in lower school, then change friends in upper school.

> Teachers need to talk to these children about their mixed race, individually — to tell them how well they can do, and so on . . . these children have to accept themselves as people of worth.

A number of comments were made about problems relating to 'West Indian' children, some referring to their origin in poor employment prospects, and racial prejudice, but others suggesting that the teacher perceived these children as exhibiting personality differences.

> What goes on outside school at home etc; black kids who go off; their willingness to learn dissipates. Motivation goes when they see what happens to their brothers and sisters; for West Indians learning becomes redundant. Asian kids keep their willingness to learn.

> West Indians are different in temperament; aggressive and loud . . . express a different life style; we have to know more about their culture. Are we trying to turn them into our ideal?

> West Indians are sensitive to touch.

> West Indians are a problem; volatile, lackadaisical, casual, 'Is it inborn' . . . a lot are lively and noisy . . . react differently when disciplined, 'confront you back', a definite skill required for handling.

One Asian teacher commented:

> There may be a communication problem. West Indians won't accept my pronunciation, especially those of low IQ.

In view of the increasingly acknowledged importance of language in the school, and especially in relation to children from ethnic minorities (Edwards, V.K., 1979), it is of interest that staff mentioned that children should be helped to improve their ability to communicate, to discuss, to reason; work on vocabulary was one way of doing this. Such reasoning power was seen as crucial to peaceful resolution of inter-personal conflict.

There was a general interest among staff, in pupil boisterousness, which was sometimes seen as a reaction to too much controlling by the school. Two teachers related boisterousness to cultural factors, the second seeing Asians as not typically boisterous:

> For West Indians it's a response to being held on a tight lead in the family. They're not given enough freedom at home . . . when they come here they erupt. Parents feel it's the teacher's fault. The children sense the teacher is a different animal — a response to freedom.

Asians are now getting boisterous.

Shaming disruptive children by, for example, reading a list of their names out at assembly was said by one member of staff to be an effective punishment and deterrent, particularly for West Indian children.

Public humiliation is not good, but it is effective for control.

Another teacher talking of dumb insolence, commented:

There is a West Indian attitude involved in this behaviour . . . this is sheer hunch.

Another, suggesting that teacher insecurity or tenseness communicated itself to pupils who behaved badly as a consequence, saw the teacher's voice as critical in this relaying of anxiety:

I'm more tense if I expect these boys to be there. If a teacher is tense, it tells and seems to escalate the situation . . . when you as a teacher are tense you pitch your voice in a special way and this gets them. West Indians are sound conscious . . . quiet teachers often do well.

In addition to referring to ethnic differences, as illustrated above, the teacher interviews contained three suggestions relating to staff of different origins. Firstly it was pointed out that since the school had so many coloured children in it, the appointment of some coloured staff to pastoral posts would improve the school's facilities for the counselling of these children. Coloured staff might have improved insight into their problems, e.g. problems of identity.

Secondly, a general increase in the number of coloured senior staff in the school was advocated (Gibbes, 1980). However, one white teacher commented:

The coloured teachers don't get on better than we do.

When the report on the interviews, containing all the above statements relating to racial origin was circulated, many staff, in particular, were angry at what they viewed as other staff's 'racialist comments', at the use of stereotypes in their quotations and at what they regarded as the misuse of the term 'West Indian' to refer to children of parents of West Indian origin, who had themselves been born in Britain. They thought such children should be called Black British, or simply Black (if such a reference was necessary), or in one case, non-Caucasian, as Negroes were called in the United States. Part of the heat generated around this issue in this school is attributable to previous problems arising from an article, published in a journal, by a member of the staff, which had been later publicised as containing racial stereotypes.

Concern was expressed lest teachers' response to disruption contained elements of racism which would be sensed by the child, from expressions and gestures, etc., and which, therefore, would exacerbate the disruption. A member of staff asked the Headmaster whether a staff discussion could be held about racial stereotyping and comments in the report in general. It was suggested, alternatively, that since the matters were sensitive, they should be discussed in small groups. It was pointed out that a large group discussion would have the advantage, that people could recognise their own attitudes as being discussed.

In view of the strength of some staff's reactions to their colleagues' remarks concerning ethnic origin, the researchers made the following statement in their second report to the school. The response of the staff to the report was at a number of levels.

The concern of some teachers centres around what are perceived as the racially-prejudiced remarks of other staff, and the fact that these remarks should have been included for staff consideration by the research team. Objections are raised on a number of issues, for example, that the term West Indian should be used (both by staff and the researchers quoting the staff) to apply to children the majority of whom are Black children born in this country. The question is whether, as some would appear to feel, this is purely a semantic problem in which case the problem seems to be an overreaction from some staff, to comments which are not in practice or intention racially-biased or whether, as is suggested, it is closely bound up with problems relating to children's identity. The matter is complicated by the absence of figures for the number of coloured children of various origins and because the children's own reaction on the question of identity varies; when relaxed they will describe themselves as West Indian but, in confrontation situations with Caribbean teachers, they may insist on being treated as English.

Reference to all groups as Black English or Black Londoner may both beg firstly the question that country of origin and ethnicity may be vital towards an understanding of the complex family group and its environment with its shared attitudes — kinship and upbringing patterns and, secondly, the identification of these members by others, as belonging or not belonging to a particular community, with its distinctive life styles and individual choices about relationships.

Ethnicity involves participation in living communities with distinctive social structures and cultural forms (Furlong, 1980). That these distinctions are clearly recognised at one level is seen in the demand that the educational system should be multi-cultural and should allow for the recognition of pluralistic values.

Recognition of cultural and ethnic differences accounts among the British for differentiations into Scots, Irish and Welsh and for regional differences — i.e. Yorkshire, Lancashire. In much the same way as it is possible to identify someone as 'a Northener' or 'a Scot' without incurring any detrimental stereotyping, it ought similarly to be possible to refer to a West Indian British, not just a Black Britisher.

Explanations of pupil reactions — i.e. references to loudness, aggressiveness, politeness, ebullience, etc., appear at least in part to be found in differences involving cultural expression. That such statements can easily involve stereotypes should not necessarily indicate that they hold no value in analysing situations. To call all such statements racialist is clouding the issue and depriving oneself of an important part of the analysis.

An alternative explanation would seek to understand the manifestations of behaviour in school as a reaction against the backgrounds from which the children come, in the case of Black children of their low employability and marginality as an economically and socially deprived group. Their behaviour is understandable as a situational adaptation to this — hence the drop-out of many intelligent children. It is presumed that in referring to children as West Indian, staff are unwilling or unable to make distinctions between children with parents from Jamaica or St. Kitts, despite the fact that several staff have direct experience of living and working in the West Indies. If there is an argument that there is a presumption in favour of staff in a multi-racial school having a greater sensitivity toward cultural differences, then it may be important that this includes an awareness of the extent to which such differences are still present, albeit modified to the circumstances of Caribbean life in London. Absence of such awareness might be as potent a reason for continuing disruption as direct reference to supposed identification.

It is perhaps also important to recognise that a large number of different arguments are being used — some of which are contradictory.

One argues for a better understanding of cultural differences as they are manifested in second generation children as a help to modifying their learning experience in the light of their particular patterning of skills and characteristics. The other argues that mechanisms structuring social organisation and influencing behavioural style are not sufficiently different to warrant consideration from one ethnic group to another and that they should not be given significance or prominence in educational planning or practice. Here the emphasis shifts to the common experience of Black children as a submerged and dispossessed economic group relating to perceived and experienced discrimination and poor employment prospects.

In explaining the strength of the reaction among the staff and the focussing on the issue of race within the report, an explanation drawing on recent events within the school and within the neighbourhood seems profitable and probably goes far to explain the hesitancy of the Head and the elaborate nature of the procedures he instituted before it was agreed to release the discussion document. Further factors are clearly the suspicion of some staff concerning the intentions of the Rampton committee enquiring nationally into multi-cultural schools, and worry at the use to which any information in this highly sensitive area might be put by politicians and others, for example, as an argument for still further cuts in educational provision.

11 THE GENESIS AND LIFE OF THE DIFFICULT SCHOOL

In this chapter we move on to consider the phenomenon of the 'difficult school'. We make no apology for appearing to change terms, for this is precisely what teachers do, in teacher language. Teachers rarely talk of a school as 'one with a high level of disruptive behaviour'; instead they call a school 'tough' or 'dicey', or very commonly 'difficult', showing that the critical aspect of such a school, for teachers, is the fact that it is difficult for them, posing problems for them — as well as, of course, for the pupils in it.

Misbehaviour in a school can be concentrated in the behaviour of relatively few children who present serious problems to the staff. In a difficult school there will be a proportionately larger number of such children. Though some socially withdrawn pupils may be hard to manage, difficult pupils in most schools are those who misbehave repeatedly or consistently 'badly', in the school's terms. Difficult children will commonly continually disobey. They will disobey regulations perhaps with regard to school uniform, or smoking in the toilets, or fulfilling homework assignments; they will disobey the teacher, refusing to respond to requests to comply with the norms of the school. This disobedience may be coupled with insolence, 'cheek', or bad language, and is often associated with 'doing no work', 'not concentrating', or 'refusing to settle down'. Obviously, these behaviours are not spectacular or bizarre; they are in the main common types of children's nonconformist behaviour. What matters is that attempts on the part of teachers to stop the children behaving in these ways have often been unsuccessful; they go on doing these things frequently or to a serious degree. They are 'difficult' pupils.

It is not only single pupils who present a problem, but groups of pupils and whole classes on occasion. Go into many schools and you will readily be told which classes are the 'worst'. Here the characteristic of the problem is a group one, on a larger scale than a single pupil. Teachers will often view with displeasure or, in extreme cases, dread having to take a lesson with that class. The problem may be comparable in difficult schools who are likely to have many difficult classes. Thus the degree of difficulty will at times be extreme.

There is a third form of misbehaviour, after the individual misbehaving child or the difficult class, and this is the level of disruptive behaviour in a school as a whole. Much less is known about this phenomenon. There are schools in which the level is far higher than in others, and these are the 'difficult schools', attractive to the media, for their high-figure of assaults on teachers.

The three phenomena of disruption: child, class and school inevitably interact. A school with large numbers of problem children will have to work very much harder than one having only a few disruptive pupils, to avoid developing into a difficult school. One or two difficult children may exert an effect on others too, which is disproportionate to their number. The class within which they are located thus risks becoming a difficult class.

What then, are the characteristics of schools with many difficult children and/or classes? One way of answering this question is to focus upon those areas where the difficult behaviour may have an impact. The most obvious is the teaching situation itself. Here there may be loss of teaching time; dealing with obstructive behaviour is a time-consuming activity. The teacher may have to stop the lesson several times, or it may never really get off the ground. Thus an atmosphere of conflict and aggression in the classroom may be generated and destroy the children's chance of concentrating. The noise or bother created by a disruptive pupil may compound the situation. We would therefore expect a lowering of the standards of attainment reached by a number of children in the class, and by the disruptive pupil himself. If it is remembered that the disrupter frequently behaves in this way, it can be seen that the loss of learning can build up appreciably over time and in some instances this can become both serious and decisive for effective learning by the children. Difficult schools can therefore have low standards thrust upon them.

In the difficult school, where there is considerable loss of pupil time, there is, as has been suggested, automatically some wastage of teacher time. This is first the time during which the teacher is actually in contact with the class. If a teacher is nominally teaching a class of thirty-two, but five pupils are regularly absent and a further three are not attending, most of the lesson, there is already a twenty-five percent wastage of his time. But a teacher's time is far more than contact time and includes time spent in the preparation of his lesson and materials. Such time often includes sessions when staff meet to discuss curriculum and syllabuses and so on. For a class such as the one just desribed, loss of teacher time can be twenty-five percent of a larger period than mere contact time. Teacher time and energies constitute a precious educational resource, which is often wasted where children opt out of the school situation.

It is easy to argue that where children opt out, either by truanting or not attending to the lesson, the teacher redeploys the same time and energies to the teaching of the remaining children, who are willing to work. This would be so, if the fact of the truanting and the lack of concentration in class were accepted by the teachers in the school so that they spent no further time and energies on them. However, where children fail to arrive at lessons, or are persistently absent, senior staff often spend considerable time in 'chasing them up', or arranging for action to be taken, for example, by an education welfare officer; and where children are attending a lesson and refusing to work, the teacher will often feel frustration, and make attempts to get them to co-operate, though eventually he may leave them to their own devices and try to 'do something about them' when the lesson is over. His frustration during the lesson may well impair his functioning vis-a-vis the rest of the class. Sessions in which such frustrations occur with a class can constitute a strain which accumulates, as the school timetable regularly repeats itself, so that commonly the 'difficult' periods — unless the difficulties are solved — come to be feared, and sap the teacher's energies. The cumulative strain of teaching a difficult class may lead to the teacher absenting himself from school and he may also suffer from psychosomatic disorders arising from it. In other words, there is likely to be a close relationship between difficult schools and teacher stress.

Before leaving the question of the use of teacher time involved in coping with misbehaviour, one should also look at the time spent by senior staff, whether these are heads of house or year, or senior tutors, or deputy heads or head of schools, on misbehaving pupils. In difficult schools this kind of work represents an enormous proportion of the total work of several members of staff. It may also co-exist with a special unit within the school, designed to assist in the education of pupils who cannot readily learn in the ordinary classroom situation. This unit may be of a 'sanctuary'-type, in which case some of its pupils may be there because they have behaved aggressively or disruptively, while others will be there because of learning or personality difficulties. Alternatively it may be a 'referral-class' unit designed specifically to contain pupils who have behaved in a disorderly fashion in the classroom. What concerns us here, is that although a sanctuary unit may be staffed by a teacher or teachers who are supernumerary to the teaching staff of the school, there are some units, particularly those of the referral-class type, which are staffed throughout the day by the regular staff of the school, obviously often senior and highly experienced staff because of the nature of the task involved. In the latter case the unit for disruptive pupils represents a considerable investment of staff for the school, in addition to the investment made by senior and other staff in the rest of the school. Difficult schools again leave less teacher time for teaching itself.

If, when serious or widespread forms of misbehaviour occur, a good deal of staff time is spent coping with these, or is wasted because pupils are not attending school or attending to their lessons, and teaching time is lost, it is precisely amongst staffs where these are highly valued that resentment at the situation may be harboured, and come to join other personal resentments.

The net result of time lost through large-scale misbehaviour in a difficult school is that its pupils suffer from a form of educational disadvantage, which is compounded by any other disadvantages to which they may already be subjected. Thus the child who by virtue of his birth and environment already has the educational cards stacked against him, who may find difficulty in learning even in favourable circumstances, is buffeted in the lesson by interruptions from his fellows, the general disorder in the class, and the constant requests of the teacher for quiet. Hopes of social mobility through education are very slim (Jencks, 1972) at the best of times, and are likely to be annihilated in such an atmosphere. If disorderly classrooms are a form of educational disadvantage, then questions can be asked about compensation for this. These questions lead directly to the issue of the supports which the Local Education Authorities and the Department of Education and Science should be providing, and to questions of the adequacy of those currently being provided by some authorities.

Another area in which difficult pupil behaviour on a large scale has an impact is on the building, its equipment and its decorations. Often teachers give up trying to put children's art work and other work on display because it is so frequently damaged and the children get upset. A vicious circle arises. The walls remain undecorated and the children never learn what it means to respect decorations on walls. Thus the difficult school is often a bleak place, with bare walls whose plaster is picked at and has holes dug in it. It is sometimes dirty, as though those whose task it is to keep it clean have given up the attempt. Doors have been kicked at and kicked into and have been patched up with hardboard or plywood, awaiting replacement. Many window panes are broken. One of the authors has entered a difficult school and on the way by two different routes to the staffroom has counted on the first occasion thirty-six broken panes of varying size, and on the second, thirty. The school has a resident glazier.

A third factor is movement by pupils around the school. Here disruption is seen in occasional commotions, around fights which spring up along the corridor or on staircases, where congestion fans the potential for scuffles. Late arrival for lessons is frequent; also frequent is non-arrival, as the pupil leaves the premises without permission or hides in a toilet or some isolated spot. Large numbers of schools now call the register every lesson, to pick up cases of this sort.

Theft may be so commonplace that stacks of empty lockers, some with doors ripped off, line the corridors neglected, and desk compartments are no longer used for anything left in them might be removed. Cloakrooms may no longer be used because coats and scarves, etc., are too often stolen. Instead, children, including small ones, carry everything around with them always — coats, bags with physical education kit, and books. Those who equip schools with cloakrooms and rows of pegs in them have not yet caught up with disruptive behaviour. (Symbolically, in one school a cloakroom unused since the school was built seven years ago has been converted to a sanctuary unit for difficult and disturbed children.) Periodically, a lesson may be interrupted while an investigation takes place into a recent theft; unless such enquiries are undertaken speedily, the chances of recovering the stolen property are small. Theft from teachers occasionally constitutes a nasty problem.

Though disruptive behaviour is commonly associated with truancy in the minds of the public, truancy constitutes only a relatively minor problem for teachers. Senior teachers spend a good deal of time working with welfare officers to get truants back into school, but for the teacher in the classroom, the truancy removes a potentially disruptive child from the sphere of his immediate concerns. Certainly, there are some classes where pupils who when younger were disruptive, then turn to truancy, thus only a fraction of the class are present at any one time. Such classes may indicate a difficult school, but they also register its past difficulties with its absent pupils, rather than by their presence.

Another characteristic of the difficult school is the contagious effect of difficult pupil behaviour. The rippling outwards of misbehaviour from children to groups of children, to whole classes, and to the school population in general is something known to many teachers. This ripple effect is noticeable in classroom groups, and when children are massed in situations like a school assembly.

The effect of the difficult school upon a child who is prone to maladjustment is a particularly serious one. In the well-ordered, stable, ordinary school, there is no reason why, as in the past, many children who are moderately maladjusted, cannot be successfully taught. There are however, school environments which for various reasons become areas of stress within the educational system, and where the successful education of disturbed children may be highly problematic.

Just as in the field of delinquency the question is often asked whether the school itself creates delinquents so, in discussions of maladjustment the belief is occasionally expressed that some maladjustment is 'school-induced', a belief fairly easily developed from the fact of the quantity of maladjusted behaviour exhibited specifically in school settings (Graham, 1967). The relationship between the behaviours and the setting is interpreted as causal. Tizard (1973) accepts that we should look at schools as institutions influencing both the incidence and duration of maladjusted behaviour patterns, and suggests that we should elicit the factors which are responsible for the difference in maladjustment figures for similar schools. One of the authors (Lawrence, 1973) replied to Tizard, and listed very briefly some of the factors which operated in a school in which she had worked, whose high maladjustment figures were in contrast to those of neighbouring schools of similar intake. The school was at that time an extremely difficult school, and though only one case is referred to (those who work in difficult schools rarely report on them), it may be useful to name the factors which seemed to feature in this one instance:

1. A large number of totally 'untreated' cases of maladjusted children (their difficulties unrecognized, and showing in a situation in which they received virtually no counselling).

2. An unstructured environment, subject to random irregularities of programme. People are not where you expect them to be at certain times. Senior school management is deficient. Communication is haphazard.

3. A number of staff who are 'bad' for all children but especially disturbed children. Blatantly racially prejudiced staff teaching immigrant children. A number of neurotic or otherwise disturbed staff. Teachers with weak personalities, with abnormally low professional standards (e.g. who fail to arrive, or are absorbed in themselves, neglecting their teaching functions).

4. Supportive services — medical and social welfare — not used.

5. An absence of home-school liaison (this is partly related to 4). Few parents enter the school.

6.   Faulty curricula. Lack of choice of subjects.

7.   Inadequate remedial assistance particularly with reading.

8.   Generally poor morale. A feeling among the children that teachers are no longer to be trusted, because they have left promises unfulfilled so often.

9.   Factors arising from the 'Social Priority Area' situation: one in four children in a school of over 700 pupils lived with only one parent. Too high a proportion of the school population was under environmental stress of one or more kinds.

10. Erratically and irrationally applied sanctions, e.g. children penalized for coming to school late when they were simply helping a sick parent.

11. High turnover of staff, leading to lack of learning and general insecurity. The appointment of staff whose English could not be understood, causing immense frustration at least in initial contact.

12. Lack of good teaching and wastage of potential. Classes out of the teachers' control.

If the factors listed above are considered in turn, one is led to ask first of all, why a school can come to have within it a large number of maladjusted children who are not receiving assistance. The head teacher's attitudes to psychology and psychiatry are critical here. There are some head teachers either totally unsympathetic to these disciplines, or who even now have not appreciated the changes, in their years of headship, of our knowledge and treatment of psychiatric and psychological disorders, and the nature of the resources now available to schools. One reason for the latter situation may be that there is necessarily a slight ambivalence in the attitude of LEA advisers, and officers towards the publicisation of psychiatric or psychological resources. I say necessarily because there would be extreme practical and economic difficulties in meeting any greatly increased demand for these resources, and further because it is not always necessary or desirable for disturbed children to draw upon them. There is a considerable range of degree and duration of disturbance, and it should be possible for many children to be helped to cope with their difficulties without specialist help.

Some teachers do not favour referring children for psychiatric help because they believe it to be ineffective. Either they refer to studies which have failed to find significant treatment effects, or they point to children who have been treated and whose behaviour has either not improved or has deteriorated. As for the former, I believe it needs to be pointed out that though 'treated' children ultimately may not tend to get significantly 'better' as a group, than 'untreated children', they may in fact suffer less during their period of disturbance than untreated children. For the latter, it is most difficult for school staffs to tolerate further or even increased misbehaviour, after the child has started guidance clinic treatment, because it is contrary to their expectations and extremely disappointing for them. They need to be warned that this in fact may happen and is part of what may be necessary for ultimate improvement to occur.

Even in schools where all the processes mentioned above have been duly carried out, maladjusted behaviour patterns may be frequently found. How much more so in schools where they are not. A large, ordinary school in which maladjusted behaviour patterns are rife and unchecked can be a very frightening and exhausting place in which to work. The characteristic of the school with a high rate of disturbed behaviour was said above to be its lack of real structure. All schools have an apparent structure whose most detailed statement is its timetable, nested within the super-structure of the curriculum which makes it 'real' and very different; it will include the 'hidden curriculum' of atmosphere, bias, attitudes and the like, so there is often a very wide gap between the stated timetable and the 'real' one. Into the real one intervene staff absences, lateness and room changes, lesson disturbances caused by emergencies and interruptions of various kinds, and actual changes of timetable. The toleration level of the 'disturbances' of the real timetable is high in most schools. Staff and children ride them, but in the difficult school with a high incidence of difficult behaviour the toleration level is not so high, as the environment has become to all intents and purposes unstructured. The irregularities of programme have become too frequent, they appear random, instead of meaningful and organised, to staff and children. This situation, anomic in character, is circular in action, the general instability triggering off incidents which themselves perpetuate the instability. Children wait for teachers who do not come, teachers for children who do not arrive, children disappear, and others are 'picked up' in odd areas of the school where they were never meant to be.

An important factor affecting the incidence of difficult behaviour is inevitably the quality of staff in a school; certain aspects of this quality are of particular significance for disorder.

One aspect of teacher quality is mental stability, and teachers include among their number an unfortunate few who themselves suffer from psychiatric disorder. The surprising fact is that disturbed teachers often cope so well with the job of teaching, which at best is demanding and is sometimes stressful. Occasionally, however, a teacher's neurotic or other disturbance is seen in his handling of incidents, or children, and where, for example, a child involved is already prone to maladjusted behaviour, the teacher's behaviour is quite likely to provoke this. A sadistic teacher can induce attacks of school phobia; a normal but disruptive child can provoke an uncontrollable aggressive outburst in a neurotic teacher who shocks a class by pinioning the child against a wall.

It is also clear that pressures upon staff in some difficult schools are considerable. These strains sometimes find their expression in physical breakdowns and mental disorders of various kinds ranging from a full 'nervous breakdown' to psychosomatic disorders leading to frequent but short absences from school for example. This latter phenomenon is well known in difficult schools, where some staff find it literally very hard to come back to school after the weekend break, or to attend for work when they have a particularly tough class to teach that day. Once again we find a vicious circle. Disturbed children and disturbed adults co-exist, each acting upon the other. As has already been suggested, perhaps in this kind of rare situation what is surprising is the commendable quantity and quality of teaching and learning which often takes place in spite of it.

What one wants to ask is how disturbed teachers can be helped towards alleviation of their own suffering, and towards good teacher relationships with their pupils. Many such teachers are already receiving psychiatric assistance; if they are not, then it is often extremely difficult for the head teacher to intervene and recommend it, when he has perceived the need for it, though a general suggestion that the teacher is unwell and should seek medical help may be acceptable. An excellent source of help in these matters are the good friends among the staff of the teacher concerned. Psychiatric assistance, even when accepted, is often long-term, however, in serious cases, and the hard truth is that seriously disturbed teachers often continue to teach for long periods because teaching is their livelihood, and because it is extremely difficult technically to relieve them of their post unless they commit an offence such as injuring a child. It appears, therefore, that what is needed are attempts to spot such potential developments at the earliest possible time, for example, by sensitising head teachers and inspectors to the signs of psychiatric disorder, and the provision of resources designed to help such teachers, at an early stage in the disturbance if possible. By this is meant that therapy should be made available to teachers — at least, initially, in Social Priority Area schools — via, for example, a counselling service for teachers, or a group therapy arrangement. Some schools already have limited access to such resources, on an informal basis, usually with a local child guidance clinic, and there are already a few group therapy schemes which number teachers among their clients, but this help is on a tiny scale compared with what is being advocated. In some cases, however, such help will not appreciably alter the situation in which the teacher really needs, in his own best interests and his pupils', to leave either the type of school he is working in, or to leave teaching altogether. In the former instance a sympathetic attitude on the part of the head teacher and local inspectorate can often help bring about the necessary change of post. In the latter there is often a need for a generous attitude on the part of the LEA towards the granting of the sabbatical leave which will allow the teacher to retrain.

Before leaving the question of the contribution of disturbed teachers to the development of the difficult school, it should be pointed out that the incidents in which their disturbance shows itself figure among the most taxing which senior school staffs, and notably head teachers, have to deal. Where a teacher's behaviour is manifestly bizarre, or exaggerated, or cruel, and the head knows that this is as a result of his being unwell, and where there is a serious complaint from a child, or her parents, coupled with their wish to have the teacher punished, it is very difficult to handle the situation in an equitable manner. Fortunately such cases are rare.

Teachers with low professional standards are a blight on any school, but they can also aggravate and precipitate maladjusted behaviours, where the potential for these is already high. They can do this through lateness and sudden absences, fail through negligence or deliberate intent to carry out instructions or to support the details of the school's policy. There is ample scope for these failures in the complex machinery of a school. One illustration of how low professional standards can create behavioural disturbance is to be seen in the area of the breakdown of trust between teachers and children. Such teachers break promises: they say that good things will happen, and they don't; they arouse enthusiasms and then let them peter out; they promise organisation and then let chaos happen. When this occurs often enough in a school, mistrust grows in children, and anxiety and misery prevail. This is a school climate in which disruptive behaviour breeds. The lack of a clearly defined and executed policy is part of the general climate, so it does not matter immediately to the children whether it occurs through the negligence or deliberate intent referred to above. Thus it is that teachers who flout agreed school policy for whatever reasons, contribute to a climate of malaise in the school in which they work.

Symptomatic of the difficult school are erratically and irrationally applied sanctions. Indeed, the whole topic of rewards and sanctions is an extremely sensitive one in relation to disruptive behaviour in the ordinary school. It is a topic upon which it is too easy to speak simplistically, when the reality is highly complex. Thus the stable school with what one could call a 'healthy' system is one in which a clear general framework, causing no unreasonable strain to the participants (in spite of the difficulty of defining 'reasonableness' of strain), still permits that flexibility which facilitates the idiosyncratic adjustment which particular situations and individuals demand. By this is meant that the overall system of rules can continue to operate, while individual teachers are able to interpret them, as flexibly as is needed occasionally; and individual children can depart from them at times, without punishment following inexorably (Reynolds, 1976). A system of rewards and punishments may be 'unhealthy' either because there is no clear framework, or because the framework causes unreasonable strain, for example by being hyper-repressive. In the latter case the child showing disruptive behaviour may be harshly punished as a consequence; in the former he may be punished when he had no reason to expect it, or may be punished by certain teachers for the same behaviour ignored by other teachers. Both types of unhealthy systems tend to disturb children.

The effect of large-scale disruptive behaviour on the quality of teaching is a seriously damaging consequence of the difficult school. Both lesson content and method are often modified, following up disruption. Previous disorder, in which the teacher has not been personally involved may force the teacher to revise what he does with a class; if he has been personally involved he may be exceptionally subdued in approach and may again find the need to modify his lesson plan. But where the disorder is continuous, this can have a drastic effect upon the quality of his teaching.

The lesson may not cohere, as steps in its logic get missed out. Or an 'active' lesson may become totally passive. Sometimes the teacher clings to an original 'active' plan, but has frequently to raise his voice above the noise, or reprimand again and again, with rising and obvious agitation. Experienced teachers sometimes state categorically that with certain classes, all they could was 'baby-mind' them, so impossible had it become to attempt normal, good teaching with them; oral work became impossible and with it all discussion of ideas except in written form. Class teaching, the presentation and clarification of new ideas by means of 'chalk and talk' and the to-and-froing of question and answer had become a thing of the past, because it provoked too many unwanted, noisy interruptions. Instead the standard teaching techniques had become 'quiet work' techniques, silent reading, and the written answering of series of questions on work-sheets. For the children in these classrooms, teaching content and technique had become dominated by misbehaviour considerations, and warped by them, so that for much of the time they were exposed to teaching, which in the teacher's opinion was less good, less interesting and stimulating, less active and less satisfying than it might otherwise have been.

In describing the ways in which the misbehaving class often creates distractions for the child wishing to concentrate and encourages inferior teaching in his teachers, what needs to be emphasised is that though it may have a deleterious effect upon the work of a stable and secure child who is coping well with the school situation and is learning readily, how much more significant its effect could be upon the child prone to maladjustment. He may already have difficulties in concentration, which disturbance around him will exacerbate. His attention span may be very short, and if excitement in the class generates emotion in him, it may so reduce it as to render it virtually useless for learning purposes. If the teacher so modifies his teaching as to over-emphasise written work, the disturbed child whose failure in school focuses upon reading and writing will be under further pressure, and if the teaching, as has been suggested above, is warped by misbehaviour considerations, then he will be taught less clearly, and in a less stimulating fashion. The child will learn less easily. The emotionally disturbed child is at an immense disadvantage in a disruptive school setting. He needs the most effective teaching possible if he is to learn. It has been found that high pupil turnover is associated with a high incidence of disruptive behaviours. If there is a direct association between these two factors, this is likely to be because disturbance is encouraged by instability of environment and because it is hard to adjust to different teaching methods, and other factors, though it may well be that both factors depend upon one or more other variables such as bad housing, which leads to rehousing, with a consequent change of school for the child. Certainly there needs to be research into means of minimising the stresses caused, when a child moves school, to both the child who moves and the groups he moves from, and into. It is too easily assumed in secondary schools where there is a high pupil turnover, that the admission and leaving of a child is a routine matter, requiring no special measures, although children are sensitive and often need help in riding these situations. When many children leave and enter a new school or class some children will become habituated to the events, but others will become sensitised and a fresh event may cause keen, if concealed, distress. Among the latter group of children one would expect to find some disturbed children. The situation in which a child moves from one school into another is psychologically a complex event for any child.

High pupil turnover is one result of environmental stresses of various kinds, and itself imposes stress upon the child, and increases the task-load of the school. Poor children may move house and school frequently. Some schools recruit children of whom an abnormally high proportion are under environmental stress of one or more kinds. These schools include the present Social Priority Area schools, but undoubtedly include others at present outside the SPA designation. Such children have been well described by Clegg and Megson (1968), Wolff (1969) and others (Schools Council 1970). As with children with learning difficulties, the need is for either a balanced school population, containing only a fair share of children with special social, personal, and educational needs or highly specialised, very adequate resources to meet a specially large proportion of such children in any one school.

Seriously disordered schools represent the apex of the problem of misbehaviour and occasionally hit the headlines, as did Risinghill, in the secondary sector (Berg, 1968), and William Tyndale (Auld Report, 1979) in the primary, but the problem of disorderliness can occur at certain times in the histories of other schools. Research is needed, to investigate when this is likely to happen, but it may be that such times are when the head teacher wishes to conceal the problems of his school, when inspectors for whatever reason do not inspect, but rely entirely on head teachers' descriptions of their schools, and when mechanisms operate in the direction of the development of slum schools. These mechanisms may include the operation of neighbourhood schools in severely disadvantaged areas, and processes of hidden selection which lead to the gathering of large numbers of potentially difficult children in one school. A disorderly school may also arise where a previously stable school has a head or senior teachers suffering from a prolonged illness associated either with depression or lengthy absence from the school. It may also occur where reorganisation takes place or the school population changes rapidly due, for example, to rehousing schemes. In the disorderly school the resources — which are largely staff stability and staffing strength, are inadequate to meet the demands made by the pupils, a large proportion of whom will have special needs. Certainly resources of staffing need to be far more generous for schools at risk of disorderliness, than for other schools.

Where head teachers require help with problems of misbehaviour in their school they can of course obtain it — in some authorities more easily than others — from the nexus of educational and social welfare services. The school doctor, the local child guidance clinic and school psychological services, and others will be in a position to offer assistance with individual pupils, or small groups of pupils. There may be need for a case study by the specialists involved. The child may have a transfer to another school arranged and so on. A lot of help is available. But when it comes to questions of more generalised misbehaviour, difficult classes, or difficult schools, adequate help and advice may not be available from local authority advisers and inspectors, or indeed her Majesty's Inspectorate. What seems to be needed here, at the central HMI level, is the development of a group of troubleshooting advisers, with specialised knowledge of problems of disruptive behaviour. This group would obviously incorporate psychologists, but it needs also advisers with expertise in the area of the relationship between administrative and organisational structures, and curriculum and disruptive behaviour. At the moment there is no such group, and indeed among HMI's there are few with experience of teaching in and managing difficult schools. There is experience of control difficulties in some Western European schools (we are at present studying these), and in others in the USA, from which the group of troubleshooters could learn, though clearly care would need to be taken in extrapolating from foreign situations to the British scene.

This section concludes with an account of a difficult school, written by a young teacher who spent a year in it. It expresses his personal, subjective view of the school, but is offered to illustrate some of the points made in the preceding pages.

A Violent School

Physically, Matchinfold School is typical of many inner city comprehensive schools described, rather flatteringly, as 'purpose-built' by the architects and educational planners responsible for their construction over the last two decades. The building is functional: that is, sparse, ill-proportioned and with a depressing, alienating pseudo-modernity. It is constructed largely of huge expanses of reinforced concrete and glass, with the odd length of brick-work and the very occasional 'contemporary' mural. The walls are sporadically covered with frequently mis-spelt graffiti and slogans celebrating local football teams, rapidly dating pop groups, rival gangs and the more notorious school celebrities. The paint work is cracked, faded, flaking and dirty. Exterior loose fittings were vandalised years ago and considered not worth replacing. Thus the disregarded empty and broken waste-paper basket holders stand faintly reproachfully as litter drifts and blows around the play areas to amass in neglected corners. Attempts to grow new grass to replace that worn out by pupils taking a short cut across the one area of green proved unsuccessful despite — or because of — frequent detentions so that during winter the one potentially friendly play area is little more than an uncomfortable mud-bath.

Inside, the school is equally run-down. Many of the fittings are missing, unusable or simply redundant. For instance, the school had been fitted with wooden lockers, along the lengths of each floor of corridors, but these have remained broken for several years. Their skeletons provide the physical base for complicated games and rituals played by most of the lower school. Again, graffiti jostles with the occasional poster or wall decoration for attention and together these provide the only visual relief to the impersonal, inadequately-lit corridors. The more outrageous slogans are dutifully painted out by a patient maintenance staff. Many of the desks and tables and chairs in the classrooms are damaged (though it must be pointed out that the school is due for refurbishing shortly) and displays hung with some care and thoughtfulness by subject teachers average a life-span of around two months before they degenerate into another eye-sore. In short, both the exterior and the interior of the school building resemble nothing so much as one of those cages simulating urban environments in which the more inhumane experimenting psychologists house their rats. It requires considerable faith to see this physical environment as the sort of geography in which learning is a priority, let alone a likely experience!

Given this structural context, it is hardly surprising that the conduct of many of the pupils is characterised by what seems to be uncaring, self-centred and rather barbaric behaviour patterns. On any journey down any corridor during break periods, it is impossible to ignore pupils shouting, arguing, running, throwing pellets, paper darts or anything that comes immediately to hand — and fighting. Sometimes this is quite vicious, more than a question of boisterousness or high spirits, and —

equally disturbingly — the girls seem to fight quite as much as the boys. Only the piercingly loud and insistent ring of the school bell manages to make itself heard above the general cacophony of noise with any ease. This atmosphere during break-time simply encourages hostility and its corollary, loneliness.

During lessons in the lower school, even the most considerate classes take a good five minutes to settle down and this can take up to twenty minutes. This apparently straightforward process appears to necessitate continuous bickering and occasionally violent arguing amongst the pupils as teachers adopt the role of arbitrators and peace-makers. The noise-level is consistently high, neatly calculated at a point just below the teacher's tolerance level. Even the strictest or the most experienced teachers face a daily barrage of petty insults, insignificant acts calculated to annoy (and of course to attract attention) and outright insolence. In general, this treatment is borne with great tolerance and forbearance.

But perhaps the most depressing element of all is the unadulterated violence of the language used by the majority of the children. Quite simply, most of the pupils swear most of the time. Some of it is affectation or swaggering, but much of it is naturally and unthinkingly incorporated into their use of language. Tacit double standards are in operation throughout the school and apply, with varying emphasis, to all the staff. The pupils are 'allowed' to swear; the teachers are not (a sample: 'Please can you sit down, Wayne?'; 'Fuck off'; Wayne sits down). Similarly, the pupils can insult the teachers; the teachers cannot insult the pupils. In many ways, it is utterly pointless for teachers to swear at or to insult their pupils: this merely provides an implicit supporting structure for their behaviour and reinforces its autonomy. Nonetheless, the crude and reductive use of language characterises the way in which many of the pupils use English and shows itself particularly clearly in the colloquialisms and short cuts which emerge in much of the written work. This brutally simplistic, blunt and wildly imprecise language is closely related to the physical grossness of many of their responses.

In comparison to the havoc in the rest of the school building, the staff room seems like a heaven. It is a repository of good, old-fashioned bourgeois values: toleration, consideration, open-mindedness, friendliness and frankness; in short, decency. To the impartial observer this blatant contrast between the staff room and the rest of the school emphasises the impression that things haven't altered very much since Disraeli first formulated the notion of Two Nations. The radical difference, however, is that the change does not centre around a split along simple class lines. It is much wider and more complex than this. Rather, there is a huge cultural divide between the respective values and assumptions of the teachers and the pupils. This, in turn, increases the gap between We and Them.

The significance of these generalised impressions of Matchinfold School lies in the fact that violence never occurs in a moral or social vacuum. The more obvious acts of violence which occurred during the period in which the writer was teaching at the school were merely the eruptions of a volcano that was constantly smouldering. The violence of the school building, the pupils' behaviour norms and their language were all essential ingredients in producing the climate for a constant backdrop of countless minor incidents and several fairly serious violent incidents.

Two in particular stand out. The first incident concerns a lower school boy who was asked to move to another seat because he was preventing another boy from working. He refused. He was asked to move again. Again he refused. This went on for some time while the rest of the class became more unsettled and distracted. Eventually the teacher (a very experienced lady respected throughout the school by pupils as well as staff) held the boy by his shoulders and attempted to move him physically. The boy turned on the teacher, punched her in the face and kicked her. The teacher had to be taken to hospital; the boy was suspended.

The second incident concerns a fourth form girl who was fighting with a boy during a lesson. The teacher (a young man with some years' teaching experience) broke up the fight by coming between the combatants and forcibly separating them. On the basis that he had interfered in her affairs instead of minding his own business, the girl went for the teacher and smashed his glasses and damaged his face. Again, the attack on the teacher involved his going to hospital. The pupil was expelled and later sent to a special school. The fact that a teacher is no less liable to physical assault than anybody else had become more obvious and the incident — news of which spread round the school very quickly — became folk-lore and another step on the road towards further violence and chaos.

Accounts of the many varied incidents with which the pastoral staff dealt daily throughout the term would literally run into tens of pages. To summarise: class-rooms were vandalised; books were completely destroyed; breaking up fights and potential fights was a regular part of a teacher's work; and extortion rackets, bullying and petty theft (the school cannot risk having cloakrooms, so the pupils carry all of their belongings with them all the time) are endemic throughout the school. Not surprisingly, staff absenteeism and illness was high, nervous breakdowns were not infrequent and several teachers claimed to maintain their sanity by near-alcoholism. Teachers at Matchinfold School are policemen and social workers as much as they are skill-instructors and pedagogues.

Of course, schools mirror the society in which they both exist and define their function while being at the same time an essential, integral part of that society in a dialectical process. Ours is a violent society. This is seen at its clearest in our large cities. It is hardly surprising that schools servicing these communities are themselves violent institutions. It is as difficult as it is unrealistic to expect teachers to impose basic standards of decency and civilised behaviour in a city whose own ethic, both economic and moral, is effectively at odds with these sorts of standards. A teacher cannot be expected to take on and reform a whole culture.

Further, it is both tempting and easy to exaggerate both the extent and the degree of the violence at any comprehensive school. Similarly, it would be quite fraudulent to pretend that genuine significant learning does not take place in any comprehensive school, including Matchinfold School; emphatically, it does. But the fact remains that the media cannot sensationalise problems which do not exist any more than educationalists can blissfully pretend that the problem is minor, irrelevant or anyway under control. Violence in some inner-city schools remains a very real problem which merits urgent attention and priority with the schools and education authorities themselves as much as, if not more than, in society generally.

Within this context, several physical and administrative structures of Matchinfold School can be seen to exacerbate the problem. It is a large school, with a roll, when the writer taught there, of 1,800. Of course, size in itself does not produce problems. But size which is physically unpleasant accompanied by anonymity, disinterest and lack of communication will inevitably help produce alienation, boredom and disaffection to which the pockets of diffident, lonely and lost children skulking in corridors away from the raucous crowds milling along the corridors provide adequate and eloquent testament. The chilling unfriendliness of the general environment creates its own criticism.

The disaffection is further exacerbated by at least two aspects of school policy in particular: almost universal mixed-ability teaching in the lower school, and the length of lessons. This is no place to argue the case for or against mixed-ability teaching. (As a side-reference, however, it seems worth pointing out that mixed-ability teaching will prove successful in a department totally committed to it in the same way that streamed or 'settled' teaching will prove successful in a department totally committed to these methods of teaching. The rest of the argument is largely a matter of teachers' personal ethics, politics, articles of faith and teaching styles. For a teacher this argument is crucial; its importance to the child is more debatable. In a potentially volatile environment like that of Matchinfold School, a policy of mixed-ability teaching demands total commitment, high standards of execution, a sense of common purpose and a unified approach from each department using it. Unfortunately, this was not the case. There was little sense of guidance from the Head of Department and the disparity of teaching styles (like the hoarding of the best text books) was enormous, with a consequent loss of coherence. Thus only the negative effects of mixed-ability teaching were in evidence. When certain children were asked to do work of which they were incapable (how, for instance, can children who can barely read or write competently be expected to study French, especially if they are in the company of children with excellent communication skills?), they compensated for their lack of self-esteem in their own and their class-mates' eyes by regularly indulging in asinine, dilatory or disruptive behaviour. Unsurprisingly they quickly ended up in serious trouble and the lesson or lessons in which they were unsuccessful in their own terms as well as the teacher's became readily identified with punishment. The result is a vicious circle: further alienation produces further failure which produces further disruption which produces further punishment which produces further alienation . . . and so on. Notoriety provides its own reward and the moral and emotional context for violent behaviour is within easy grasp.

Like many schools, Matchinfold uses a policy of three double lessons of eighty or ninety minutes each daily. One apparently cogent argument commonly cited for this practice is that it minimises disruption during lesson-changes. However, most of the lower school and middle school classes taught found it difficult to maintain concentration for more than forty minutes and each change of activity within the double period lesson took at least five minutes (which it was circumspect to allow for in lesson plans). This inability to maintain concentration quickly manifested itself in the tendency to become easily distracted, bored or disaffected and, again, the appropriate geography for violence was so much nearer.

The writer believes that there is a tangible causal relationship between violence in some inner-city schools and the architectural nature of the buildings, the received behaviour and language patterns of the pupils and certain educational practices currently fairly common in secondary schools. The writer has attempted neither to discuss the vexed and vexing question of discipline and the implications of its rigid implementation, nor the fact that some of the problems stem from the simple fact that schooling is compulsory and that a large minority of schoolchildren feel that they are unlikely to learn anything which they consider, whether rightly or wrongly, to be relevant. However, the fact remains that violence in schools is ignored at the peril of parents, teachers, society and the children themselves. A determination to reduce school violence does not necessitate the re-introduction of the birch. But it does involve conceding the scope and degree of the problem and placing its solution above educational ideology, white-washing liberalism or face-saving stone-walling.

Part Three

TECHNIQUES FOR COPING
WITH DISRUPTIVE BEHAVIOUR IN SCHOOLS

12 INTRODUCTION

In this section we present firstly accounts of three linked studies of techniques for studying and coping with disruptive behaviour. They will be of interest to students and teachers in all types of school, and all the details are given which make it possible for the techniques to be tried out by the reader or his colleagues.

The first of the three studies is of women teachers' reactions to their most difficult and unusual boys and girls, and leads to description of a systematic check-list approach to the handling of difficult children. The second study shows how it is possible to analyse and measure the difficulty of a class of children, while the last describes an 'encouragement project' in which an attempt was made to improve the behaviour of a difficult class of third year boys in a secondary school.

Analytical research into the factors which predispose to disruptive behaviour and trigger it off is clearly of the utmost importance. Side by side with this we need to develop simple techniques which will help schools to analyse their own particular situation and to modify it if they wish, using the tools and resources which are at their disposal.

If we look at Barbara Wootton's *Crime and Penal Policy*, we find in it the very serious suggestion that children of compulsory school age should eventually not be subject to criminal jurisdiction at all. Instead, offences of schoolchildren should be dealt with in the educational, not the penal system, with the help of counsellor/social workers and a 'comprehensive conference' of teachers, parents, etc. We could therefore look to an expansion of the teacher's role in relation to deviant behaviour, with a consequent even more pressing need for the development within teacher training at all levels of teachers' skills in this field.

Practical self-help techniques are badly needed, as is shown by the Schools Council Project initiated in January 1981, which hopes to produce a self-help guide for teachers coping with difficult pupil behaviour. Over and above the help which these techniques can give, the very fact of the analysis, and the taking up of a research stance, can be of benefit to a school and to its teachers. All too often disruptive behaviour is dealt with in an atmosphere of aggression and acrimony, rather than one of rationality. Of course anger can be useful, but all too often in incidents of disruption it becomes destructive, rather than constructive. To use an analytical approach, and to use planned techniques in coping with disruptive behaviour may also reduce the sense of impotence which teachers sometimes experience in dealing with it, the feeling that they have 'tried everything', have come to the end of the road, and that the end is a sense of failure or degradation, or the total rejection of the child in a form of exclusion. There will be failure at times; there has to be, particularly in this area, where criminologists also fail. But the failure can be less frequent if we utilise our resources, and realise indeed how extensive they are.

The following three small-scale studies of disruptive behaviour are linked in that some of the findings of each study led on to the next and are embedded in it, so that they form a group. They also have this in common, that they rest upon a belief that a central factor in the handling of disruptive behaviour is the way in which the teacher sees the child and his actions, that we need to understand this, and take it as one starting point in any attempt to modify the situation. This is not to say that we should deny 'reality' — a broken window is a broken window and will need to be repaired.

13

A CHECK-LIST
REACTING TO DIFFICULT AND UNUSUAL BEHAVIOUR IN TEN TO THIRTEEN YEAR OLDS

We do not yet know in detail how teachers' perception of the difficulty and unusualness of certain pupils develops; we do not know how quickly certain children stand out as 'difficult' to newly trained teachers of varying personality types. Young teachers, student teachers, quickly spot 'awkward customers' in their classes, but we do not know how durable these first impressions are and what changes occur in the child characteristics which students and young teachers find difficult, as they become more experienced at teaching. But what is fairly clear is that after a few years of teaching, teaching skill — though it may still be improved upon, like other skills, for a very long time — is usually such that the teacher can control and cope with most children that he is likely to meet in the ordinary school situation. The first study therefore focused on the reactions of experienced teachers to seriously misbehaving children — these were almost all teachers who had been teaching for a minimum of five years full-time; with one exception, they had been through a course of teacher training. Many of them also held posts of special responsibility in a primary or a secondary school.

There were thirty-one teachers taking part in the study, all of them women, as it was suspected that the two sexes might differ in their responses to misbehaviour, and they came from twenty-three different schools, six secondary and seventeen primary. In most cases the primary schools acted as feeder schools to the secondary schools, and all the schools were scattered in different areas of a large city. Of the secondary schools, one was a grammar school, four were comprehensive (all different in history, character and size, which ranged from 750 to 1,700 pupils) and one was a Roman Catholic secondary modern school. Of the primary schools, thirteen were non-denominational, one was Church of England and three were Roman Catholic. Not only were all the schools mixed, but all the teachers taught mixed classes; this was essential because it was necessary to know what their responses were to children of both sexes. The teachers had an average of over thirteen years teaching experience, and over half had taught in their present school for four years or more, so that they were a 'stable' group, whose difficulties could not be attributed to a recent move into a new school. They included two primary head teachers, four primary deputy heads, two secondary senior mistresses who also carried out head of department functions, and various other senior secondary teachers, and primary teachers with graded posts. All the teachers had taught the children they were talking about for at least two terms, though the secondary teachers would of course have a shorter period of contact with them each week than would most of the primary teachers.

The research set out to explore not only what sort of children these teachers found to be their most difficult or unusual pupils, but also what techniques these teachers of high competence had used with these and similar children, when they behaved particularly disconcertingly. This seemed to be very valuable information for other teachers to have.

To obtain this information a questionnaire was prepared in which the teachers were asked to pick out first the girl in their top class (in the primary school) or first or second year class (in the secondary school) who was the most difficult or unusual girl in the class, or who showed the most signs of being so later. (This meant that most of the children were aged ten to thirteen years.) The teachers were then given a list of twenty-four types of behaviour, which teachers often find among their pupils and were asked to tick those types which described the girl they had chosen, and say which types had created the most frequent and serious difficulties. After this they were given a list of some forty steps which teachers take, and techniques which they commonly employ to deal with such behaviours, and they were asked to pick out the ones that they had actually used with this girl, in dealing with the behaviours which caused them the most serious and frequent difficulties, and to say how often they had used these techniques. Teachers were also asked what else they had done to cope. This constitutes the first section of the questionnaire; the second section was identical to the first, but asked about the teacher's most difficult or unusual boy.

The types of behaviour which played a key role in these two sections were compiled by modifying a behaviour scale used as a screening device in the diagnosis of maladjustment and whose validity and reliability had been tested (Rutter, 1967). The list of steps and techniques was derived from the researcher's experience of working with teachers in secondary schools, and from pilot interviews with secondary and primary teachers. The third and fourth sections of the questionnaire investigated how the teachers would handle behaviour which was specifically anti-social and specifically neurotic as these are the two most common types of maladjusted behaviour, and for this purpose two hypothetical boys were described, John, an anti-social boy, and Paul, a neurotic boy. The description of these two boys was arrived at by combining, in the profile of each, symptoms which previous research had found to discriminate between anti-social and neurotic children. Once again the teachers were given the same list of possible responses to the behaviour as they had had for the sections on the boy and girl whom they taught, and this time were asked which they would definitely, or possibly use, for a child like John and like Paul.

In this way, each teacher was speaking about four children, two real and two hypothetical, but even in talking about the 'hypothetical' children it was clear that such cases were on the whole familiar to the teachers concerned. This was particularly so of John, the anti-social boy.

Study of the way in which the teachers ticked the types of behaviour describing their boy or girl yielded some very interesting findings. As had been suspected, the way they saw the child dominated the way they answered the questionnaire. The teacher response seemed to be emotional in character. The boy's behaviour called forth an even more emotional response than the girl's; the teachers were often very worried indeed by his behaviour. If we remember that these were all female teachers this finding becomes extremely interesting, particularly as it was found later that the primary teachers' anxieties, greater than those of the secondary teachers in any case, centred particularly around the boy, whereas the secondary teachers were more worried about their girl. Why were women primary teachers so anxious about deviancy in boys? Is this over-anxiety? And what effect does over-anxiety have on the boy's behaviour? Can it propel him towards delinquency or greater disturbance? These are important questions, especially since most boys of primary school age are taught by women in this country. Analysis showed again and again that the teachers were responding in a rather different way to the girl and the boy, in their descriptions of them, and emotional reactions to them. How can we interpret those clear differential sex findings? Why should female primary teachers be more concerned about deviancy in boys, yet female secondary teachers be more concerned about deviancy in girls? There may be a clue to the reason in the finding, which reached a low level of significance that as a group the teachers spotted signs of miserableness and unhappiness less often in boys than girls. If female teachers, because of their sex, are less sensitive to signs of unhappiness in boys than in girls this may be because they cannot empathise so easily with boys, and also because they cannot recognise the unhappiness behind the masculine 'stiff-upper-lip', culturally dictated role which boys in our society have taken on, certainly by the age of ten. If to this we add the teacher's culturally-derived notions of delinquency and criminality being mainly masculine, coupled with her basic sexual notions of the overpowering male, we have a fine psychological 'mix' which could very easily explain over-anxiety concerning deviant boys.

Teachers perceptions of deviancy and intelligence in their pupils are frequently related. J B W Douglas (1964) found a negative evaluation of boys' potential by their primary teachers, most of whom were women. More recently, Sula Wolff (1969) has picked up this finding, adding to it by wondering whether the excessive number of behaviour disorders among boys is related to it.

Why then does the picture change from primary school to secondary school, so that in the latter women teachers come to regard deviancy in girls as more worrying than that in boys? Perhaps in the secondary school, the young boy is seen with older boys, and is therefore seen by the teacher as male with a difference: he is now an attractive male. He is developing adult characteristics, and his view of himself, in relation to the female teacher, may affect his behaviour, thus further influencing her perception of him. The boy's propensity for delinquency is now a fact of life, which has to be accepted, as with the increasing age of the child it is no longer easy to reverse. Because delinquent trends are less easy to reverse, anxiety-rousing attempts to counter them are more seldom made. Besides, delinquency is more easy tolerated when off-set by arguments of masculinity. The female teacher, however, teaching pre-adolescent girls who are deviant, sees in them a distortion of the female role which is her own, so that the distortion is painful to her.

This perceptual similarity: 'We are both female', accentuated by the presence of the male, increases anxieties on both sides. Added to this there is, of course, the association of deviancy in adolescent girls with illegitimate births, and possibly long-term promiscuity. All this may make the female secondary teacher more sensitive to girls' deviant behaviour and more emotionally roused by it.

The second interesting group of findings in this study relates to the types of behaviour which the teachers had witnessed in their sixty-two most difficult and unusual children. The most frequently mentioned behaviours were very clearly, disobedience, poor concentration, fighting, and quickness to fly off the handle. When however, it came to designating those behaviours which had caused the most frequent and serious difficulties, the pattern is rather different. Disobedience is mentioned almost twice as often as its nearest two rivals, poor concentration and quickness to fly off the handle, and all other types of behaviour fall well behind these three. It seemed that these three behaviours were especially important for the group of teachers in this study and that when a teacher found one or two or all three of them in a child, she might put a specially large effort into coping with the child, and be particularly worried about him or her, and she might even spot a particularly large number of deviant types of behaviour in the child. The questionnaire scores were therefore analysed using one-tailed Mann Whitney U-tests and ample evidence was found of what had been anticipated with the differences in the important scores of children with and without these behaviours becoming more and more apparent as first one, then any two, and finally all three of the behaviours were found in the same child (Lawrence, 1970).

Basically, these behaviours were 'out of control' behaviours. If we remember that many of the teachers held senior posts, it is easy to understand that as a group they were likely to want to control. But there is another way of looking at these findings; we can look at misbehaviour in schools as a series of problems requiring solutions. If we do this, we can see that whereas a single important form of misbehaviour could constitute a problem to a teacher, if the child shows two forms the problem could multiply considerably in size, and if he shows three forms it could become enormous. Take disobedience, and temper. By itself temper may be something of a problem. But if the child shows temper and is disobedient, he will resist attempts to calm him down and so his temper problem becomes more acute. If to temper and disobedience he now adds poor concentration, he will not settle to work when told and in periods of not concentrating there will be more opportunities for his flare-ups of temper to occur. In these results we see in microcosm the enormous difficulties which can be experienced in attempts to control and teach children with multiple behaviour difficulties, as one form of misbehaviour rebounds from the other, exacerbating several-fold an already problematic situation.

We now come to the ways in which the teachers handled the deviant behaviour of their boy and girl, and here it was interesting that there were a few cases in which there were statistically significant differences between the secondary and primary teachers. The secondary teachers suggested more often that a girl should be referred to a doctor or child guidance clinic. This could be because primary teachers, in the case of their ten-year-olds, prefer to leave referral in abeyance in the hope that the child's behaviour may improve, on the change to the new secondary school.

The primary teachers more often gave their boy special help with his work, and when telling a child of either sex off, they took the child more often to one side. One wonders whether it is easier, in the primary classroom, to use techniques such as these. It may be easier, in the more fluid primary classroom, to take a child aside, but surely secondary teachers too would try particularly to help a misbehaving child in his work from difficulties in which obviously some misbehaviour itself stems? Primary teachers more often told both their boy and girl that they were sure he or she was going to improve. Does this reflect a more optimistic attitude to the future of misbehaving children in the primary than in the secondary school? Or are both secondary school teachers and pupils simply more realistic? Perhaps the deviant child of secondary school age would reject as untrue a teacher's statement of her confidence in his improvement.

If we combine the information concerning what the teachers did about all the four children in the questionnaire and list the steps they took, or would take, with very difficult or unusual children, in their order of frequency, we arrive at the following series of techniques and behaviours used by highly experienced teachers for the handling of seriously deviant behaviour.

ACTION TAKEN BY TEACHERS	**Percentage Frequencies**
1. I have communicated with other staff about him.	90.3
2. I have given him special help with his work.	83.9
3. I have looked at his school records.	81.4
4. I have had a chat with him.	80.6
5. I have had to give him special attention, to settle him to his work.	79.0
6. I have reasoned with him.	73.4
7. I have been extra gentle in handling him.	68.5
8. In the midst of teaching, I have had to concentrate on this pupil for several minutes.	65.3
9. I have jollied him along.	64.5
10. I have advised contacting, or have contacted, his parents or guardians.	63.7
11. When telling him off, I have taken him to one side.	62.1
12. I have ignored his behaviour, on occasion.	60.5
13. I have told him off.	58.1
14. I have had to stop the lesson for a minute or two.	56.4
15. I have asked him why he behaved like this.	56.4
16 I have pointed out to him that the rest of the class are getting on with their work.	52.4

ACTION TAKEN BY TEACHERS	Percentage Frequencies
17. I have changed his seat.	50.8
18. I have praised his work more than was due.	50.8
19. I have given him different work to do, from what I had intended.	50.8
20. I have suggested that he should be referred to a doctor or child guidance clinic.	49.2
21. I have regarded getting him back to his work as my first priority.	48.4
22. I have modified my teaching approach to him.	46.8
23. I have told him off in front of the class.	46.8
24. I have told him that I have had better behaviour from him at other times.	45.2
25. I have got a suitable friend to help settle him to his work.	44.4
26. I have separated him from the others.	42.7
27. I have considered that he should be referred to a doctor or child guidance clinic.	41.9
28. I have regarded getting the class back to work as my first priority.	40.3
29. I have asked him whether he would like to apologise.	36.3
30. I have referred to rules of classroom behaviour.	34.7
31. I have told him I am sure he is going to improve.	29.8
32. I have thought it best to steer clear of him, for a while.	29.0
33. I have asked another member of staff, or the head, to have a chat with him.	24.2
34. I have told him what would happen to him if he repeated or continued with this sort of behaviour.	24.2
35. I have been aware of this boy's behaviour damaging my relationships with the class.	23.4
36. I have sent him out of the room.	22.6
37. I have referred to the action the community takes, to protect itself against behaviour of this kind.	21.0
38. I have altered my plan for that lesson.	20.2

Spearman rank order correlation coefficients were calculated for the four sections of the questionnaire, to check that the ranking of the techniques just listed was a fairly stable one, so that items towards the top part of the list for the handling of the boy would tend also to appear towards the top for the handling of the girl. The coefficients were all high ones, being exceptionally high (0.923 $p < 0.01$) for the relationship between the lists for the real boy and the real girl. In other words, there was a great degree of agreement between the use of techniques for these children. In answer to anyone who is inclined to say 'Those teachers aren't saying what they actually did; they're saying what they think they ought to say', it should be mentioned that occasionally teachers commented in the margin of the questionnaire that they had used a certain technique but that it had been useless, or unsuccessful. Where teachers can admit failure in this wasy, it is fairly certain they really have tried to use the technique. Besides, there is a good deal of evidence scattered through the study that their responses to at least the sections on the real children, were 'true'.

Probably the most interesting aspect of the ranked list of techniques and behaviours called forth from teachers by deviant children is the first place, in importance, given to communicating with other staff about the child. No one who has been in a school staff room for any length of time could fail to recognise the truth of this finding. When teachers are worried about children they talk about them. From observations in the staff rooms of difficult schools it could be said that talk between teachers about misbehaving children ranges across a whole continuum of styles, from the distraught fury and panic talk of the teacher who bursts into the staff room after a set-to with a child, through the controlled, loudly expressed exasperation of the confident, experienced teacher who has experienced unwonted difficulties with a class, to the quiet, muted tones of the young teacher in serious difficulties with a group of children.

The need to communicate concerning misbehaving children is great for several very good reasons. Teachers are vulnerable in the area of controlling children; it is a key part of their task as the child who misbehaves may not be learning, as a result, and is likely to stop other children from learning too. The teacher who cannot control children is traditionally considered to be not much use in a school, and so misbehaviour rouses anxieties, and a lot of anger, which often bubble into speech. A lot of 'misbehaviour' talk is defensive, blaming the child to decrease the teacher's feelings of guilt at his inadequacy. Another part of such talk is 'off-loading talk' — talk to teachers who can offer practical assistance in handling the child or group of children concerned, and direct and indirect requests for advice. Much young teacher talk is of this kind. A related purpose of some misbehaviour talk is to gain information about the child; 'What do you know about him?' 'What's he like in your lessons'. The questionnaire included a series of questions about who and for what purpose the teachers had communicated, and would do so, the answers to which provide ample evidence of all the purposes mentioned above as well as evidence of frequent use of communication for the purpose of giving information about this child. This is interesting, as it suggests that teachers feel that misbehaviour talk is not just 'selfish' but in fact helps other teachers, including assistant staff, the better to carry out their work.

There were some interesting comments about the sort of staff to whom the teacher would choose to talk: 'Anyone who had had a good relationship with him', 'Those who know him and are compassionate', showing selectiveness. The responses to this part of the questionnaire raise the question of whether teachers need counsellors to help them through their problems, among which the handling of misbehaviour may well figure, more frequently at an early stage in their career than later, and more commonly in certain schools than in others. One could deduce from this study that the emotion generated by serious deviancy makes the availability of counsellors desirable. But one could also deduce from the answers to the communication section that counsellors could not offer some of the benefits which talk with other teaching staff clearly does offer: information, advice, and practical assistance. If we reflect on this study, it emerges that teachers, particularly experienced teachers, have a large number of ways of dealing with a very difficult child and that it is possible to list these ways. A school staff could pool its list of coping procedures, and the very making of the list would clarify those which were generally acceptable, within the ethos of the school, and those which were not. Young, inexperienced staff might well have novel, worthwhile steps to suggest, and the incorporation within a working party of parents or pupils or ancillary staff, or indeed of a local education authority adviser or officer could enrich the list and the discussion. Distinctions could be made between short-term steps, to deal with the immediate situation, and the longer-term measures. The limitations of the list might suggest the need to add to the school's resources (staff, facilities, etc.) and the list would therefore constantly be open to revision.

The school list or a teacher's own personal list could be used by a teacher, or an assistant teacher in conjunction with a senior teacher as part of an overall strategy to help an individual child, in a systematic way. Thus starting with the group of steps most likely to help this child, one or more steps could be tried for a given period. At the end of this period, a review would take place, and either the same steps could be followed for a longer period, if they were proving useful, or a further step could be added, or could replace one which was not proving fruitful. It is obvious that where a list in itself contains many steps, the different permutations of all these, the combinations, make the list potentially enormous. A great deal will of course depend upon the insight, experience and skill of the teachers concerned, and in their diagnosis of the child's situation, personality and needs. In a sophisticated programme, psychological testing might underpin the work but most schools will not have the resources which this requires. The approach being described is in some ways similar to that advocated by Roberts (1977) when he recommends a 'think tank' group who will consider and carry out remediation strategies with problem children. The differences between our suggestions are several however. In our terms 'listing' can be used by individuals, and the list should include all available strategies not only those which appear useful. Particularly where behaviour is resistant to strategies which are well tried, it may be valuable to attempt a 'fresh' approach, of little obvious utility.

An objection which can quickly be raised to the 'listing' approach is that it reduces the subtlety and spontaneity of inter-personal communication to arid cipher-dictated manipulation. The issue is debatable. Do we not plan, and employ strategies even in the fast-moving *va-et-vient* of 'natural' interaction? Even if one accepts that the cold manipulation of 'listing' is different in kind from the latter, is it not less painful to the child than the alternatives and can it not be a door to better forms of relationship?

The following Behaviour Problem Check List is one that has been developed recently by one of the authors in discussion with several groups of teachers attending courses on children with special needs, or disruptive behaviour. As can be seen, Section A lists steps commonly taken (with the exception of behaviour modification, steps 2 and 3) by classroom teachers who are finding a child difficult. Section B lists other procedures, which senior staff commonly consider, when dealing with such a child. Space is left at the end of each list, so that the teacher and the school can list their idiosyncratic techniques. In general teachers have accepted the lists, commenting that they have never seen the procedures listed in this way, and a number including headteachers, have commented on the potential utility of such a check list. Not only can it help to systematise work with behaviour problems, but it is helpful to teachers who cannot be expected to remember all the possibilities open to them, and all those they have tried. Furthermore, it points out to teachers the very wide range of procedures open to them, singly and in combination, and can thus be a source of considerable encouragement.

Behaviour Problem Check List

A. Classroom Procedures

1.	Apology — give opportunity for
2.	Behaviour modification: Encouragement, etc.
3.	Behaviour modification: Contract
4.	Causes: inspect records
5.	Friend/s: get friend/s to help him
6.	Gentle: be extra gentle
7.	Ignore misbehaviour
8.	Increase attention
9.	Increase praise — private/public
10.	Jolly along
11.	Leader: use as
12.	Medical reasons? e.g. sit near board
13.	Monitor: use as
14.	Place change: seat/group
15.	Point out others behaving well
16.	Previous good conduct: refer to
17.	Private chat
18.	Reasoning
19.	Reprimand: private/public
20.	Rules: reminder
21.	Sanctions: minor (e.g. detention)
	....
22.	Send out of room
23.	Send to other staff
	....
24.	Special help with work
25.	Teaching approach: modify
26.	Work: change work
	....
	....
	....

Behaviour Problem Check List
B. School Procedures

1. Attach to influential staff
2. Class change
3. Communicate with other staff re. areas of good behaviour, preferred subjects, etc.
4. Counselling — formal (counsellor)
5. Counselling — form tutor/other
6. Counselling — preferred teacher
7. Curriculum revision
8. Medical?
9. On report
10. Parent contact — letter
11. Parent contact — invite to school
12. Parent contact — visit
13. Records. Check general record
14. Records. Check medical record
15. Sanctions. Major
    (a) cane
    (b) suspension
    (c) exclusion
    (d) expulsion
16. School: transfer of school
17. Sibling: contact
18. Social services?
19. Special educational treatment
20. Special unit: referral to
21. Supplementary tuition
22. Testing — School
23. Assessment — Educational psychologist

    ....
    ....
    ....

14 A DIFFICULTY GRID: MEASURING THE DIFFICULTY OF CLASSES IN A SECONDARY SCHOOL

The difficulty of classes is a concept which is used a great deal in discussions among secondary school teachers, who, unlike primary teachers, are specialists who teach their special subject or subjects to a large number of different classes, so that they quite naturally compare them for difficulty. Not only can individual teachers tell you which of the classes they teach they find most difficult, but a fair quantity of teacher talk centres around the 'fact' that one class in the school is overall more difficult than others. Recently one of the authors happened to visit a student in a difficult school when an emergency offered her a chance to teach for a period a class left without a teacher. At the end of the period she came into the staff room, where a teacher started to talk to her and elicited the fact that she had just been teaching 3C. In awe-struck tones she told her that she had just taught 'the third most difficult class in the school'? In this school, at least, there seemed to be some consensus as to the rank order of difficulty of the classes. All the talk that goes on in schools round the point, that senior long-established staff often allocate themselves the 'easier' classes, leaving junior staff and newcomers to the school to take the 'tougher' ones, serves to confirm that the concept of class difficulty is a very common one. There have, however, not been any attempts specifically to measure class difficulty. Incidental attempts have been made, in behaviour modification experiments which try to modify the behaviour of the whole class, as distinct from that of individual children. In these experiments, the 'base-line' behaviour patterns of the class are measured by observational methods, in which child after child is systematically observed, and his 'out-of-seat' or other deviant behaviours are counted. The behaviour modification techniques are then employed, and during their implementation, further counting takes place, so that any modification of the behaviours can be assessed. The difference between the technique of this study and the behaviour modification measuring technique just described, was firstly that the technique of this study was to be non-observational, and secondly that it was to be unrelated to any attempt, initially any way, to modify behaviour.

A great deal has been written on observational research techniques, their complexities and advantages and disadvantages. It is said that observational techniques are 'stronger', more valid than other techniques; after all, if you want to study children's running around in a classroom, when they've been told to sit down, the best thing you can do is to get into the classroom and watch what they do, and count how often they do it. But in choosing to try to develop a non-observational technique, the researcher was prompted by several ideas. Firstly, teachers are sensitive about being watched at all, unless they have got used to it, for example, by being involved in team-teaching. They are particularly sensitive about their difficulties in handling non-conforming children, and so observational techniques, though in some respects better techniques, might not be entirely and always acceptable in the study of misbehaviour. Secondly, observational techniques, even where only a sample of behaviour is observed, can be expensive of personnel (some one has got to sit and observe), and time-consuming. This is particularly important if one wants, for example, to survey a whole school or series of schools. For these reasons it seemed useful to try to elaborate a paper-and-pen technique.

The starting point was offered by the finding, in the questionnaire project described earlier, that when describing a child on a profile of items of behaviour, teachers who found certain critical behaviours in a very difficult or unusual child became highly emotional, their emotion colouring their response to many parts of a long questionnaire. In particular, where a child showed the critical behaviours (disobedience, poor concentration and quickness to fly off the handle), the teacher ticked large numbers of other deviant behaviours on the profile. It was thought that the same sort of mechanism might operate for behaviours which teachers value positively, behaviours like co-operation, even-temperedness, and ability to settle to work, behaviours which were the opposite of those concentrated on in the study just described in Chapter 13. If this was right, then by giving teachers a mixed list of items of behaviour, half negatively and half positively valued, it would be found that the ticks on such a list would describe a child as one whom the teacher found either 'difficult' or 'easy'. If, in a secondary school, all the teachers who taught a particular class were to describe all the children in the class, one would end up with a comprehensive picture of the class. Not only would one see patterns in misbehaviour emerging, perhaps one or more children being seen as 'negative' by lots of, or all the teachers teaching them, or certain teachers seeing lots of children as negative, but one could also calculate the ratio of 'positively' seen children to 'negatively' seen children, and this ratio could in fact be a measure of the overall difficulty of this class.

It was possible to do just what has been described. When completing the 'mixed' profiles, most teachers in the project described most pupils in either a very negative or a very positive way. The 'P' for positive descriptions compared with the 'N' for negative descriptions yielded a ratio of N : P descriptions which became the measure of difficulty for the classes concerned. But before going into the details of the study itself, one or two of the thoughts behind it should be drawn out. Children and things are only 'difficult' to people, if they see them as difficult. Some interesting ideas follow from this; for example, if we want teachers to find children less difficult than they do, one way would be to raise their level of tolerance, so that they did not register as 'disobedience' what other teachers would almost certainly register as such. What therefore would be very interesting is to combine this profile measurement technique with observation of the same children, as this would bring to light those cases in which children were misbehaving but were not regarded negatively. Why should this be so? Studies of this kind would add to our knowledge of the psychology of misbehaviour. But secondly, why this preoccupation with the measurement of class difficulty? There were two main reasons for it. With measurements one can compare and with measurements one can investigate factors which bring about change. With a measurement of class difficulty, we can compare classes, and if class measures are combined into a school measure, we can compare schools. The field of misbehaviour in schools is at present bedevilled by generalisations based on rumour rather than fact. We need to know the epidemiology of misbehaviour, so that we can estimate for example the scale of resources needed to cope with it. If we can measure class difficulty we can also isolate those factors which relate to it; with longitudinal studies we can see which factors precede the disturbance in schools or follow as a consequence of it, and we can also systematically deploy resources (staff, curricula etc.) in an attempt to reduce the difficulties.

For the purposes of this 'Grid' Study, then, a pupil profile was devised (see below), containing thirty randomly arranged items, fifteen 'favourable' and fifteen 'unfavourable', which were in most cases approximate opposites of the favourable ones, and which were derived mainly from the list of types of behaviour used in the questionnaire of the earlier study of teachers' perceptions, plus UNCOUNTED item 25.

PUPIL PROFILE

Name of BOY/GIRL (Initial and first 3 letters of surname)

Sex of pupil (ring)   M / F

Please tick *only* those descriptions which ON THE WHOLE describe the above pupil when you TEACH him/her. Please don't think for TOO long! But be sure to tick ALL the items which apply.

Tick Here

1. Settles well to work   . . . . .
2. Not much liked by other pupils   . . . . .
3. Popular with a variety of pupils   . . . . .
4. A disruptive influence   . . . . .
5. Mixes satisfactorily   . . . . .
6. Contributes to classwork   . . . . .
7. Will progress   . . . . .
8. Unlikely to progress   . . . . .
9. Even tempered   . . . . .
10. Quick to fly off the handle   . . . . .
11. Is a potential problem   . . . . .
12. Irritable   . . . . .
13. Miserable or unhappy   . . . . .
14. Poor concentration   . . . . .
15. Prone to lying   . . . . .
16. Physically aggressive   . . . . .
17. Peace-loving; likes a quiet life   . . . . .
18. Fussy   . . . . .
19. Co-operative   . . . . .
20. Disobedient   . . . . .
21. Is easy-going, in a pleasant way   . . . . .
22. Insolent or truculent at times   . . . . .
23. Tends to bully other pupils   . . . . .
24. Is working steadily   . . . . .
25. Probably the most difficult pupil in the class   . . . . .
26. A pleasure to teach   . . . . .
27. Reliable   . . . . .
28. Able to accept criticism   . . . . .
29. Cheerful   . . . . .
30. Is a satisfactory influence   . . . . .
31. Very restless   . . . . .

In order to assess whether a pupil was 'P' (viewed positively) or 'N' (viewed negatively) by the teacher describing him, a difference of at least two, had to be found, when the smaller number of items (either favourable or unfavourable) was subtracted from the larger number. To take an example: if a pupil was given three unfavourable items and eight favourable, the difference between these was five, in the positive (i.e. favourable) direction, so he would appear on the final grid as P5, for that teacher. Where he was given six unfavourable items and three favourable he would appear as N3. When the difference was only two, or fewer than two, he would appear as V (for Vague). The profiles were analysed the more quickly, by the use of templates; this is an important point if the technique is to be used by schools, in which time is at a premium.

The first school to be asked to use the profiles was a 'difficult' five-form entry girls' comprehensive school in a large city; the profiles were completed by the staff teaching three second-year, non-remedial classes. Class A contained pupils of somewhat higher ability than B or C which were parallel. Twenty-eight teachers (four male, twenty-four female) out of the thirty-two teachers involved with these classes co-operated, although one teacher's profiles were not analysed, as he misunderstood the instructions. Eight hundred and sixty-seven profiles were analysed. Some teachers taught only a few of the children in each class, where the children were setted for their subject; several staff were new to the school and felt they did not know some girls well enough, to complete their forms; where staff taught two or all three classes, for more than one subject, they completed profiles relating to only one subject. All these factors reduced the number analysed but the resultant grid remains of considerable interest. It is important to mention that the teachers were asked to work through the profiles 'reasonably FAST' so that their basic attitude to each child could be ascertained; slow completion might have involved more rationalising.

The results were as follows. In class A, the 'more able' class, 14% were negative, 72.8% were positive and 13.2% were vague. In Class B, 21.6% were negative, 59.5% positive and 18.9% vague. In Class C, 20.7% were negative, 66.2% positive, and 13.1% vague. If we now calculate the ratio of negative to positive profiles, we can calculate the overall difficulty of the class. The easiest class appears as A, with a ratio of 1 : 5.1. The next class, in order of difficulty is C, with a ratio of 1 . 3.2, and the most difficult class is B, with a ratio of 1 : 2.8.

In the second school in which the profiles were used, a mixed 'difficult' urban middle-school, the ratios for the two third year, parallel, non-remedial classes were 1 : 4.5 and 1 : 3.4; in the third school, a 'difficult' urban secondary modern just turned comprehensive, in which a difficult class of third year boys were studied, the ratio was 1 : 2.2, rising to 1 : 2.5 at the conclusion of the behaviour modification project which was carried out with these boys. (This is the school in Chapter 15). It is interesting, and promising that in all these three urban schools the range of ratios was 1 : 5.1 to 1 : 2.2. Knowing the schools and their problems, these ratios may possibly be representative of fairly difficult inner city schools, but the way is open for more research, to test this hypothesis, in schools of different kinds and in different areas.

To return to the first school, it was important to test the validity of the N : P ratio, as a measure of class difficulty, and this was done by obtaining independent ratings of the three classes, from the head teacher, the head of the junior school, and the head of second year, who would know all three classes. The deputy head was newly appointed to the school, so her rating was not requested. Along a seven-point scale ranging from point one: 'A very pleasant group to teach', to point seven: 'A very difficult class', ratings from all three senior staff were identical, for all three classes. Class A was rated on point two: 'A pleasant group to teach', and both classes B and C were rated on point five: 'A fairly difficult class. Presents quite a few teaching and/or class management problems'. It can be seen that the order of difficulty rated by the senior staff, corresponds well with the three ratios derived from the profiles.

One interesting point which emerged from the analysis of the profiles, was that a very large percentage, 48.8% of all the profiles, were entirely favourable (with not a single unfavourable item ticked), and 11.9% were entirely unfavourable. One could deduce from this that the rapidity of the completion really has tapped attitude and that teachers find it very easy to categorise children in this way as on the whole co-operative or uncooperative. It could further be deduced that simply asking teachers to describe children as co-operative, or uncooperative or neither would serve the same purpose as the completion of a lengthy profile. The profile measure is however, more useful because it is more refined, so that one can detect small changes, if one wishes to; a change from N to P or vice versa is a big change in one's perception of the child. Also, in studying teachers' perceptions of individual children, it is valuable to know just how positive or negative is her perception of each child. The profile analysis shows the range of each teacher's perception (e.g. a teacher may use the range P5 — N4), and therefore shows, because of its detail, how close a child stands to the extremes of the teacher's range.

The grids for the three classes revealed, as had been expected, patterns in the clustering and scattering of the P's and N's. Thus, although classes B and C had similar N : P ratios, their patterns were different. In class B the N's were more widely scattered through the class, while in class C they were more concentrated on certain pupils, four pupils alone accounting for 58.1% of the N's. In class A, the 'easiest' class with the fewest N's, three girls account for 57.4% of these. To try to understand the relationship between the staffing of these classes, and the patterns of the grids, their relative staffing strengths were measured. The measure of strength was composite and based on the teacher status of the staff, teaching experience and their length of teaching service in the school. The strength of the staff of class C, the most difficult class, with a concentration of difficulty upon a group of girls, was found to be very slightly lower in status, and lower in respect of the other two criteria of strength. The details are given in Table A.

TABLE A			
Class	**Average status score (scaled)**	**Average experience score (scaled)**	**Average number of years in school (completed years)**
A	3.4	4.8	1.6
B	3.2	4.6	1.6
C	2.6	2.3	0.9

We can thus see that class A emerges as an 'easy' class, in which a few difficult pupils are isolated. Class B, a fairly difficult class, with stronger staffing shows more scattered difficulties: no pupil is difficult with more than a few of the staff but the difficulties are widespread. Class C, a fairly difficult class with weaker staffing than class B, shows both a concentration of difficult pupils plus scattered difficulties. It will be remembered that B was slightly more difficult than C in terms of ratio. This is so, in spite of rather stronger staffing.

Thus, in this study we have two classes, similar in difficulty, different in two respects: strength of staff, and presence of a cluster of difficult pupils. Weaker staff are associated with clustering, stronger staff with scattering of N's. Is the association significant? This is the sort of question research in this field could pursue. Do small groups of difficult children, difficult to most teachers, develop as a result of an overall weak staffing of the class? Longitudinal studies on this question are needed and studies of ways of matching staffing strength to class difficulty, which in the case of this school seems to have been done.

An expectation that the grids would reveal children who, though viewed negatively by most teachers, were seen positively or in mixed fashion by one or two, was borne out. This is an extremely important finding because it might be possible for a head teacher, with this information, to form a special link between a very difficult child, and the teacher who perceived him in a fairly positive way if, of course, the child reciprocated the positive perception. Thus this teacher could take over a tutorial role with this child or might agree to have the child with him for part of the school day, so that his work with him could act as a growth point for the child, in the improvement of his attitude towards work with other staff.

Table B gives the relevant details for seven of the children in this study.

TABLE B					
Class	**Pupil No.**	**No. of staff describing pupil as N**	**No. of staff calling pupil 'probably most difficult pupil in class'**	**No. of P's**	**No. of V's**
A	1	10	2	0	2
	2	9	3	1	2
	3	8	1	1	2
C	4	9	5	1	
	5	10	3	1	
	6	9	3	1	
	7	8	0	1	1

When the school records of these children were looked at, it was found in some cases that the primary school had mentioned as the child's favourite or 'best' subject, the subject of the teacher who was viewing this difficult child as 'P' or 'V'.

Were the children who were often called 'probably the most difficult pupil in the class', really 'the most difficult' in these classes? To test the validity of this item on the profile, the head of year was asked to name the most difficult girls in each class. She named eight; independently, working from the grids the researcher named nine, of whom seven appeared on the head of year's list. Agreement was thus 70%, on a rigid test, involving three classes. It was also wished to ascertain the extent to which the patterning of N's and P's and V's was true, and so for a hundred of the children there was summarised in writing, the pattern for each child in terms of 'OK' (i.e. positive on the whole), 'difficult' (negative on the whole), 'mixed', 'mixed verging on positive', etc. The head of year, without anyone revealing the summaries to her, was asked to state in her own words her view of each child, explaining what the terms 'OK', 'positive', etc. meant. Thus a rough measure of agreement could be calculated, This validation session took place three weeks after the profile completion by which time four girls had left the school and two had not been attending, so ninety-four pupils were commented on. For these, agreement between the head of year, and the profiles was 89.4%, which is high.

Several points of interest arose from the validation discussions. For example, a wide range of types of designation for a child occasionally indicated a child's volatility, or a disturbed child. Thus, of the ten cases of disagreement between the profiles and the head of year, nine were in the direction of the head of year thinking the child more difficult than the grid suggested. It could well be that the technique was showing the head of year's over-anxiety; she herself volunteered that this might be so, saying 'I needn't have worried' and 'perhaps I have been expecting too much of that child', etc. The school also said that the grid information was useful in giving, for example, support to the school's favourable opinion of one child, in the face of parental pressure to regard her as difficult, and also in suggesting, in the pattern of designations for one child, that her absenteeism might be due to school phobia.

The information obtainable from grids such as those developed in this study might be useful in many ways to head teachers. Of course there is the cost in teacher time and effort, and this is a big factor, particularly in schools under stress. But if the grids add to the head's picture, to his overview of his school, they may well be worth the outlay, in helping him the more effectively to deploy the school's resources, in coping with its situation.

It could be argued that school staffs use a form of gridding technique when teachers discuss with others which children in a class are 'OK' or 'difficult', and that of course teachers know which classes are more difficult than others and there is no need for the sort of analysis described above. It can be argued however that a lot of apparent 'gridding' in schools is partial, incomplete, and vital information goes missing because it is not systematically sought.

15 AN ENCOURAGEMENT PROJECT

A programme to reduce the difficulty of a class of third form boys in a secondary school, through the use of positive behaviour modification techniques.

There is no shortage of reasons offered to explain disruptive behaviour in its various forms. Thus a recent article on the causes of violence (Pritchard and Taylor, 1975) using a list of causes drawn up by teachers and social workers, lists no fewer than sixty-six. Most people would feel that causes are easier to find, in this area, than effective means of controlling the behaviours themselves. It is partly for this reason, that techniques of behaviour control appear to be so few in number, that behaviour modification techniques are worth consideration in attempts to control deviance in school. There exists already a large volume of research in behaviour modification in the United States. Some has been undertaken in this country and there are several practical guides for teachers in the application of these principles published in this country (Poteet, 1973; Westmacott and Cameron, 1981). Almost all this work is, however, done with children in primary school classes, mainly for practical reasons. These are that daily observational sessions are a typical feature of the research programme, and daily periods of work with the same teacher are the norm in the primary school, and rarer in the secondary school, and secondly that the primary teacher teaches pupils for much or all of their school week, and has far more opportunity for the practice of any techniques with specific children or a whole class, than the specialist secondary school teacher who may teach any one group for as little as an hour per week.

Current behaviour modification work with secondary school children is tending to be restricted to maladjusted children, and to be mainly of the 'contract' type in which a contract is agreed between teacher and child within which appropriate behaviour is rewarded, and rewards are withheld or penalties imposed for breach of the contract.

Aware of the very hostile reaction which is provoked in some quarters at the mere mention of 'behaviour modification', where it is equated with clinical manipulation of a depersonalised child, we would ask that the study reported here be considered in its own right, both outside the theoretical framework in which it is rooted, as well as, necessarily, within it.

The results of behaviour modification research are impressive, and the principles are simple enough to make them easy to teach, if not as easy to apply. One of the authors, therefore, decided that, as the need for behaviour control techniques was great in secondary schools, she would try to introduce some of the techniques to a group of staff in a secondary school, in an attempt to modify the behaviour of a difficult class. This meant working if possible with all the teachers who taught the class, for a period, and trying to detect any change in the class's behaviour which might occur. She would go into the school, meet the boys, teach the techniques to the staff, and see each of them individually each week, to discuss their progress in the use of the techniques. She would thus take on the role of adviser on deviancy, and this would be interesting, as one can foresee the development of this role, in the albeit far future, as local education authorities come to regard the handling of deviancy in school as a specialist matter. The project would also be useful in mirroring the situation which secondary schools have to work in if they wish to affect whole classes — the corporate initiation and following through of measures designed to modify the class. What was artificial in one sense in the project was that the author 'brought in' the idea of using the techniques; in another sense this was not artificial, as the head or a senior teacher or adviser might equally well bring in a series of techniques, and suggest their application in the school. The idea of applying certain techniques, to modify behaviour, it was hoped, would arise from the staff themselves, and grow gradually, through staff-room discussion, into a request for action to be taken.

One decision that was arrived at early on, was that the researcher would not actually observe the teachers but would rely upon what they said had happened in the class. In typical behaviour modification experiments the teacher is trained by being observed in the classroom, and then being offered a feedback and discussion period, in which he is shown, on a graph, how he is succeeding in reducing certain unwanted types of behaviour and in increasing the quantity of appropriate behaviour. It was decided not to observe the teachers mainly beause they were working with a difficult class, in a difficult school, and the pressures on them from these factors and from sheer co-operation in the project would be great enough (e.g. they had to give up a free period each week for three months) without adding to their strain, by observing them.

The techniques the teachers were to use were basically controlled, systematic 'rewards' (of praise, attention and encouragement) for appropriate behaviour, and the ignoring of unwanted behaviour, except when it was dangerous. The project was described as an exploration of encouragement techniques with the class, and it became known as the '3W Encouragement Project'. An explanatory sheet issued to staff is reproduced on page 197. Collaboration would be entirely voluntary: any teacher could opt out at any time. In fact not one of the twelve staff did so.

The school was a recently reorganised mixed, urban, secondary modern school. The class selected by the headmaster for its volatility and consequent potential for improvement, under appropriate influence, was a third year boys' class, the middle stream of three. The staff were asked to rate the difficulty of the class on a seven-point scale, from point one: 'A very pleasant group to teach', to point seven: 'A very difficult class'. Of the thirteen staff currently teaching the boys, eight rated it 'a fairly difficult class' (point five) or 'a difficult class' (point six); three thought it 'a straightforward teaching group' (point four), only two 'a pleasant group to teach' (point two). The head and two of his three senior administrative staff thought that staff found the class 'fairly difficult', and the other 'difficult'.

The above ratings need to be considered in conjunction with the staffing strength of the class, which was good. All thirteen staff who taught it (eleven men and two women) were qualified teachers, with experience averaging twelve years. No fewer than nine held a graded post or head of department post. Only one was a probationer, and only one part-time.

All thirteen staff had taught the class for at least one full term before the research began. One teacher was held as a control, an accidental circumstance allowing this to be done without his knowing it, or the other staff being aware of it.

Thirty-two boys were on roll for most of the research period, but two were excluded from the results, because one had joined the class only just before the research began and one shortly after. Both had been transferred from another class for reasons of psychological disturbance. Records were not complete, but of the thirty boys in the study sample, six had appeared at least once before the courts and one had attended a Child Guidance Centre. All recorded IQ's were low average. There were no quoted parental occupations in social classes I or II. The class was racially mixed.

The boys followed an ordinary secondary school curriculum, with a craft emphasis and without a foreign language. With only one exception, in which two staff shared the periods, each teacher taught the class for all the periods in his subject. For the three craft subjects the class was taught in two halves, so that boys had only fortnightly instruction.

The researcher wanted to measure the difficulty of the class before and after the project, and for this purpose used the profile grid technique whose development has been described in the study reported earlier. To check on reliability one week after the pre-test profiles had been completed, twenty-five percent of the profiles were redistributed in a randomly rearranged format, though only sixteen percent were used in the reliability test, owing to teachers' delays in completing them. The reliability of the profiles was tested by calculating the percentage of the profiles which changed category from N to P or P to N (V = vague was used in this study where the difference between the number of favourable and unfavourable behaviour items was less than two). Reliability after one week was high: 96.4%, only a single profile changing in either direction, and here the swing was only N2 to P3 and P3 to N2. This figure of 96.4% can be compared with the 77.4% of profiles (i.e. 233 of the total of 348 profiles) which still had not changed from P to N or N to P by the end of the eleven-week project period.

The following is the paper given to all staff involved in the project, explaining it and suggesting guidelines.

3W An Encouragement Project — Paper to Staff

This is a brief account of the ideas which research has provided for the basis of our 3W project. Many are so obvious that they will seem to be hardly worth stating; indeed, they will already be basic to your approach to teaching. Others will perhaps seem controversial, and others may seem 'bunk'. I talk of 'boys' only because this is a boys' class; the principles hold good for either sex.

1.   'Encouragement' is a very powerful means of improving both a boy's behaviour and the work he does.

2.   The *more* encouragement for appropriate behaviour and work he receives, the *better* he will behave and work.

3.   A teacher may *think* he is encouraging a pupil a great deal but in practice he does not, for various reasons, e.g. what he considers encouraging may not be what the boy considers encouraging, or the encouragement may not be expressed in terms which are absolutely clear to the boy, or — quite often — the *degree* of encouragement may not be sufficient to influence the boy.

At this point, can it be said that 'encouragement' includes:

● Praise of all kinds, for the boy's work and behaviour.

● Attention to the boy.

● Interest in the boy.

● Help to the boy.

● Increasing a boy's self-respect, or self esteem.

4.   When a teacher observes misbehaviour he often reacts with repri-
      mand or criticism, to bring about correct behaviuor. However,
      if attention is 'encouraging' then the reprimand 'encourages'
      further misbehaviour, and thus produces the opposite of what the
      teacher wishes. This is very important where the misbehaviour is
      designed by the boy to attract the teacher's attention so that he
      will have the other boys' attention too (and interest and praise
      and help, i.e. all types of encouragement!)

5.   Misbehaviour can often be 'cancelled out' if when it is observed,
      the teacher ignores the boy, but simultaneously praises another
      who is behaving correctly. The teacher than returns to encourage
      the first boy *as soon* as he is behaving appropriately (e.g. by say-
      ing 'That's more like it!' or 'I'm pleased to see you're behaving
      like an adult now!').

6.   Another way of handling inappropriate behaviour is simply to
      ignore it, but (as under '5') to praise as soon as appropriate
      behaviour is seen.

Miscellaneous implications of the above, for practical classroom issues

1.   The major exception to 'ignoring misbehaviour' is obviously
      dangerous behaviour.

2.   Quick moving about the class, saying 'That's right', or 'good',
      'That's what I like to see', is a way of settling the class to work
      fast, partly because it distributes a large quantity of
      encouragement.

3.   Small groups of sections of the class can be similarly encouraged, e.g. 'Well done, those boys over there', and of course the whole class: 'Well done 3W'. Group praise will raise the self esteem of the group.

4.   Encouraging a boy can include 'catching' him before or after a lesson, to show interest in him.

5.   Boys of this age want to be treated as adults, and to be thanked for something raises their status and makes them feel more adult. It is often useful to create situations in which the teacher has to thank the pupil, e.g. 'Williams, give me a hand with this, will you? . . . Thanks a lot'. 'Jones, I've got a problem . . . etc. Got any bright ideas? . . . Yes, well done, I could try that'. The difference between making a job a source of encouragement or just a chore may rest in how the teacher asks for it to be executed. 'Would you mind straightening the chairs — Thank you', encourages. 'Straighten the chairs, Brown' may be a chore.

6.   All the work discussed during the lesson, e.g. homework can be included, for encouragement purposes. Praise for what is correct, is a powerful incentive to improvement. Even when mistakes have to be pointed out, it is possible to encourage by emphasising what is right (e.g. 'These answers are good') and phrasing further instructions in a positive way (e.g. 'Now try and get the others as good as those', or 'This is all right but you'll get more right next time if you . . .').

7.   Because the boy must know quite clearly that you really are encouraging him, it is safest to 'spell out' your praise etc., at the risk of 'over-doing it', e.g. 'That is very good', 'You've got through that *extremely* fast'. It is helpful to face and look directly at the boy, catching his eye while praising him because then, in addition to being praised with words he will 'see' the praise in your facial expression and gestures. (If you turn the TV sound down, you will see how much praise, pleasure, etc. are conveyed by gestures, etc. which will be missed if the boy is not looking your way).

8.   It helps to use words which are the boy's own words or at least are meaningful to him. At present 3W recognise the words 'great' and 'smart' as meaning 'excellent' (e.g. 'There's a smart new comic out').

9.   A visible sign of praise is displaying pupils' work. Good work can be quickly displayed by, for example, showing it to the boys sitting near him, or saying, e.g. 'John's just done a very good answer to that question. He'll show it to you later, if you ask him, I expect'. Encouragement by display not only raises a boy's self-esteem, in relation to the teacher, but also in relation to his group, which is an additional source of esteem. Sometimes teachers acknowledge the value of displayed work by putting some work on display, but then do not fully utilize the display for encouragement purposes because they do not add recently done work to it. There is little reason why 'display' should become a source of competition — if plenty of changing work is put on display. A boy sometimes produces work which is on the whole poor but is praiseworthy in one or more respects. This can be displayed with a note on it, pointing out what is particularly skilful in it.

10.   Interest in a boy's own interests or problems is often highly 'encouraging'. This is why the teacher who knows of a boy's recent problems or triumphs (e.g. a fall in PE, the loss of a personal possession or a good piece of work, or progress made in another lesson) and refers to it, is 'encouraging' a boy towards appropriate work and behaviour in his own lessons.

11.   A willingness to spend time helping a pupil over a hurdle in his work will be regarded as encouragement especially if put as an offer of help ('Would you like to give me a hand for three or four minutes . . . etc.'). Even the offer may be encouraging apart from any benefit which may accrue from the help itself.

12.   In view of the boy's desire to be treated as adult, not only will praise such as 'That's what I call adult behaviour' be a high form of praise but person-to-person chat at an adult level is often appreciated, e.g. a chat on a topic of adult interest.

Important

13.   With boys of 3W's age a clear statement of the teacher's intentions with regard to suitable and unsuitable conduct can take the following forms: 'I'll come and have a word with you when you're quiet enough for me to hear myself speak' or 'I know you're stuck; I'll come and give you a hand with your work as soon as you quit fooling around'. Such statements make explicit to the boy that *correct* behaviour and *attention* are related.

14.   The relationships between all that has been said above, and the work that the boys are asked to do, are so many and obvious that they will not be dealt with here in detail. But it will be clear that school work which is seen to be of adult value will give encouragement. A task which is absorbing and seen to be 'worthwhile', e.g. 'masculine' will increase the teacher's chance to praise and reduce the very need for criticism.

The 'Action Weeks' of the Project

We will be trying out the approach outlined on page 1 with individual boys, to see how it works.

The project does not try to provide a 'blanket' answer to every classroom situation. It recognises that boys are different, and that teachers are different, that the types of encouragement favoured by one teacher may not be favoured, or may even be disliked, by another. It does, however, rest upon the premise that if a clear and consistent positive approach is adopted by the teacher to the pupil, to obtain what the teacher requires in relation to work and conduct, then the chances are high in favour of results in the desired direction.

Because the project does not involve any observation of the teacher, while he teaches the class, it is necessary for the teacher to record his own information about his use of the technique. I attach copies of the sheets on which this information can be quickly recorded. Recording which cannot be done during the lesson should be done immediately after it, or as soon as possible afterwards, otherwise it will tend to be inaccurate.

You may find you can record just the frequency and success/failure of your encouragement etc., immediately after the lesson, and can add details shortly afterwards.

The numbers 1 - 6 on the record sheet refer to separate 'incidents' of when you praise a boy or assist him etc. It will be fastest, if you are recording in this column during the lesson, just to put a ring round the number, and a tick or cross next to it, to show the outcome. You may like to think of the six possible 'incidents' as being spread out roughly over five-minute intervals in the lesson, but this is not necessary and you may prefer to concentrate encouragement at any point or points in the lesson. Do not panic if you find yourself left with a blank sheet or a sheet with one ring round it at the end of the lesson! But aim at

as high a level of encouragement as possible. Continuous encouragement over a period of about three minutes or more counts as two
incidents. If you want to score more than six, note it under 'remarks'.

As with the previous form-filling, the recording may need practice, becoming progressively quicker. I have included some spare forms
on which you can practice recording with any pupils you wish.

I will suggest a few 3W boys out of whom you choose a couple to
start with, but we will also decide on 'spares' because one or more of
your 'target' boys might be absent. Recording for three boys may be
too much to start with; you may prefer to start with one or two, moving
on to the 'next on the list' when you are ready for it.

It is vital that when you teach 3W you have a form with you! A supply
of emergency forms has been left with Mrs Brown.

In brief, what the teachers were asked to do was to apply a clear and
positive approach to the work and conduct of individual boys, who they
had themselves selected in their weekly discussion with the researcher.
They would then record the details of their encouragement and its success or failure on a record sheet, which they would start to fill in during
the lesson and complete later. Each encouragement 'incident' would be
separately noted. The selection of his 'target' boys was assisted by the
information the teacher had supplied on his profiles. Thus, especially
in the early stages of the programme, the boys to be 'targetted' were
not that teacher's most difficult ones, the exception to this being where
the teacher expressed a particular wish to work with such a boy. The
teacher could carry on 'encouraging' his target boys for as many weeks
as he felt this was profitable or interesting, and would then make a
change of one or more boys. The discussion periods lasted usually fifteen to thirty minutes; as the project progressed they became informal
and relaxed, and were held over a cup of tea in the staff room. This
confirms the potential of such a project for use by senior school staff
in the normal course of their work with staff in their school. None of
the staff opted out, or threatened to opt out, at any stage, in spite of
their reservations about the principles being used (one teacher favoured
a punitive approach), or about their success (a newly qualified teacher
ran into difficulties). Part of the reason for this was that the head master
was sponsoring the project, and the researcher was thus viewed as
something of an authority figure. But this was also so because of the
large measure of self-determination which the teacher was permitted.
To a considerable extent he 'ran' his own exploration, changing his focus

as he became bored or dispirited. His feedback was self-monitored, that
is to say, he stated on the record sheet (see below) or in discussion, his
success, or failure. It was these factors that appeared to help to maintain staff interest and cooperation.

	RECORD SHEET (Chapter 4)							
	Encouragement			**Inappropriate Behaviour**				**Remarks**
	✓ or X	Type of Encourage-ment		✓ or x	Ignored (details)		✓ or x	Cancelled (details)	
Lesson	1			1			1		
No:	2			2			2		
Boy's	3			3			3		
Name	4			4			4		
_____	5			5			5		
_____	6			6			6		

Latitude was also allowed for in the completion of the record sheets; indeed, teachers soon developed characteristic modes of reporting. In all, 75% of all the lessons taken with 3W were reported on, timetable alterations and staff absences, etc accounting for the rest. The thirteenth member of staff who took the class was ill at the beginning of the project, though he had completed the profiles; he was left out of it and was thus able to be used as a 'control'.

The pupil-profile scores allowed for the arrangement of the boys in a rank-order of difficulty, and for a comparison of the pre-test and post-test order, for each teacher. For the control teacher, rho (a rank-order correlation coefficient) was $+.833$ ($N = 20$) and for all twelve project staff high positive rhos were general, all significant at the 0.01 level.

It appears that a teacher's perception of the relative conformity of individuals within a group may tend to be very static over a period such as that covered by the present study, i.e. three months.

Inspection of the details of the pre-test and post-test rank orders shows, typically, small or very small changes in rank for most of the class, but also large changes (i.e. of ten places or more) for two or three members of the class, these changes being in both directions, i.e. cases of both improvement and deterioration.

It is of interest for future studies that the two teachers with the lowest correlation coefficients, i.e. whose perception of the relative difficulty of individuals within the class was the most labile, were from our observations, the two who differed most in their acceptance of non-conformity, the one being almost totally accepting, and the other being rigidly authoritarian.

A study of the liking of the boys for each of their school subjects before and after the project, which also gave a chance to meet them, showed that the control teacher was the only one of the thirteen to show no case of increased liking. He also gathered a somewhat greater percentage of decreased liking than any other teacher. Too much should not be made of this, as only one teacher was involved, but the findings are suggestive.

Staff morale appeared highest half-way through the action period of the research, possibly because the routine had by then been established, and evidence of results, and interesting facets of the project, were coming to light where there had been low expectation of this. A dropping of morale in the final fortnight of the project is attributed partly to anticipation of its conclusion, but also to the increase in difficulty in controlling the class because it had lost its security and routine during the three-week Easter holiday, and because of the disruption of one disturbed boy.

The record sheets were used regularly by ten out of twelve staff. The probationer teacher found it possible to complete the sheets only at the expense of other teaching/control priorities and so he reported orally, and one highly experienced teacher, using encouragement techniques possibly more than any other, preferred to report orally. Verbatim accounts of staff's statements, elaborating the record sheet information with all their staff were recorded as far as possible. Styles of reporting on the record sheets varied from meticulous, very detailed reporting, to brief reporting, supplemented during the discussion period.

The encouragement columns were used the most heavily, and encouragement was usually marked as successful, by a tick, though this was sometimes qualified by a statement such as 'for a time only', or by a stroke across the tick ($\not\checkmark$) to show the success was partial. Ignoring was more frequent than 'cancelling', (i.e. ignoring inappropriate behaviour and as soon as possible afterwards praising, etc., appropriate behaviour) and for both, there were many examples quoted of both successful and unsuccessful use, and of partial success.

The final free comments on the project were frank and mixed. Seven staff ranging widely in length of experience and status took a clearly favourable or very favourable view of it; three had mixed feelings or were non-commital, while one expressed considerable doubt concerning its value. One teacher, whose difficulties with the class had increased during the project, questioned whether it had contributed to his difficulties.

The intensity of application required by the project techniques was referred to by four teachers. One felt 'pressurised' by them — though qualifying this statement by adding that '3W was certainly a difficult class to try a project out on' — while the other three commented favourably on the intensity required: 'The results more than repaid the time spent on the project'; 'It forced me to think more carefully about my teaching and my treatment of the class in general'. Opinion concerning the relationship between the use of project techniques and normal school practice ranged from *(a)* a belief that they were the same, through *(b)* the feeling that they were ordinary teaching techniques, used intensively, to *(c)* a feeling that their use involved insincerity.

Of the ten staff who completed record sheets only two, in their conclusions, mentioned difficulty in completing them during the lesson; of these two, one had difficulty in remembering to fill in the forms, and not in filling them in. One teacher was even led to comment that recording had become 'just another classroom job'. Eight staff mentioned that the project had been of benefit to individual boys; fifteen boys (i.e. half the class) were mentioned by name, and there were in addition references to the benefit obtained by 'certain individual pupils' and 'many of them'.

In a section of the questionnaire on 'the project and 3W as a class' seven out of nine staff who commented thought it had improved the class, and one that it had deteriorated. In this section the terms used were often enthusiastic: *(a)* 'It definitely made a better atmosphere in the class', . . . 'Response of whole class better'. *(b)* 'There is no doubt that the class gained considerably from the project as a whole'. *(c)* 'Now the group is viable . . . there is little conflict'. *(d)* 'There has been an all-round and marked improvement in the behaviour and attitude of the whole class. They are now more easily managed and have a greater desire to cooperate and to succeed with their work'. *(e)* '3W as a whole benefited . . . became more friendly and co-operative. More boys remained to tidy room, etc . . . at end of lesson, without being asked'. *(f)* 'I approached the project with some scepticism especially with 3W as the target class. I feel, however, the project has been extremely successful with the most difficult boys in the class. The latter have responded "beyond my wildest dreams" even though they were not always my target pupils . . . The short term results were excellent'.

The hoped for softening of the teachers' perception of the class, using the N : P% ratio as the criterion did not occur to any marked extent, though the trend was in this direction, the ratio improving by .3%. Either the N : P ratio is a particularly stringent measure of class difficulty or it may be that the potential for greater softening was cancelled out by the effort required by the techniques, and/or more realistic or detailed perception of the class which came from using them. The 'effort' explanation is endorsed by teacher comments (e.g. 'my first reaction on meeting 3W once the project was over was "Thank God I haven't got to try any more!" — *enormous* feeling of relief'), and by the findings of other researchers. Thus Withall (1956) has pointed out how difficult redistribution of teacher attention is, and Barrish *et al* (1969) report on the difficulties of the teacher who has to be alert to teaching and target behaviours as well. It may also be as Waetjen (1970) suggests that the teachers did not perceive their pupils more favourably, because their improvement was seen as the result of teacher behaviour rather than as the result of internal pupil motivation. Equally well, it may be that the pupil-profile, from which the N : P% ratio is calculated, measures the effective or emotional component of attitude towards pupil deviancy and that this is not readily amenable to shift.

There was, however, clear evidence that the class was often affected by the severely disruptive behaviour of a disturbed boy who had joined the class just before the research began (e.g. at post-test he was three times designated 'probably the most difficult boy in the class'). In another project, improved results might come from coupling the approach followed in the present study with a concentration of the approach, at an agreed point in the project, by as many staff as possible, on any such disturbed boy.

It appears feasible for a senior teacher, trained to administer such a project, to do so. A period of four to six weekly 'sessions' might be useful, with more widely spaced follow-up. If scepticism is felt about the value of such a short period, Bandura's (1969) suggestion should be borne in mind that extinction phenomena primarily reflect the operation of cognitively mediated inhibitory sets. This statement could suggest that where cognitive control is strong (as with many normal, intelligent, secondary school pupils) relatively few repetitions of the absence of aversive consequences may be all that is needed for the extinction of an inappropriate response, and that relatively few reinforcements of appropriate behaviour may serve to establish the latter.

Weighed against the benefits which may be derived from such a project should be set the risk of task-overload especially for the teacher who is in the first or second year of teaching. In the light of the present study, it is advocated that additional support and/or reduced project 'work' (e.g. oral reporting rather than reporting on record sheets) should be offered to inexperienced staff.

In arguing for a continuation of the study of teacher-pupil perceptions, and further projects exploring positive reinforcement techniques, one is doing no more than reiterate Morrell's (1969) statement:

> It is a waste of time to fuss about what we think that children should learn if we do not understand how to organise a system of pupil-teacher relationships which is productive of our intended learnings.

We do not feel that teachers need be frightened by positive behaviour modification techniques. Not only are they well-known, much used techniques of help and attention but they will be effective, not because children are 'conditioned' by them or 'manipulated' by them, but for 'good' reasons. It must often be a relief to an unappreciated child to receive appreciation, and what opportunities a change in the teacher's approach to him must give him to modify his own behaviour in a direction he may basically have wished very much he could travel in!

We have deliberately taken enormous liberties with the use of the phrase 'behaviour modification'; it is a far cry from the study described above to the traditional behaviour modification experiment. This is inevitable: if, as is believed by the writers, the principles are sound and useful, they will require adaptation if they are to be used in the contact of the free-flowing situation of the hectic secondary school.

A school wishing to carry out an Encouragement Project might wish to consider the following programme.

1. Initial moves by staff interested in such a project, to interest others in the possibility by means of circulated papers, and staff meetings, (formal or informal) on the project, behaviour modification in general, relevance to the school's situation etc. Invitations to speakers (e.g. Educational Psychologist). Full staff meeting upon which a decision to go ahead can be based, and to discuss the means for deciding which class/classes the project should focus on.

2. Project co-ordinator to discuss with those involved the feasibility of the project focussing upon their class/classes. This group to formulate the project programme. Opportunity to be given to individual staff to opt out of the programme if they wish it. Where several staff opt out, the group may wish to consider the feasibility of continuing to operate without them. The possible role of outside agencies in the project to be considered (e.g. Educational Psychologist, School Social Workers, Education Welfare Officers). The decision to go ahead with a certain class will involve group discussion but may also involve discussion with other senior and assistant staff, and the use of the difficulty of class grid described in Chapter 14.

3. Planning of programme in detail with reference to:

   (a) Dates.

   (b) Assessment of difficulty of class at the beginning of the project, during the project period, and at the conclusion of the project (including short-term and long-term follow-up procedures).

   (c) Consideration of pupils requiring a special programme, e.g. pupils diagnosed as 'needing special schooling'.

   (d) Possibility of weekly 'support' tutorials for staff involved.

   (e) Selection of pupils. How many should be worked with at one time? Should all staff have a similar selection to work with? What should be the bases upon which a decision to change the selection of pupils be made?

(f)   Mid-project reporting. Should a report form using tallies (see page 203) be used, or should reporting be by means of an informal written or oral report to the co-ordinator or other designated person?

4. Series of meetings to evaluate progress, and the project as a whole, and to consider the dissemination of the findings, and the possibility of extending the work.

Clearly the above programme is only one possible framework. Schools operate very differently and there is scope for considerable variation depending, for example, on the role of the head teacher in any such project, and the existing administrative structure in the school. In some schools a committee may well exist into whose work such a project would fit quite neatly.

16 CONCLUSIONS.
ON STRATEGIES FOR COPING

Techniques are utilised within strategies. We would hope that those described in the previous chapters would be used within a strategy that is humane. Certainly it would be analytical, hoping to capitalise on as much information as possible, and flexible, open to change as the situation changed and more information became available. The difficulty grid should not be used to 'fix' a class but to measure change, to look at the future, as should listing procedures, and any programme of behaviour modification.

A strategy for disruptive behaviour needs also, in our view, to be many-sided. Particularly where the behaviour is intractable, an approach from several directions may be needed, a programme, i.e. a battery of techniques, rather than a single procedure being brought into operation. Monitoring the success of a complicated programme is difficult, and implicit in such a programme lies the need for team-work with all the problems and opportunities which this involves, and the need for a responsible co-ordinator with the necessary expertise. The need for training courses for teachers who can return to their schools with the expertise required for such work has only just been recognised in the course started recently at the University of Cardiff.

Strategies for disruptive behaviour use resources of staff, premises and other kinds. It is possible to discern in current developments a strong trend towards a 'unit' strategy, an approach to disruptive behaviour which consists in funding special units of various kinds for difficult children who have been suspended from school, or who have engaged in severely anti-social behaviour. The units may be on-site, off-site, varying in ethos and programmes, and length of stay etc. Such units are a current concern of the DES and the Schools Council (1978). Although clearly it is very helpful at times for teachers to be able to remove disruptive pupils from their classes, and given individual or small group tuition in a unit many children can be helped, we need to ask whether a 'unit' strategy uses resources which deprive schools of the chance to develop alternative techniques. For example, teachers could be available in schools to act as crisis staff or 'disruption preventors', who would go *into* classrooms when need arose to work where possible with a difficult group or difficult child, without their being excluded from the classroom. Alternatively a counsellor could be afforded, who could run a staff support group, or funds could be made available for such groups to operate at a local Child Guidance Clinic. Similarly, the cost of training one or a group of teachers for work in the field of disruptive behaviour could be met from funds not deployed on a unit. A few local education authorities already favour this strategy. Funds devoted to units for suspended pupils could pay the salaries of staff developing programmes to reintegrate such children into normal schools.

The involvement of the Schools Psychological Service in any strategy for disruptive behaviour is an important issue seen at its starkest in the decision by at least one large authority not to involve the service in the placement of pupils in their planned units for disruptive pupils, unless the school wishes to consult on a child. This may be a dangerous practice if it puts the onus on schools of differentiating in placement between the 'disturbed' and the 'disruptive' child, without ensuring that schools have staff with the expertise to make such a differentiation. If schools are to develop sound programmes and practices in coping with disruptive behaviour more help from educational psychologists will be needed than the above decision implies.

Finally strategies for disruptive behaviour should be based on an acknowledgement of its integral nature in the life and work of all schools. This acknowledgement could see its most useful expression in the incorporation within the wide-ranging researches of, e.g. the National Foundation for Educational Research of questions relating these researches to matters of disruptive behaviour, as a matter of routine. We badly need information concerning the relationship between disruptive behaviour and issues of curriculum, teaching methods and styles, etc. and could obtain this at relatively small cost if the important questions were built into the planning of major projects.

Part Four

THE LOCAL EDUCATION AUTHORITY
AND CENTRAL GOVERNMENT

17 LOCAL EDUCATION AUTHORITIES' POLICIES AND DISRUPTIVE BEHAVIOUR

Introduction

Disruptive behaviour in schools is not new. There is well documented evidence of this from public and elementary schools in the nineteenth century. From time to time, unacceptable behaviour in schools has been examined by the mass media (Toxteth, 1982). The focus of interest has been, for the most part, the school. This is understandable given the legal requirement of head teachers (by articles of government and rules of management) to be responsible for the discipline of their schools, the implied contract between parent and teacher concerning the pupil, and also societal expectations of the task of the schools in socialising their pupils.

Little attention has been directed towards the activities of LEAs in the matter of disruptive behaviour in schools. From material obtained from LEAs (minutes of meetings, memoranda to schools, etc.) there is evidence to suggest that many have a disruptive behaviour policy. This is borne out by the DES Survey referred to in the next section which suggests that sixty-nine LEAs operate one or more Special Units. The sources indicate that many disruptive behaviour policies can be dated from 1973 onwards, with a 1974 peak. One key policy indicator is the establishment of Special Units for Difficult Pupils, which is often attributed to the raising of the school-leaving age in 1972, with the consequent retention of unwilling mature students in school. This is too simple an explanation. It is more likely that the activity coincided with the incidence of 'need' for the service, the disposition of the authority to provide the service and the availability of resources with which to provide it.

The 'need' had its origins in the five years prior to 1974. During this period there appeared a wide range of literature including clinical (Rutter, 1975) criminological (e.g. Marshall), ideological (Boyson, 1972), philosophical (Wilson, 1971), and teacher/professional (Lowenstein, 1974), approaches to the discussion of disruptive behaviour. It is not surprising that these, combined with pressures from teacher committees, unions and so on, created a climate of thinking about disruptive behaviour to which the LEAs responded. LEA activity changed in that period from keeping the topic under review at a low temperature 'administrative' level to an active interest in strategies to deal with disruptive behaviour. Discussion papers were circulated within education committee circles and working parties established, with a remit to examine identified 'problems'. The 'problems' concerned pupil absence, vandalism and behaviour in the classroom.

Without individual case studies, the origin of these activities remains obscure. Limited evidence indicates officer initiatives in articulating questions for discussion, for example: 'What should the Authority do to support the school?' 'Does the Authority have a coherent policy for disruptive behaviour?' The policy outputs of the LEA as an outcome of such discussions were varied and included the provision of off-site teaching units, peripatetic teachers and home tuition. The LEA documents provide extensive evidence of such provision, although evaluation on our part is problematic where the activity is so varied and the outcome so difficult to measure (DES, 1978).

There was evidence in the LEA material to indicate a growing concern of teachers' associations with the problems teachers were meeting. Teacher stress and the disproportionate amount of staff time demanded by work with problem children were frequently referred to along with a 'need' to provide more fully for disruptive behaviour in schools. This concern was probably reflected in the publication of the NAS survey findings (Lowenstein, 1975).

Prior to 1973 there were few indications that LEA's were willing or able to respond to this growing concern. The LEA's were, however, prepared to redefine the suspension procedures and to give guidance to headteachers as to how they should proceed in such matters. Some authorities very early on fostered the establishment of special sanctuary units (Jones, 1973).

It seems possible that LEA officers noted teacher concern but continued to see the matter as a routine administrative matter rather than a positive policy issue. The impetus to deal more positively with problems in classrooms may well have come from 'a strong impression that misbehaviour has increased' (DES, 1975). 'Impressions' of this kind were frequently mentioned in some of the LEA material in support of a policy for disruptive behaviour in schools, but little evidence in the reports was offered by the LEA officers. In one instance, the increase in suspensions was cited, but the same report doubted the validity of this as a support for the contention that misbehaviour had increased in schools. In another, the incidence of truancy was mentioned. Again this was not regarded as an indicator of misbehaviour, but associated with the raising of the school-leaving age to sixteen.

The reorganisation of local government in 1974 reduced the number of local education authorities but increased the average size of the remainder. Metropolitan and non-metropolitan authorities emerged with differing wide-ranging responsibilities for education. Size has proved to be a structural constraint in the past for some authorities. Their smallness had prompted a 'fire-engine' approach to individual problems rather than tackling their causes. Thus it was unlikely that these new larger authorities, with their increased responsibilities for education, were able to make an appraisal of the services offered. Thus a fresh opportunity was afforded to examine policies for disruptive behaviour and much else in the education service. The financial climate in 1974 was more propitious for an investigation into misbehaviour than in subsequent years. It was possible to set up pilot schemes and engage in modest research into the problem. The outcomes, described later, were interesting.

Defining Disruption

The character of an authority's policy, it is contended, is related to its perception of, and hence definition of, the problem of disruption. Where the definition is global, then it relates to a conglomeration of a large number of behaviours of different kinds. The LEA can either separate them out for thorough treatment (e.g. vandalism or truancy, and talk of 'a policy for vandalism', 'a policy for truancy'), or it can take an extremely broad view and publish, as do several authorities, a large booklet, ranging widely over the spectrum of school activities and making recommendations along this broad front. Where, however, an authority views the problem of disruption as one of disruptive pupils, the emphasis may be on the identification of such pupils. This may take the form of either early identification through screening or other procedures, or identification at a later stage in schooling, equating disruptive pupils with suspended pupils (or pupils warned of the possibility of suspension, where there is a procedure of 'stages' leading ultimately to it). Commonly an authority uses a 'double definition' of disruption, identifying it as both a cluster of behaviours which it will try to avoid by broad in-school and out-of school measures, and a pupil phenomenon which it will try to treat by special placement, perhaps in a unit or centre.

An interesting question for LEAs is whether emphasis should be placed on a general lack of effectiveness on the part of schools in coping with disruptive behaviour through normal school processes, or whether emphasis should be put on the need to remove the disruptive child. Where pressure comes through the union representatives or from teachers, we might expect a greater emphasis on 'pupil' characteristics and on those aspects of school which are largely concerned with control elements, and indeed several authorities itemise the range of sanctions available. Where the problem is identified by officers of the authority from suspension figures, it could well be taken as an *ad hoc* indication of schools where arrangements for coping are less sophisticated or flexible, and thus as a gross indicator for LEAs of less effective schools (Reynolds, 1976; Rutter, 1979). In this case an appropriate administrative response, given financial stringency and concern for legal liability, might be to tighten up current procedures, for example availability and liaison with social services, to provide a unit and to emphasise in-school procedures adopted by identifiably 'good' coping schools (DES, 1978).

There are several contrasting features between a policy which rests on the description of disruption as a wide-ranging set of behaviours, rooted partly in school practices and relating potentially to large numbers of children, and a policy which equates 'disruptive pupils' with 'suspended and pre-suspension pupils'. Where disruption is described as a wide-ranging set of behaviours, preventative strategies such as the modification of the curriculum, or the appointment of a school counsellor are adopted. The difficulty for those authorities who decide to initiate this kind of policy is to show how the situation subsequently improves as a result. The establishment of an off-site unit for suspended or pre-suspension pupils in an area on the other hand can be shown directly to deal both with the problems of such pupils failing to receive education and remaining untaught at home for long periods, and with the problem child who is stopping the learning of other children in the class. The 'broad front' school policy competes unequally with the 'pupil' policy in the matter of serious crisis intervention. As part of school policy there will almost always be an in-school 'place' to which particularly difficult pupils can be moved as a temporary 'crisis' measure. However, where the difficulty is violent behaviour threatening bodily harm to another pupil or a member of staff, no in-school placement or other in-school measures are seen to be capable of dealing with such a crisis, and appropriate to it. Segregation in a unit for severely disruptive pupils is, on the other hand, generally acceptable. As one authority expressed it: 'No school will want to admit a pupil who has assaulted members of staff'. In the words of another: 'The idea of separate centres is now acceptable'.

LEA Responses

We have argued that 'broad-front' measures may be less easily proved effective, and to be less helpful in crisis situations than 'disruptive pupil' measures. In addition, they lack the character of 'dramatic action' which the establishment of a special unit has. The message running through the major booklets on disruptive behaviour published by a number of LEAs is that the school should above all improve its current practices in areas such as classroom control and organisation, school administration, pastoral care, curriculum etc. There is nothing new here, and in terms of evidence (to a committee, for example) that the authority is 'acting' on the problem of disruption, a booklet of advice may be less persuasive than the dramatic action of the establishment of a new type of centre or unit. Where such action has, in addition, the important advantage of helping the authority to meet its legal obligations with regard to the provision of education, it is easy to see why it recommends itself and why so many authorities are now engaged in establishing special units for disruptive pupils. In some cases they seem to be affected by the ready availability of buildings, in itself a side effect of falling rolls.

Commonly, certain aspects of 'broad-front' in-school policies for the minimising of disruption receive greater emphasis than others, and there is often a pledge from the LEA that it will support the schools in their development of these aspects of their work. While some responses are seen by LEAs to be supportive of heads and senior staff, other policies by contrast adopt a broader approach to include the classroom teacher. The need for pastoral care staff to have plenty of time for their work, and the critical importance of remedial education in preventing frustration and a sense of failure in potentially disruptive children are often mentioned. Occasionally the extension of work experience schemes and of link courses in colleges of further education is seen as helpful in improving the attitudes of older secondary pupils and the general importance of a relevant and interesting curriculum is often stressed. Not surprisingly, perhaps, the overall emphasis seems to be on the pattern of institutional response with more EWOs/counsellors/remedial staff/units, but with rather less emphasis on the quality and nature of the work undertaken.

Policy recommendations made by working parties often refer to the need for the authorities to improve supporting services, e.g. to provide in-service training for teachers, to increase the number of educational psychologists and psychiatrists or to improve the advisory service by the appointment of an adviser for Special Education. More rarely, but importantly, there is reference to loss of teacher morale and the exploration by the authority of a teacher welfare service with the reduction of teacher stress as one of its aims. In contrast to such an innovatory practice, a review of suspension procedures is more frequently advocated, along with a more than occasional statement or re-statement of the authority's views and regulations relating to corporal punishment and rewards and sanctions. LEAs also frequently emphasise that teachers' skills are the significant factor in the solution of problems of disruptive behaviour.

Most clearly the impression emerges that disruptive behaviour is an area in which LEAs and schools are seen as needing to keep under review developments, to inspect relevant statistics frequently, and to initiate inquiries as and where this appears to be appropriate. Units, for example, are often portrayed as experimental. More remarkable is the growing popularity of the off-site 'special-unit' in which children are separated from a school's ordinary classrooms for varying periods of time. This appears to be a favourite strategy adopted by the LEAs for dealing with disruptive behaviour, despite the mounting pressure, as exemplified by the Warnock Report (1978) towards the integration of children with special needs with the ordinary school. Any such units may be established by analogy with special units (e.g. tutorial units) for maladjusted children, but they would serve offending children, not those who are disturbed. An alternative strategy, where teachers are appointed to work in normal classrooms alongside a class teacher in whose class there are some difficult children, receives only an occasional mention yet could probably be much more cost-efficient.

How do LEAs reach the decision to establish a unit or units?

The decision to establish a unit is the culmination of a series of processes, of which the first group concerns the statement of a problem or group of problems, the second group usually comprises a period of suggested solutions, explored through a variety of enquiries, and the third either an immediate acceptance of a unit strategy, or a postponement of a decision until further information and experience is available, with subsequent acceptance of units.

The first group of processes, involving definition of the problem, can arise in the context of different groups of people. Sometimes a head teacher consultative committee will raise the problem of provision for disruptive pupils, at others a group of officers will initiate discussion of the topic, each group quickly referring the matter outwards for joint consideration by a combined group of those who will be interested. Concern for children and their behaviour difficulties is not nessarily confined to the Education Service. In one instance the local members of a magistrates Association expressed concern over the level of truancy and juvenile crime and requested discussion with interested parties. The outcome of these discussions was the establishment of units in the authority. The broader context against which the problem is raised varies. Thus in one authority, the County Council passed a resolution requiring the Director of Education to prepare a report on educational standards in the county. Following on from this, 'it was later decided' that three reports would be prepared, on literacy, numeracy and behaviour. The preparation of the report on behaviour was facilitated by the setting up of a working party to consider behaviour problems in schools. The local association of secondary school head teacher at this period also reported on their own survey of disruptive pupils. It was in the context of these events that the decision to establish off-site units in this county evolved.

The problem is usually seen as one of relative lack of provision; some forms of provision are already there, for example the variety of in-school measures commonly deployed for instances of disruption: temporary withdrawal from lessons, pastoral care procedures, etc. as well as transfer between schools and suspension. The problem is the lack of provision relative to the felt need for it. Thus one authority which in 1975 considered a unit but rejected it, three years later agreed to establish one, partly because more information was now available, but also because there was 'greater unanimity about the need to strengthen measures'.

It is quite clear from the LEA materials that have been inspected in our research that it is suspension procedures which create the kind of difficulties for the authority which the units are designed to solve. One finds, for example, in a set of Education/Social Services Committee work party minutes, that Item 88, on Suspension of Pupils from School, reports on the proposal to set up a unit for disruptive pupils. The same minutes refer to a central problem relating to suspension: 'the danger of a trend towards permanency', i.e. the difficulty of bringing to an end a period of suspension by the reabsorption of the pupil into the school system. The reabsorption may be made difficult because of the strong reluctance of the pupil's school, or some other school, to have him/her back either because of the violent nature of his outburst(s) which make him a danger to staff and pupils, or because he has been so chronically disruptive that his rehabilitation in an ordinary school environment is highly unlikely. Placement in a special school may be difficult to arrange without a long delay, and is unlikely to be sought for older secondary pupils. Given this situation, a suspension may become 'permanent', so that the authority which does not offer home tuition on the grounds of expense or appropriateness for the case, may be shown to be in contravention of its legal requirement to educate. The provision of an off-site unit avoids the authority's dilemma. No ordinary school need be asked, at least in the short-term, to receive the pupil, though he/she can remain on the school roll. The authority meets its statutory obligation, and can with some justification, argue that it is meeting the special educational and socialisation needs of the pupil in the unit.

The main problem, which the unit is expected to solve, is that of pupils who cause disruption in school, but the unit is also often seen as helping with the problem of serious non-attendance cases, including cases of school phobia. Although the unit appears at first sight to be as expensive, where it is used in lieu of home-tuition, it may in fact be more economic than it appears to be. One authority, for example, in its Co-ordination Subcommittee minutes, gives estimates for the cost of setting up a pilot unit, and points out that the effect would be to cut expenditure on the home-tuition of pupils who were school-phobic or excluded from school for disciplinary reasons. The figures quoted are Home Tuition two hours per day = £150 per term, per pupil. The minutes suggest that the unit could take twenty pupils and that, apart from educational considerations, the economic advantages would be great. Another authority suggested they were cheaper in the long run than borstals or treatment centres!

Having defined its problem, the LEA usually engages in the second group of processes, the enquiries which will help it reach a decision. It is at this point that some authorities devote an enormous amount of work to the problem, carrying out surveys of various kinds, and setting up working parties whose deliberations and enquiries culminate in the preparation and publication of comprehensive and extremely impressive reports, some of which are generally available (Staffordshire CC, 1977). In other cases a committee may do no more than ask for information about off-site units, and the chief officer will arrange for information about them to be gathered from various sources (e.g. reports, or an HMI), and often for visits to be paid to units already established and functioning in neighbouring authorities. Thus one of the Greater London Boroughs reports 'Recently officers of the Education Department have visited five centres established by other authorities in the

Greater London Area. On the basis of these visits and a study of the evidence from other authorities throughout the country it is recommended . . .' etc. It is clear that a good deal of visiting of early established units has gone on. It is equally clear that the York conference on disruptive pupils, held in 1977, exerted an influence on the establishment of units, those attending reporting back to their authorities and pointing out that area units were one of the answers put forward to 'this difficult problem.'

The response of LEAs to disruptive behaviour is thus diverse, but the thread which seems to run persistently through reports and working papers is concern about the level of suspensions from schools, related closely to the statutory requirement on authorities to provide full-time education for all and to the insistent pressure from teacher unions to make special provision for children whose behaviour disrupts the education of the majority and interferes with the normal running of the school. What triggers off the response varies between authorities. For some it is concern with the police or magistrates.

For others it is the existence of large, powerful and organised pressure groups articulating a wider concern in the press and the media. Among pressure groups it is possible to identify those of parents, head teachers, local teacher associations, teacher unions, the Social Services and health authorities. The extent to which particular events have increased the authorities' sensitivity to such pressures is difficult to assess, but events such as the Maria Coldwell case have led to wide discussion of related education/health problems, to reviews of the adequacy of services to cope and to discussions on the advantages of a more integrated approach. For some the key factor seems to be the inability of educational psychologists to cope with the mounting pressure of work — itself perhaps an indication of the trend within schools to make use of outside help. The influence of initiatives taken by neighbouring authorities and the encouragement of University and Institute departments is also clearly apparent whilst the availability of money from Urban Aid Programmes and the stimulus of boundary revisions have provided for some the opportunity.

Given the complexity of disentangling the threads in accounting for the response of the local authorities, it remains a problem to explain why for so many, the preferred strategy of coping appears to be the off-site unit — particularly where so much of the discussion in documents acknowledges the disadvantages of such a unit, the problems of reintegrating children into schools and the risks of stigmatisation. Clearly LEAs are not unaware of the penal implications or of the distinctions between the manifest and latent functions of the new disruptive units which they are funding. The rhetoric of reports emphasises that the problem is an educational one. Many explore exhaustively the potential within the school to respond appropriately without invoking additional provision. Schools are urged to provide an explicit framework of discipline and to review the appropriateness of curricular and organisational arrangements; close home-school links are advocated and special provision within the school in adjustment classes, sanctuaries, remedial classes where the emphasis is firmly therapeutic and remedial; heads are urged to take initiative in providing help to probationary teachers, in stimulating staff discussion and involvement in courses provided by Universities and Institutes; they are urged to make full use of transfer possibilities with other schools. At the level of the authority, initiatives have variously encouraged co-ordination and development of all the helping services to set up groups of peripatetic 'trouble-shooting' teachers, to extend the availability of home tutors, and to explore the possibilities of an early warning system in co-operation with the junior schools. But having explored all the possibilities within the system to respond, many LEAs seem to accept, albeit reluctantly and with misgivings, the need for additional provision in the form of the off-site unit.

18 THE DEPARTMENT OF EDUCATION AND SCIENCE'S RESPONSE TO DISRUPTION

There has been a noticeable lack of response from DES in the area of school disruption apart from a survey in 1972 assisted by Education Committees and two HMI survey documents published in 1978. This lack is understandable in that the DES has a tradition of respect for the autonomy of LEAs and is not eager to get involved with what it regards as details of the running of the service (Pile, 1980) like policies for disruption. Even secondary reorganisation (1970-74) was regarded as primarily a local matter.

The absence of policy initiatives did not mean that the DES was not interested in the issue. A public disagreement about levels of school violence between the National Association of Schoolmasters (NAS) and the National Union of Teachers (NUT) led the Secretary of State to commission a survey in 1972. The figures were collected for the DES by the now defunct Association of Education Committees. In the House of Commons (November, 1973) the Secretary of State for Education, Mrs Thatcher, reported that from sixty percent of the completed questionnaires incidents of violence were proportionately very low. A good deal of anecdotal evidence on misbehaviour being published at that time was not reflected in the findings.

In 1976 a conference was convened by the DES at which representatives of LEAs, teacher associations and other interested bodies were present to discuss problems of non-attendance and disruptive behaviour in schools. One outcome of the conference by the DES was to undertake a survey of the existing provision of special units for disruptive pupils in ordinary schools, excluding those provided through special education procedures.

The DES survey was undertaken in two stages. The first was to discover from all LEAs in England by questionnaire how much special provision existed and where it was situated. After the questionnaire returns were analysed a team of eight HMIs visited a sample of almost half of the units, to assess the facilities available and the methods of dealing with pupils referred to the units.

At the same time a further DES survey was undertaken to examine practice and procedures which were found helpful in dealing with truancy, problems of non-attendance and violent and disruptive behaviour in a sample of schools. The exercise was limited to a small number of urban secondary schools suggested by their local education authorities because they appeared to be achieving greater success in dealing with these problems than might have been expected from their situation and the conditions under which they worked.

In the conclusions of these two surveys suggestions made by head teachers in schools indicated that a growth in the number of units for disruptive pupils was required. They gave as their reason for desiring an increase the general social decline (itemising such issues as family breakdown, lack of respect for authority, a fall in moral standards, and a widespread lack of self-discipline) as a major contributory factor. A second reason linked causes of greater school disruption and need for units, with the apparently increased difficulty experienced by schools in dealing with deviant behaviour and non-conformity.

Specific recommendations by HMI to LEAs with units included more in-service training provision for unit staff, the safe-guarding of career prospects in these somewhat isolated positions and the secondment of teachers from ordinary schools to work in units. The two reports did not categorically encourage the establishment of units but recommended that, should they be established, the local authorities should pay more attention to the importance of educational aims, the avoidance of staff and pupil isolation from parent schools and the provision of adequate resources, equipment and buildings.

19 SPECIAL UNITS: COSTS AND BENEFITS

What are the perceived advantages of units?

Some of the advantages of units have already been mentioned in Chapter 18 but the central advantage of the unit is that it is thought to solve what are seen as urgent problems. Many LEA reports point out that the disruptive pupil harms the education of other children and that removing him/her is thus beneficial to others, but they also point out that the disruptive pupil, on the school premises at break and during the lunch-hour and non-teaching time exerts a 'continuing disruptive influence upon others in the school community'.

One advantage of a unit is that it is a 'different', i.e. an additional type of resource. Thus one working party recommended units because they felt 'that there was much to be said for a diversified approach and that for some children a central unit may be appropriate'. The impression given is that the LEAs see the problem of disruptive pupils as complex and to an extent intractable, and that given the extremely problematic nature of the topic and the children, provision should be very varied, in the hope that somewhere within the provision, all or at least most of the types of case will be catered for. A unit adds to the variety of provision. To illustrate further, one authority's study group, having recommended a unit (to be called an 'exclusion centre'), comment that in doing so they have now offered 'a variety of practical arrangements', and another talks of its unit as an 'additional resource'.

The unit is generally seen as being beneficial as a place of last resort, a 'long-stop' area, abnormal in character in that it is 'for cases where normal sanctions have failed', as one authority puts it. It may be seen as useful as a place where 'certain children with difficulties . . . are contained within the educational system and in receipt of education even though not within the mainstream'.

Different types of unit structures are seen as having their own advantages. Thus one LEA commends twin units, where the two teachers can support each other, share resources and ancillary staff, and provide a wider programme and more flexible organisation for the children. Another points out the advantages of units situated in Youth and Community Centres, where youth staff could help during the day, and premises already exist as well as equipment. And through the LEA reports runs the theme that the units make available to the child experiences that will help his socialisation and side by side with this afford educational benefits. Typical is the comment of one LEA considering the establishment of a unit, that other authorities have found that pupils 'attended regularly, became far less disruptive, and began to settle into regular routines of work and behaviour'.

The establishment of a unit is also seen as giving the authority more experience and data concerning the management of disruptive pupils, which would 'help to guide the continuing appraisal which would be needed of the best ways of dealing with (them)'.

Within an LEA the style of units can vary. Thus one LEA has a 'Suspended Pupils Project', a 'Learning Centre' (established under the Urban Aid Scheme), a 'Tutorial Class' and, 'Secondary Tutorial Units' located within each school where difficult or disaffected pupils could 'cool-off' for short periods.

What are the perceived disadvantages of units?

The costs of establishing and maintaining a unit are often mentioned as a disadvantage, including the high cost in terms of pupil/teacher ratio, although it is often pointed out that 'against this must be set the time and efforts of schools in dealing with seriously disruptive pupils, and the damage to the education of other children'. In other words, there is already a wastage of resources where there is disruptive behaviour in schools.

An important disadvantage of units, for some authorities, is that their long-term effectiveness has not yet been proven. It is pointed out that, for example, a neighbouring authority has established a unit which has run into difficulties. A further more radical objection raised by some LEAs is that the notion of an off-site unit runs counter to the present policy of the Education Committee which is that wherever possible children should be educated in ordinary schools. One authority, in saying this, adds that 'recent research would tend to support this view since it has been shown that generally the prognosis for children with behavioural disorders is better in the ordinary school than in special settings'.

One serious objection raised to off-site units is the difficulties which arise when attempts are made to transfer some pupils back to their own school or some other ordinary school. Schools are said not always to be prepared to co-operate with the readmission of these pupils. The pupil is divorced from the life of the school, and re-entry to normal classes is made very difficult. Other objections relate to the fact that a central unit can cope with only small numbers of difficult children from each of its feeder schools, and to the fact that in a central unit all the most difficult cases would be brought together.

The disadvantages of off-site units are often compared with the advantages of an on-site sanctuary unit. It is pointed out, for example, that units within a school 'can start to deal with a disturbed child immediately and can blur the edges where necessary between work in the unit and in the main school. It also makes it possible for the staff of the unit to have the support of professional colleagues and for them to offer expertise to other members of staff.'

An additional disadvantage is the unsuitability of off-site units for the pupil in the final year of school. There is the danger that such pupils may be deprived of the course variety and work experience offered elsewhere in schools.

Careful distinctions should also be made between clienteles. The units might be used as an intermediate stage for the child with psychiatric disorders while other provision is made. The personnel of the units are sometimes not equipped to deal with children having special needs. Commonly, unit leaders are teachers secure in their approach to teaching but without any other training.

What is the nature of the unit?

Many authorities show an awareness of the dilemma inherent in the establishment within the educational system, as an off-shoot of normal school provision, of a unit for children who have disrupted and disturbed. The dilemma rises in the need to provide an educational regime within a structure which is itself a form of sanction. As has been stated earlier, the unit is a place of last resort, the bottom rung of the ladder, the place for pupils on whom all normal sanctions have failed. In itself it is thus a sanction, with conditions of entry which refer to the children's failure to cope with normal schooling and/or the school's failure to cope with the child. Typically, one authority calls its units 'Stage 5 centres' for children who after reaching 'Stage 4' and being transferred to another school 'still did not conform to acceptable standards of behaviour', and for a very small number of pupils who at Stage 4 'were considered to present such serious problems that no normal secondary school should be asked to take them'. For other pupils the unit is the last stop before court action for non-attendance: failure to attend or disruptive behaviour at the centre such as to warrant exclusion 'would probably lead to court action for non-attendance'. It is quite clear that here the unit is seen as a last resort. Almost all the authorities prefer however to emphasise the educational component and potential in the work of the unit, and some are explicit in denying its 'negative' aspect. One states: 'Establishments which are penal are outside the ambit of the sub-committee', and another that its centre 'should not be punitive or a dumping ground'. But closer inspection reveals that some of the thinking behind the decision to establish a unit may well in fact be punitive in character. Thus one LEA states that its unit was set up with three aims: to offer relief to schools of particularly disruptive pupils, to facilitate education for the pupils referred; and as a deterrent to mildly disruptive pupils still in the school. This last aim is a clear declaration of the use of the unit as deterrent punishment. Similarly, and ironically, the same authority which declares that establishments which are penal are outside the ambit of the subcommittee, has a working party on provision for dealing with disruptive pupils which recommends that a unit should be established along the following lines:

> Such centres should be single-sex, inconvenient, uncomfortable and offer less freedom than normal schools. If the local centre fails to correct this hard core, large houses should be purchased around the county, each catering for about fifteen of these pupils. They should, in the panel's opinion, be sent away from home to these special centres and not allowed home at weekends, though it is appreciated that there are important legal implications to this.

It is clear from this description that in the minds of this group the transition has been made, in the off-site unit, from school to penal institution. Not only is there to be an environment which is unpleasant, but the correctional function of the unit is explicitly referred to and it detains its pupils in a residential setting, if needs be.

Other authorities recognise but reject the identification of their purpose as penal. One sees the danger of their being seen as mini-borstals and 'sin bins' but lays the stress firmly on prevention; similarly another sees them as therapeutic, not 'dumping grounds' and a third as 'supporting schools in containing disruptive pupils'. Others express concern for the continuous education of disruptors and see the units as a 'relief for the parent schools' or argue for the provision of 'interim help and guidance'. One LEA aims in its units to provide a 'completely alternative set of relationships . . . in alternative education . . . within and separate from normal school'. The policy is seen as an extension of the notion of special education, 'a positive contribution to the educational needs of a minority of children whose needs cannot be met in any other way, who might become educationally handicapped and who, by their disruptive behaviour might deprive others of educational opportunity'.

Even where the unit is not envisaged as punitive, it is often conceived of as a special environment. Sometimes it is explicitly said to have non-school norms, or an adult approach, or a practical work bias. Although it usually serves pupils of an age to be entering for external examinations, while it frequently allows pupils who have been entered to complete the exams, it is commonly seen as not a place in which pupils are prepared for examinations. It is also a place for cooling-off, offering a period during which decisions concerning the pupil can be arrived at.

The unit's brief varies in range, from one concerned with the pupils it is immediately serving, to a wide ranging brief which can include assisting schools in the identification of children with special needs, supporting schools in internal attempts to resolve the problem, and the provision of in-service training for teachers on an area and a within-school basis.

LEA responses appear to indicate a number of different continua. One ranges from seeing units as temporary and experimental to seeing them as a permanent addition to the range of educational provision — a logical extension of the argument that disruptive children are yet another category of children with special needs; or as another continuum with units seen as ranging from penal to therapeutic and preventative measures. LEAs also differ in their degree of reluctance in acknowledging a need for units — from those which emphasise that normally schools will be expected to cope within their existing arrangements to those who acknowledge units as an extension of their coping strategies.

For what type of child is the unit designed?

The children to be placed in a unit are seen typically as very few in number, but significant nonetheless. In his embryonic stage the pupil is a 'child under stress' or a 'problem child', but he is later a 'chronic and persistent disrupter', requiring a different form of rehabilitative provision from therapeutic day classes for maladjusted children, although in the description of the unit's schooling this distinction is sometimes rather blurred. One authority talked of a 'gradient level of disturbance from occasional episodes of truancy or outbursts in the classroom, to totally disruptive behaviour in any group situation'. Certainly the unit is usually seen as catering for 'extremely disruptive children for whom formal education has proved unsuitable'. However, though the unit takes those who are extremely disruptive, quite often it is also stated that there are some children who should not be placed there (e.g. 'placement of acutely disturbed or aggressive children within the centre would be undesirable and alternative treatment outside of the centre should be available'). Similarly, one head of unit makes a plea that he should be allowed to refuse to admit a child to the unit, if he deems him incompatible with the group of children there.

In general the children are seen as having special needs, in that they require 'rehabilitation': their needs are in the area of social and learning skills, with some emphasis upon 'socialisation', though they may constitute a group with apparent differences between them (e.g. crisis referrals, suspended pupils and 'early warning' or 'potentially disruptive' pupils).

As has been pointed out earlier, the unit may be specifically designed, as one LEA puts it, for pupils (in this case, fourteen to sixteen-year-olds), 'for whom fulfilling the legal obligation with regard to education has been a problem. They have caused difficulties to schools and have therefore been shunted from one school to another'.

The pupils are those who have manifestly 'failed to cope in schools' and who, it is hoped, will in the unit learn the skills 'that will enable them to return quickly to normal school and an acceptable pattern of behaviour'. In some cases such re-integration in fact occurs; in others it does not.

Is the LEA evaluating the unit and modifying it in the light of the evaluation?

The units are typically established first on an experimental or temporary basis so that they are subject in one sense to 'evaluation'. The progress of the unit is monitored over perhaps a period of a year so that the permanent establishment of the unit can be considered on the basis of a report on its 'success'. However, the unit's progress is commonly monitored by the head of the centre who submits periodic reports so that the evaluation could often be said to be open to bias, as the head's post depends on the continuation of the unit. As one LEA puts it 'the success of such a centre is difficult to monitor' and 'it is difficult for those closely involved to be entirely objective'.

The temporary nature of the first establishment of a unit can itself cause problems. One head of unit comments: 'The uncertain future of the annexe leads to insecurity for pupils and staff . . . We are under pressure to "prove" ourselves, although definitions of success are as yet unclarified.' The insecurities are illustrated by the following account of two unit projects, set up by another LEA: 'Since the projects are experimental and the capacity of units very limited, the procedure relating to referral to the units must also be regarded as provisional. They are, therefore, subject to amendment at any stage during the operation of the pilot schemes in the light of experience gained and comments received.'

These projects were later regarded as a success and made permanent, their success being exemplified by the high proportion of pupils successfully reintegrated into normal schools, and of other pupils who on leaving went into employment. Other quoted criteria of the success of a trial period include the benefits to the secondary schools in the area, and the progress of the children admitted to the unit.

Authorities not using units

Where an authority has no units, and having considered them decides against their establishment, this may be on a variety of grounds, some of which have already been mentioned above, notably that there is a preference for dealing with disruptive children on the school campus, and that an in-school sanctuary system seems preferable to off-site units, on the grounds of greater flexibility, and less cost etc.

Authorities without units often point out that the solid positive evidence of their viability and success is not yet available. As one put it: 'It was recognised that there was only a thin scatter of experimental units for disruptive pupils in operation in the country at the present time, many of which had only recently been set up and it would therefore be difficult to draw too many conclusions about their success or otherwise.' The same LEA points to a further ground for caution: 'Many such units would have been created in response to local needs and might not be easily or successfully duplicated.'

Some authorities not using units have produced impressive handbooks of guidance for their teachers detailing preventive and crisis strategies. One such authority concludes, in spite of this, that heads have little alternative except to suspend in some extreme cases; it states that home tuition would not be appropriate for these pupils, but that variation of their work programme might be profitable if this increased their contact with teachers with whom they had a good relationship. It reminds its schools that the police could be called in cases of violence. Other authorities without units provide home tuition where suspension lasts more than a few days.

Units set against other preferred strategies

Consideration of units is set in two different types of context in the LEA materials. The first is the context of disciplinary procedures: suspension procedures, corporal punishment regulations and notes on authority and discipline in schools. The second is the context of broadly based measures which are designed to be preventive. These include early school identification of behaviour problems (e.g. with the suggestion that the Child Guidance Service should provide notes of guidance to schools and short-term courses for classroom teachers) and the strengthening of Pastoral Care staff, especially in schools with the greatest number of difficult childeren, as well as closer links with the Social Services than formerly and with other agencies (e.g. police). Other preventive measures include home liaison teachers, the improvement of facilities for the under-fives, and that the relevance of curriculum and school organisation should be kept under review especially in Social Priority Areas.

It appears that many authorities would favour informal transfer of pupils between schools as a strategy which would avoid long suspensions and perhaps the need for a unit. However, the LEA often expresses regrets that such transfer systems are difficult to work because: 'some schools press for transfer of children but will always have a good reason for not admitting a child with a similar behaviour problem. There appears to be an increasing tendency for the Heads to reject the idea of admitting an additional problem child on the grounds that they already have enough in their school'.

Occasionally, an LEA shows keen interest in a strategy less heavily emphasised by most others. Thus many authorities refer, though briefly, to the stress and strain caused by disruptive pupils, amongst other factors in teaching, upon school staffs. One, however, held a conference on stress in schools as part of its consideration of how best teacher support could be given, to meet what it saw as an important teacher welfare problem.

A few other authorities have adopted the strategy of deploying a group of teachers with a range of experience and an interest in disruptive pupils, to go into schools which have problems in their area, and so supplement the schools' efforts in dealing with them.

The most favoured alternative strategy to the off-site unit is, however, the on-site sanctuary, sometimes used as a 'cooling off' area for the disruptive child. Rejection of the establishment of a unit is frequently accompanied by a declared intention to strengthen sanctuary provision within the authority.

Implications

The establishment of off-site units for disruptive pupils needs to be appreciated as a significant, serious development within the educational system. Units developed as part of special schooling (e.g. tutorial units) have an ethos which is clearly defined, relating to educational handicap. Although the Warnock Report (1979) very briefly refers to disruptive pupils as a group of pupils with special needs, the ethos of off-site units for these pupils is more problematic. This arises from the notion that the units cater for pupils with whom schools have been *unable to cope;* they are *unsuitable* for *normal* schooling; their behaviour cannot be *tolerated.* (The italicised words are found in various of the LEA materials). It is clear that authorities are themselves worried about the penal implications of the units, stressing, for example that 'the role of the Centres is not one of containment', yet a letter from an LEA to parents saying that their child is being considered for admission to a unit, gives as the reason, that 'his/her behaviour in this school cannot be tolerated any longer' though it is added 'and I consider that a period in centre would be in his/her best interests'. The juxtaposition is common, as in this example of 'his behaviour is impossible for the school to cope with' and 'it is best for him to enter the unit'.

One important characteristic of the units is that they are removed from the school. One authority reports 'those favouring an area unit outside the school are exemplified by one head who wrote: disruptive pupils must be removed from normal schools; it is these pupils who are tarnishing the image of the comprehensive schools'. The removal is clearly important in the minds of staff of the school from which the pupil is sent; an LEA describes it thus, when problems have arisen in respect of pupils' re-entry to normal school: 'difficulties might occur if widespread within any school there was the mistaken impression that referral to the centre implied the final removal of the pupil from the normal school system'.

A second characteristic of the units is that, as has been said earlier, they constitute a form of sanction. This comes out clearly through the penological flavour of some of the vocabulary relating to them, e.g. 'a central reporting centre', 'an exclusion centre', a unit 'involving segregation and isolation', 'a strict regime of diversified activities which will keep the younger interested, occupied and subject to a firm discipline', 'it is felt that it should have a highly structured and industrious regime', etc. The language here is very reminiscent of Borstal and prison. It is relevant too that occasionally an LEA will express concern lest attendance at the unit carry a stigma. One authority establishing a Remedial and a Disruptive Unit comments: 'We must consider that the siting and staffing of the suggested Centres must be undertaken with great care. Particular attention must be given to ensure that the remedial, or disruptive children, and their families do not carry any stigma as a result of attending units at the Centre.'

The anomalous, potentially dangerous nature of the unit as a structure within the education system is clear from the indication of one director of education to his Schools and Special Services Sub-Committee 'that the Unit would not come under the control of any governing body'.

Finally, in considering the future of the units within the system, it appears that in offering a quasi-penological alternative form of treatment for difficult, anti-social adolescents, they would fit in well with Barbara Wootton's (1978) suggestion that all delinquency should be dealt with in an educational context, through 'informal' discussions under an educational umbrella covering parents and school staffs. Units for disruptive pupils are a bridge structure between education and penology and thus open to use, and abuse, by both systems.

20 INITIAL TEACHER TRAINING

There is a consensus that teacher education should be flexible, and up-to-date; as changes occur in educational processes within schools, courses of training for teachers whether these be initial courses, or induction courses or later in-service training courses, must reflect such changes and support and develop relevant skills in the staff upon whom these changes will impinge. Clearly the above is true of the substantial changes in structures and attitudes towards questions of disruptive behaviour which have occurred in the last decade and are on-going. The relevance of these changes to initial teacher training is different in some respects to their relevance to induction courses. The differences occur in the area of length of time allotted to the training. In spite of the pressure on initial training courses due to the demands made on an education course, it could be argued that there is more time there, than in in-service training courses.

The need for induction courses to concern themselves with matters of appropriate behaviour in the classroom appears more urgent than in initial courses, and since for LEAs the former is the prime concern and an area in which they have a main influence, the bulk of the data on teacher training in the LEA material studied, concerns the induction course. It should, however, be noted that many authorities refer briefly at least to the need to improve initial training, and some show considerable concern about this. One authority, for example, talks of the need for colleges to provide more realistic training in classroom management, administration, and self-awareness and an awareness of the types of situations and attitudes which teachers normally encounter' and says that 'this training should emphasise not only the pupils' contribution to disruptive situations, but the teacher's also'.

Another authority points out that the provision of resources and special facilities meets only part of the need — there is also the 'need for teacher training to take cognizance of the current situation'. Yet another couches its recommendations as a criticism, 'Some teachers are not given initial courses with adequate attention to the problems of controlling children in groups and dealing with children with problems,', and one suggests, related to this, that colleges need to involve educational psychologists and child psychiatrists in initial (as well as in-service) training courses (the last is an authority whose schools have strong links with a university human development research unit). One LEA working party on the disruptive child underlines, in black for emphasis, the following recommendation on 'Colleges of Education placing a greater emphasis on the handling of the disruptive child, and the broadening of the whole area of social education in training courses'.

As well as containing some specific references to initial training, the LEA materials contain much of direct relevance to initial courses. These materials are largely in the area of topics related to work with difficult children, some of which already figure in many courses, others which are treated relatively lightly at present but which, if the various working party reports are heeded, will warrant greater emphasis. No authority, however, mentions the issue which from a college of education point of view will be of major importance: the need to maintain a balanced perspective of the teacher's role and work. It would be only too easy for initial courses, should they be planned too much with behaviour problems in mind, to present a morbid view of teaching. This would be at variance with the overall situation in school and far removed from the best interests of the teacher in training. Matters of balance however, are mentioned in statements such as one that a school's resources should not be 'unduly distorted' in 'attempts to handle disruptive and difficult elements'.

There are clear pointers from other materials not presented here that disruptive behaviour is an area where factual information about facilities is required, and also an examination of related concepts so that these may be fruitfully and accurately differentiated. This is a field in which colleges can do useful work, so that a student enters teaching with knowledge of what is meant by a 'sanctuary' or a 'nurture group', with the ability to analyse the cluster of terms often subsumed under the word 'truancy', and with an acquaintance with the differences between terms such as 'expulsion', 'exclusion' and 'suspension'. At college the examination of the differences and relationships between names such as 'disruptive', 'difficult', 'maladjusted', and so on, can be introduced and important information concerning the role of the agencies concerned with deviant behaviour can be imparted.

Basic, however, to discussions of this area of teacher training, must surely be the development of the student's critical faculties. If this is true of a student teacher's work in general, it is particularly important in work on deviant behaviour where there are no God-given truths, nor easy solutions, and where sensitivity and flexibility of attitude and behaviour may be immensely valuable. Should this be acceptable, then there is a strong case for matters of deviancy to run as a thread through the basic elements of the initial course, particularly in subjects such as the philosophy and sociology of education, though there will also be a demand for separate treatment of specific topics. In this way the problematic nature of the issue will be kept to the forefront. In terms of current literature, for example, the recent Department of Education and Science report (DES, 1978) on behavioural units would be studied not only as 'information' (e.g., in a short course on units of various kinds, by speakers working in them) but from the point of view of discipline and how it relates to political decisions, assessment procedures, penology, and other matters. Similarly, if as occasionally happens, courses on behavioural approaches to the modification of pupil behaviour are organised in colleges on a diversity of scales, they would appropriately be set against the debate concerning the ethical issues involved in behaviour modification.

There are many areas dealt with in initial courses into which consideration of issues related to disruptive behaviour can be integrated. Table I illustrates some of those which received frequent mention in the LEA materials.

TABLE I	
Area	**Relationship with disruptive behaviour**
Language	Teacher-pupil language discrepancies. Verbal abuse. Problems of dialect of non-English speaking child, etc.
Teacher/pupil relationship	Teaching styles and leadership styles in relation to confrontation situations, aggression and frustration, etc. Rewards and sanctions including corporal punishment.
Curriculum	Criteria relating to a curriculum which the adolescent sees as 'good'. Vocational and educational guidance.
Pastoral care	Prevention of disruption. Counselling and children's problems. Social work support.
Multi-cultural education	Prejudice leading to disruption. Specific language and other problems.
Remedial education	Low self-esteem leading to deviant behaviour. Importance of basic skills, and success in them, to adjustment to school as a whole.

Many authorities refer to the need for teachers to develop good observational skills, with reference to the early screening of children, so that children with minimal difficulties can be appropriately helped and the development of more complex and serious difficulties avoided. In terms of initial courses, this would mean training students to be alert to child behaviour, on film or in schools. Much can be done whether through the use of observation schedules, or child study work, and through seminar or tutorial follow-up sessions of observation of teaching.

This issue of LEA interests brings us to a consideration of the role of teaching practice in the training of students for work in the area of deviancy. In the LEA papers considered, it is clear that authorities anticipate that many teachers in the course of their career will engage in some work with disruptive children for a period, though such teachers are likely to be experienced, and often have a related higher qualification. In the light of the integration of such work within the ordinary career structure, it could be useful if, during initial training, at some point, a student has an opportunity to meet with some 'very difficult' children. Such an objective could be accomplished by a short visit (e.g. one or two days) to a 'difficult' school, or (more rarely) by a teaching practice period in one, or by arrangement whereby a teaching practice includes teaching classes of a range of difficulty. An opportunity to teach difficult children in a one-to-one situation or in a small group, and to teach in a remedial education situation might be particularly instructive.

Finally, on initial training, one would hope to develop students' capacities to see teaching as a series of puzzles whose attempted solution is a fascinating and worthwhile exercise. As one LEA put it, 'all solutions depend on the quality of the individual teacher and the professional skills with which he is able to tackle the problems posed by disruptive children'. This echoes in interesting fashion the belief of Hoghughi (1978) that a central quality in those working with extremely difficult children is a capacity to view the child as a puzzle to be teased out. Any initial training course which demands a thinking, enquiring, problem solving approach from its students, thus prepares them for work with disruptive behaviour.

Implications for teacher training

What then are the implications for initial teacher training? Most courses in some measure reflect the concerns of the past decade: curriculum development, integration, team teaching, individualized learning, mixed ability, slow learners, remedial work, language across the curriculum, community schools. To this list must now be added a worked-out understanding of the implications of multi-cultural education, the special needs of schooling in urban areas, the educational needs of special categories of children previously the concern of special schools but since Warnock (DES, 1978) the province of the ordinary comprehensive school — children with learning difficulties, the partially sighted and hard of hearing, and the delicate etc. Added to this, is the insistent pressure of the unions to equip teachers and provide them with support in dealing with the problems of disruptive children.

Decisions on priorities involve complicated assessment of the needs for immediate action, i.e., to reduce teacher stress caused by violent behaviour among children as against long-term planning, for an informed and effective teaching force with skills to implement comprehensive education aims. The danger lies in isolating each of the problems so that LEA policies follow and react to events as they occur rather than precede and shape them. There is some evidence to suggest that this is what is already happeniung with respect to the LEA's response to disruptive chiledren. There must be concern that *ad hoc* responses to pressure groups — parents, teachers or unions — and to pressures arising from campaigns in the media, will dissipate energies, misdirect efforts at amelioration and create more differentiated and separate bureaucracies for coping.

Some of the work so far suggested for initial training programmes in Colleges of Education can at best be dealt with only at a superficial level. This is particularly true when one considers the average length of a PGCE course which is nine months. However, initial training is not confined to the college-based course, but extends into the probationary year when the new teacher is working full-time in the classroom. It might prove helpful to examine what the LEAs themselves provide in their induction programmes to deal with disciplinary problems experienced by the probationer in the school setting.

There are clear indications from the material that LEAs do not see their induction programmes in terms of a 'deficit model of a teacher'. Although the authorities expressed concern for the topic of misbehaviour in the context of initial training programmes in Colleges and Departments of Education, they did not suggest that existing programmes failed to produce competent probationer teachers. The courses examined concerning teacher centre programmes of induction reflect this feeling; they are not premised on the idea of a 'mini-college top-up course' but are seen as building upon practical skills initially acquired on college-based courses. This attitude to teacher centre programmes seems to be something for those concerned with initial training to consider: the complementary nature of LEA courses as a means of avoiding the kind of morbid view of teaching referred to earlier in this section and also as a source of information when planning the content of courses which intend to take account of behaviour problems experienced by the probationer teacher.

One authority for example, describes subsequent stages of training as 'Adaptation, Development, Assessment and Review' each to be undertaken in the three terms of the first year in teaching. The phase of Adaptation would be marked by a formal session with the delegated staff member to discuss any unexpected problems. Discussion topics would include school aims, guidelines in professionalism, school reporting systems, teacher unions, parents' evenings, audio-visual aids, the disadvantaged, disturbed, handicapped and epileptic child. The Development stage would include discipline, the role of the LEA advisers and teacher centres, the curriculum, the Education department, examination procedures and governors. The third state — Assessment and Review — would examine the contributory schools, the role of Her Majesty's Inspectorate (HMI), the discussion of reports produced by the DES, Schools Council, Careers, in-service training and external services including child welfare and social services. Throughout each stage there would be opportunities for case studies and to discuss self-development and to observe examples of 'good' teaching in school. The responsibility for this programme would be shared between the headmaster, a designated teacher-tutor and the head of department.

As well as school training some authorities suggest the value of attachment for varying periods of time to experienced teachers in the school, to teachers in disruptive units, to Education Welfare Officers and to child welfare workers. It is also suggested that it is valuable for probationers to visit other schools. In the light of the acknowledged reluctance of many teachers to admit to their colleagues that they are experiencing difficulties where these may be seen as reflecting on their competence these suggestions are particularly interesting as alternatives or as supplements to an in-school in-service programme.

In respect of initial teacher training it is clear from the LEA documents studied that they are requiring elements of teacher education which are modest and feasible, much of which are already incorporated in college and institute programmes, but which will require staff who are up-to-date *vis-a-vis* disruptive behaviour.

21 THE CONTRIBUTION TO INSET OF ACTION RESEARCH

In the prolonged period of nil economic growth facing the economy in the eighties, the prospects for education are poor. Local authority spending is being pared to such an extent that even essentials such as teachers' textbooks are at risk. In such a climate there seems little hope of any belated implementation of the James Report (1972) but, arguably in this situation, in-service education offers the best hope for making the fullest use of existing resources. Official reports and statements make acknowledgement of the need for INSET particularly where fifty per-cent of the teachers in the future will come from the short route of PGCE training (DES, 1981) which all acknowledge is too short effectively to train teachers for the complex task of teaching in the eighties. However, they are wary of promising that any funds will be made available.

It seems unlikely that there will be any extension of the existing pro-vision for teachers to be released for INSET courses, whether long or short, and the nature and viability of existing in-service provision is itself an important and unresolved issue. Past provision has been, and the effect of HMI reports from monitoring by the Assessment of Perfor-mance Unit (APU) may reinforce the trend, mainly in the area of short courses in subject areas. Whilst there can be little doubt that specialist further training of this kind is necessary and should continue, it has long been recognised that there is a largely unmet need for teachers, at every stage of their career, but particularly for those new to the pro-fession, for more general training and enlarged understanding of classroom and management skills. The rate of change and the range of new problems created by organisational, curricular and pedagogical innovations in schools have created a situation where, for many teachers, the skill and knowledge acquired, the attitudes formed during training and the experience gained in re-organised schools, is inadequate to meet the changed circumstances and the new pupil population in the eighties. This is especially true in the schools serving mixed race populations in the inner cities where tensions and difficulties of adjustment are most apparent and create a level of strain and stress which is unacceptable to many teachers. Outwardly the manifestations of these tensions are teacher breakdown, increasing concern for the disruptive nature of pupil behaviour in many schools, low levels of achievement and high levels of truancy.

In such a period of financial stringency, it might seem that the best and most cost effective way forward in education is by an extension of in-service training and an implementation of some of the recommendations of the James Report of 1972. The present stage in education with the on-going debate about curriculum and teaching strategies and more particularly the concern about levels of misbehaviour in schools suggests that there might be a richer pay off for schools in projects which involve the whole staff in development projects and planning.

In Part Two we have described two pieces of research in schools which explore the possibility of institutional and organisational change and development as one possible response to disruption. There are also implications for using such research projects as a means of staff development and as a way of enabling staff to cope with and to contribute towards necessary change. School-based research can thus be a powerful form of INSET. It provides a mechanism for involving and training staff in schools in research procedures and in particular, in procedures for looking at problems of children's behaviour in the whole context of the school. In both schools, the level of involvement of staff and the degree of co-operation was remarkable. Given the framework and procedures adopted and the availability of researchers to explain and talk through the project, it was possible in the limited time available, to dispel anxieties and doubts and to act as a catalyst in bringing together the concern and vast resourcefulness of the staff in coping with difficulties. Only one member of the staff in the two schools initially refused to co-operate in the monitoring exercise and he subsequently agreed to write a critical note to the final report (although this was not in fact forthcoming).

Equally important, the project provided the occasion for fruitful discussion at a number of levels; between researchers and individual teachers, between researchers and senior staff and between staff, Local Authority officials and researchers at different levels. Whilst it is difficult to quantify, it might reasonably be assumed that such focussed concern would be helpful in clarifying ideas, identifying problems, exploring appropriate strategies and in providing a stimulus and incentive for action.

At the staff level, the potential is greatest. Probably the greatest gain is in terms of staff morale and the feeling that there is an appropriate machinery for staff to make clear their anxieties and problems and to be influential in affecting change in the overall structures of the school. Whilst it may be argued that such machinery already exists through committee structures, staff meetings and clearly established lines of communication, in practice it would appear from the comments of junior staff, that many feel that the bureaucratic structure militates against any genuine or effective involvement. Such a situation runs the risk of a division between the senior management of the school and the junior staff and the feeling that problems experienced in the classroom are not fully understood by those who are responsible for overall school organisation and curriculum. The problem of devising a manageable form of participatory democracy in school is not new but it would appear, from this experience, that a project undertaken involving the whole staff, has a considerable potential in terms of staff morale and efficiency and in unlocking the considerable resourcefulness of teachers which is too often locked up in separate subject departments or role separation.

What was most noticeable was the alacritiy with which staff responded to the opportunity to talk about the problems they were experiencing; the expressions of relief from realising that it was possible to talk about them, and admit to difficulties without incurring the slur of professional incompetence. Unintentionally, as researchers we found ourselves cast in the role of teacher counsellor and what was unavoidable in all staff descriptions of incidents involving disruptive behaviour in which they had been involved, was the level of emotional intensity with which they were invested. Teachers feel strongly about children's misbehaviour; often they feel demeaned and drained of energy; frequently they feel compelled to cope on their own and unable to refer for help outside. In this situation, the importance of help and advice being immediately available in the situation where the problem arises, is apparent (Lawrence, 1980). Such help is both more immediate and related to the specific, and often quite complicated situation, which gives rise to problem behaviour, than any course providing for the in-service needs of teachers in the teacher centres. And it should be noted that the need for such advice and support is not restricted to probationary and inexperienced teachers; both the projects uncovered a range of problems experienced by teachers at all levels — not least by senior teachers who had been unable to adjust to the changes in organisation, curriculum and new styles of pedagogy required, in teaching in mixed ability comprehensive schools. The strength of a project approach was again shown in the ability to bring in staff at different stages of their career, especially those whose seniority might have made it difficult for them to seek help or to avail themselves of the teachers' courses designed primarily for probationary teachers. The characteristics of the two projects — notably an analytical approach to problem solving and the incorporation of teachers' ideas elicited through interviewing, potentially offer help at a number of levels but mainly it helps in the verbalisation and articulation of problems and offers the possibility of amelioration through rigorous analysis. From this point of view it is possible to claim that, apart from any benefits derived by the teaching staff, a project might be of assistance to the senior management and the head and where the Authority is new to such an enquiry, to the members and officers of that Authority.

Problems arise, however, precisely because such INSET takes place within a project rather than through a course. It places a heavy reliance on staff involvement which at any stage may be no more than partial and runs the risk of staff refusing to co-operate. The two projects ran into problems typical of all INSET courses — staff failing to pick up forms for reporting incidents, limited attendance at the staff meetings called to explain the project initially and later to discuss the findings, failure of some staff to read the reports which we produced. It should be pointed out, however, that in both schools, the remarkably high return both of incident forms, and of questionnaires relating to staff experience in the first Project school, indicated a strong measure of support and interest.

A second difficulty relates to problems of follow up. Despite the expense involved, we felt it essential to circulate every member of staff with the two reports in the second projct. More important, the level of contact we were able to achieve was partly the result of having three members of the research team available so that during the Autumn term and in the Spring term week of monitoring at least one member of staff was always available to make contacts with teachers and to follow up speedily on the incident forms which had been returned. Clearly part of the success of such a project depends on how easily it can mesh in and not interfere with school routines. This requires careful planning and some skill.

What became clear to us in the course of our research was that such action research is itself a powerful and effective form of INSET. Critical to its success clearly is the role of the headmaster. The motives for encouraging the adoption by the school of such a project might be various (Brent Davies, 1979); they could be no more than a public relations exercise or they could be influenced by submitting to the wishes of the County Education officer or the Educational Advisers. Equally they could stem from the desire to devolve authority and provide ways of involving staff at all levels in decisiion making. It is possible also that such motives may be subject to change and development in the course of the project, so that potentially, at least, by withdrawing co-operation a project could stop at any time.

For Local Authority officials, the response to such projects will in part be influenced by the ways in which they perceive their role; research information will clearly be relevant to their role as inspectors; equally as teacher educators, they may perceive the possibilities for INSET and as schools' helpers, see the project as a technique for assisting individual schools.

This raises the question of who carries out the project, and in what ways they are perceived as being able to offer help. In the two project schools, the researchers presented themselves as having, on the one hand an expertise developed in recognised disciplines relating to education — i.e. in Psychology, Educational Administration and in Sociology, and as teacher educators all of whom work in institutions of teacher education and have long and varied experience in teaching. Such a background it was hoped would be regarded by teachers in the 'difficult' schools in which the projects were carried out as a relevant and suitable background for working with and advising teachers on the problems relating to difficult pupil behaviour.

The nature of the help is often difficult to determine. Most probably it is related to the offer of an opportunity to verbalise problems and discuss difficulties in an acceptant context of informed analysis; such discussion might indicate that, whilst such problems are not easily or completely soluble, it is possible through such analysis, identification and co-operative effort to take steps towards their solution. It is also possible that a recognition that problems are shared with other schools, is helpful in suggesting that they are sufficiently widespread to warrant the development of special schemes and processes for tackling them. In particular the recognition of the centrality of problems of pupils' behaviour and motivation to every aspect of the school organisation, curriculum, grouping, timetabling, pedagogy is itself an important step to locate such problems within the system, aspects of which are capable of modification and change, rather than just within the psychological or motivational make up of individual disruptive children (Gillham, 1981; Rutter, 1979; Steed, 1982).

With the support of staff, the second project undertook small scale exploratory studies of pupil attitudes to disruption through childrens' writing in the first year and through a number of structured interviews of pupils involved in reported disruptions.

It is important to recognise that there may be strong resistance among teachers to research which attempts to incorporate the pupil view because of the implied criticisms this may level at teachers. Many, however, appreciate the importance of the pupils' perspective and any research which relies heavily on the subjective expression of feeling related to disruptive incidents, (irrespective of the objective nature of the disruptive act) must clearly give attention to how such incidents are perceived and experienced by the pupils. Clearly the potential for the further training of teaching in this area is enormous in extending sensitivity towards non-verbal behaviour, in examining stereotyping, in exploring the use of language and gesture and more generally in understanding some of the dynamics of groups and classes (Lawrence *et al.,* 1980 (iii)). In particular it might be of value in acquiring relevant social or pedagogic skills relating to teaching in a multi-cultural classroom (Little and Willey, 1981).

A further INSET aspect of such project work relates to the possibility of working with and incorporating the views of ancillary staff-school helpers, secretaries, cleaners etc. At present this is an unexplored area because the focus of our concern so far has been on the teachers' problems. Within the whole school community, however, questions of the relationship of the ancillary staff to teaching staff and their degree of involvement in decisions relating to school management are clearly important and could be incorporated.

The question which has to be asked at the end of such a project, given that there is a desire that it continue in some form, is who should be responsible for such work? Should it be the responsibility of the school or the local authority? Should work continue within the school or be formalised into a more general teacher course at the local centre?

To go a stage further, would it be conceivable for such projects to be developed, generated and staffed from within the school or the authority without the assistance of outside researchers? Whilst it is probable that there would be gains and losses from undertaking such a project on a 'Do It Yourself' basis — losses most notably perhaps in the reluctance of staff to admit to other colleagues their problems which would diminish the area of staff counselling and therapy which was a feature of our research — it is clear that, in principle at least, there need be no obstacle to such an undertaking. Indeed we would think that a school policy to systematically monitor, regularly and routinely, the incidence of behaviour using the kind of instruments which we have developed in the two projects would be desirable and administratively straightforward. Many schools already do similar exercises on a limited scale. The advantages in having available regular and systematised information over a period of time is that it could be fed into discussions and be used to inform decisions taken for example, in curriculum planning, timetabling revisions, planning optional courses, staff recruitment etc. The question who should or could initiate such a regular (perhaps once every two or three years) monitoring exercise is more difficult to answer. It might be expected that officials of the authority might encourage schools to undertake such an exercise and, in the first instance, might themselves be responsible for the planning, executing and administering the initial monitoring to make teachers familiar with the procedures and to train them in the relevant research methods. From such a beginning, it might be expected that, within schools, individual teachers, either on the basis of position (i.e. the school counsellor, tutor deputy head) or of experience or recognised skill, could be identified as the link and the initiator for subsequent monitoring. We already know of a few, recent 'self-monitoring' exercises in schools.

22 PARENTS AND DISRUPTIVE BEHAVIOUR IN SCHOOLS

It is an unpleasant shock for some parents to learn that their child is regarded by teachers as a disruptive influence in the school he attends. For other parents, such knowledge is greeted with indifference and even hostility when they remember their own school experiences and look at what they see as an acceptable pattern of behaviour in their child at home. However, the news of their child's disruption is received, this may be a parent's first contact with the pastoral organisation. Thus an understanding of how a school defines disruption and copes with it may be crucial in coping with the circumstances. It is bewildering for example when school suspension proceedings are involved with what may seem to a parent great speed. The onus is upon the schools to inform parents about all aspects of school organisation and most do so in the form of a short document circulated when the child first enters the school. The requirement in the 1980 Education Act (Section 8) that schools must publish information about themselves may go some way to establishing a clearer comprehension on the part of parents as to how schools operate. For example, parents will learn that teachers do not control all the school factors influencing the classroom.

A classroom teacher's concerns are two-fold: the teacher must be able to control disruptive pupils and involve them in learning; in some ways this is a simultaneous process. Secondly, the teacher wishes to help pupils move upward through the stages of discipline, i.e. the ability to listen and follow directions. Hence the teacher has both immediate and developmental concerns. Certain other factors are the responsibility of the administration (head teacher, school governors). How an individual school is organised, what class size is decided upon, and what kind of support for teachers is given (materials and media, as well as an internal referral system when misbehaviour occurs in the classroom, corridor or playground) — all are factors in determining the quality of classroom discipline.

Obviously parents are more concerned with the immediate situation and how the school deals with it rather than the local authorities. What this section has also tried to show is the part the local education authority plays in determining broad guidelines for disruptive behaviour in its area. There is also a consideration of initial training and the in-service training needs of teachers where disruptive behaviour is concerned that can indicate to parents some of the issues and dilemmas facing teacher educators and teachers.

Part Five

CONCLUSIONS

23 CONCLUSIONS

Conclusions will be presented here in the form of a series of propositions. They are:

1. That disruption in schools is sufficiently serious to deserve extensive study and research.

2. The indicators of its seriousness are different from those highlighted in the media. The picture we have presented focuses less on pupil violence and assaults on teachers and pupils, although these are very serious and a matter of concern, than on the frustration and irritation which arises from the constant interruptions.

3. Such disruption is ubiquitous and suggests the need to revise considerably the estimates of its extent and its nature.

   The evidence we have presented is partly objective, in that we have attempted to count incidents but also qualitative in that we have attempted to show the levels of intensity of emotion involved for participants — both teachers and pupils.

4. That difficulties teachers experience with pupils should be more open to discussion and cease to be a cause of shame and embarrassment or regarded solely as an indication of professional ineptness or incompetence. Staff support and development can probably best be achieved in an atmosphere which acknowledges that disruption is normal in situations where teachers and pupils may not share the same intentions and expectations.

5. To achieve this, we believe that it would be desirable for disruptive behaviour, together with language across the curriculum and multi-racial education, to become a subject for serious and sustained staff discussion and research. Every school should have an agreed school behaviour policy.

6. That schools should undertake ongoing school based monitoring of behaviour.

7. Such an approach is within the resources available to them; it is practical and cheap and can be achieved without serious interruption to the school or adding to the existing pressures on teachers.

The benefits of such a policy might be shown in:

a) Improved staff morale and confidence in the classroom from an acknowledgement that problems have been recognised and understood.

b) The existence of information collected routinely, which over a period of time could give indications of the effectiveness of measures taken, and of the need for further development and change in the classroom and in the curriculum and in aspects of the school organisation.

c) Involvement of staff in research and development could contribute importantly to the understanding and cohesion of staff — most particularly it might meet the criticism of those at the chalk face — classroom teachers, that their problems are not understood by their colleagues at senior management level.

d) Schools with a developed and agreed Behaviour Policy might be expected to keep constantly under review aspects of the organisation and curriculum which could contribute significantly to disruption experienced in the classroom.

e) Change and development within schools might under these circumstances be seen as less threatening and related specifically to the achievement of agreed educational aims within the constraints and opportunities of the particular circumstances of the school and its resources.

8. The implication of such an approach is that a single educational package available equally to all children will no longer serve to meet the needs of an increasingly diversified school population.

9. That change is inevitable and to be welcomed but in adapting to change it is important to devise new ways in which staff, pupils and parents can increasingly be involved in and affect decisions relating to school.

10.   That control of disruptive behaviour whilst important, need not and in our view should not, rely primarily on punitive measures; disruption is an educational problem.

11.   That continuous disruption is serious because of the strain and stress to teachers, pupils and parents alike. It is something we cannot afford to ignore.

It is not easy to draw conclusions from discussions on disruption, partly because it is difficult to agree about the nature, adequacy and significance of the evidence but more importantly perhaps, because of the danger of being seen as wanting the last word.

There are no simple answers or easy solutions, nor is there any single cause of school disruption and the sooner we recognise this and stop looking for one, the sooner we can get down to the real problem of re-examining features of the school environment and demands teachers make which provoke disruptive behaviour. Such reviews may well indicate that schools, however well they are organised, may never be disruption-free but that whilst some is unavoidable and acceptable, some we can and should do something about. Disruptive behaviour can then be viewed as an invitation and opportunity to review the adequacy of educational aims and the appropriateness of the means available to achieve these.

REFERENCES

Aries, R. (1962) *Centuries of Childhood,* Cape.

Armytage, W.H.G. (1970) *Four Hundred Years of English Education,* 2nd Ed., Cambridge University Press.

Auld, R. (1976) *William Tyndale Junior and Infants Schools Public Inquiry,* ILEA.

Bandura, A. (1970) *Principles of Behaviour Modification,* Holt, Rinehart and Winston.

Bancroft, J. (1970) *Behaviour Modification in a School Classroom,* Paper to R.M.P.A. (Children's Section) Annual Conference.

Bamish, H.H. *et al.* (1969) 'Good Behaviour Game: Effects of Individual Contingencies for Group Consequences on Disruptive Behaviour in a Classroom', *Journal of Applied Behaviour,* Annals 2, 10-15.

Becker, H.S. (1964) *The Other Side: Perspectives on Deviance,* Collier: McMillan.

Belson, W.A. (1975) *Juvenile Theft: The Causal Factors,* Harper Row.

Bender, M.P. (1976) *Community Psychology,* Methuen.

Bennett, N. (1976) *Teaching Styles and Pupil Progress,* Open Books.

Berg, L. (1968) *Risinghill: Death of a Comprehensive,* Pelican Books.

Bernbaum, G. (ed.) (1979) *Schooling in Decline,* McMillan.

Blishen, E. (1969) *The School that I'd Like,* Penguin Education with the Observer.

Bowles, S. and Gintis, H. (1976) *Schooling in Capitalist America,* Routledge and Kegan Paul.

Boyd, W. (1973) *History of Western Education,* Black.

Boyson, R. (ed.) (1972) *Education: Threatened Standards,* Enfield, Churchill.

Brent Davies, K. (1979) *I.L.E.A. Contact,* 17th November.

Burns, T. and Stalker, G.M. (1961) *The Management of Innovation,* Tavistock Publications.

Carroll, H.C.M. (ed.) (1977) *Absenteeism in South Wales,* University College of Swansea.

Centre for Information and Advice on Educational Disadvantage (1977), *Identification of Children with Special Educational Needs, Conference Report,* March.

Central Policy Review Staff (1978) *Vandalism,* H.M.S.O.

Clarke, D.D., Parry Jones, W.L.L., Gay, B.M. and Smith, C.M.B. (1981) 'Disruptive Incidents in Secondary School Classrooms — A Sequence Analysis Approach,' *Oxford Review of Education,* 7, 111-117.

Clegg, A. and Megson, B. (1968) *Children in Distress,* Allen Lane, Penguin.

Cohen, S. (1979) 'Crime and Punishment', *New Society,* 1, 15; 29 March.

Cope, E. and Gray, J. (1978) 'Figures and Perspectives on the National Problem of Truancy, An Opening Discussion', *Collaborative Research Newsletter,* Centre for Educational Sociology, University of Edinburgh.

Corwin, R.G. (1965) *A Sociology of Education,* Appleton Century Crofts, New York.

Cox, C.B. and Dyson, A.E. (1968) *Fight for Education,* (Black Papers), Critical Quarterly Society.

Davie, R. (1980) 'Behaviour Problems in Schools and School-based Inservice Training', in Upton, G. and Gobell, R. (eds.) (1980) *Behaviour Problems in the Comprehensive School,* Faculty of Education, University College, Cardiff.

Dawson, R.L. (1980) *Special Provision for Disturbed Pupils,* Macmillan Education.

Department of Education and Science (1972) *Teacher Education and Training,* (The James Report), H.M.S.O.

Department of Education and Science (1975) *A Language for Life,* (The Bullock Report), H.M.S.O.

Department of Education and Science (1978) *Special Educational Needs,* (The Warnock Report), Cmnd 7212, H.M.S.O.

Department of Education and Science (1981) *The School Curriculum,* H.M.S.O.

Department of Education and Science (1981) *West Indian Children in Our Schools,* (The Rampton Report), H.M.S.O.

Devonshire County Council (1975) *Disruptive and Violent Behaviour in Schools,* Devonshire Education Department.

Donahue, G.T. and Michtern, S. (1965) *Teaching the Troubled Child,* Collier-Macmillan.

Douglas, J.B.W. (1964) *The Home and the School,* MacGibbon and Kee; also Panther.

Douglas, M. (1966) *Purity and Danger,* Routledge and Kegan Paul.

Dunham, J. (1977) 'Stress of Working with Maladjusted Children', *Therapeutic Education,* 5, 2, 3-11.

Edwards, V.K. (1979) *The West Indian Language Issue in British Schools: Challenges and Responses.* Routledge and Kegan Paul.

Ellis, T. *et al.* (1976) *William Tyndale: the teachers' story,* Writers and Readers Publishing Co-operative.

Erickson, E. (1965) *Childhood and Society,* Penguin, Hogarth.

Etzioni, A. (1964) *Modern Organizations,* Prentice Hall.

Finlayson, D.J. and Loughran, L. (1975) 'Pupils' perceptions in low and high delinquency schools', *Educational Resarch,* 18, 138-45.

Ford, J., Mongon, D. and Whelan, M. (1982) *Special Education and Social Control: Invisible Disasters,* Routledge, and Kegan Paul.

Furlong, J. (1980) 'Black Resistance in the Liberal Comprehensive', *Brunel University, Disaffected Pupil Study,* Unpublished paper.

Galloway, D. (1981) 'Exclusion and Suspension from School', *Trends in Education,* 1980/82.

Galloway, D., Ball, T., Blomfield, D. and Seyd, R. (1982) *Schools and Disruptive Pupils,* Longman.

Galloway, D.M. *et al.* (1978) 'Absence from School and Behaviour Problems in Schools' (Sheffield School and Home Project), *Therapeutic Education,* 6, 2, 28-33.

Galloway, D.M. and Goodwin, C. (1980) *Educating Slow Learning and Maladjusted Children,* Longman.

Gibbes, N. (1980) *West Indian Teachers Speak Out: their experience in some of London's Schools,* Caribbean Teachers' Association and Lewisham C.C.R.

Gillham, B. (ed.) (1982) *Problem Behaviour in the Secondary School: A Systems Approach,* Croom Helm.

Graham, P. (1967) 'Perceiving Disturbed Children', *Special Education,* 56, 29-33.

Hammersley, M. and Woods, P. (eds.) (1976) *The Process of Schooling,* Routledge, and Kegan Paul and Open University Press, 217-229.

Hargreaves, D. (1968) *Social Relations in the Secondary School,* Routledge and Kegan Paul.

Hastings, N. and Schweiso, J. (1979) 'Practices, Prejudices and Prospects: Behaviour Modification and Teacher Training', *Psychology of Teaching,* (APT Bulletin) 7, 2, 137-142.

Heal, K. (1978) 'Misbehaviour Among School Children: The Role of the School in Strategies for Prevention', *Policy and Politics,* 6, 321-332.

Henderson, G.S. and Perry, G.W. (1981) *Change and Development in Schools,* McGraw Hill.

Her Majesty's Inspectorate (1977) *10 Good Schools:* A secondary school inquiry. Matters for Discussion Series, D.E.S.

Her Majesty's Inspectorate (1978) *Behavioural Units,* D.E.S.

Her Majesty's Inspectorate (1978) *Truancy and Behavioural Problems in some Urban Schools,* D.E.S.

Her Majesty's Inspectorate (1979) *Aspects of Secondary Education in England:* H.M.S.O.

Hoghughi, M. (1978) *Troubled and Troublesome,* Burnett Books.

Hoghughi, M. (1980) *Assessing Problem Children: Issues and Practices,* Burnett Books.

Inner London Education Authority (1978) *Disruptive Pupils,* Report 8058, January.

Illich, I. (1976) *Limits to Medicine: Medical Nemesis, The Expropriation of Health,* Boyars.

Ingvarson, L.C. (1970) *Training a Teacher in Classroom Control,* (Unpublished MA (ed.) Thesis, University of London).

Jarman, T.L. (1963) *Landmarks in the History of Education,* Murray.

Jencks, C. (1972) *Inequality: A reassessment of the effect of family and schooling,* New York: Basic Books.

Jones, N.J. (1973) 'Special Adjustment Units in Comprehensive Schools', *Therapeutic Education,* 1, 2, 23-31.

Jones-Davies, B. and Cave, R.G. (eds.) (1976) *The Disruptive Pupil in the Secondary School,* Ward Lock.

Kennedy, I. (1981) *The Unmasking of Medicine,* Allen and Unwin.

Kogan, M. (1978) *The Politics of Educational Change,* Fontana.

Kolvin, I. *et al.* (1976) 'Maladjusted Pupils in Ordinary Schools', *Special Education:* Forward Trends, 3, 3, 15-19.

Kounin, J. (1970) *Discipline and Group Management in Classrooms,* Holt, Rinehart and Winston.

Kyriacou, C. (1980) 'High Anxiety', *Times Educational Supplement,* 3338, 6.6.80.

Kyriacou, C. and Sutcliffe, J. (1978) 'Teacher Stress: Prevalence Sources and Symptoms', *British Journal of Educational Psychology,* 48, 159-167.

Kyriacou, C. and Sutcliffe, J. (1979) 'A Note on Teacher Stress and Laws of Control', *Journal of Occupational Psychology,* 52, 227-228.

Lane, D., (undated) Hungerford Education Guidance Unit, Inner London Education Authority.

Lawrence, J. (1970) *A Questionnaire Study of Female Teachers' Self-Reported Responses to Real and Hypothetical Deviant Behaviour,* Unpublished MA (ed.) Thesis, University of London.

Lawrence, J. (1973) 'Maladjusted Children and the Child Guidance Service', *London Educational Review,* 2, 2, 22-27.

Lawrence, J. (1980) *Exploring Techniques for Coping with Disruptive Behaviour,* Goldsmith's College.

258 References

References

Lawrence, J., Steed, D. and Young, P. (1977) *Disruptive Behaviour in a Secondary School,* Goldsmiths' Educational Studies Monograph No.1.

Lawrence, J., Steed, D. and Young, P. (1978a) 'Monitoring Incidents of Disruptive Behaviour in a Secondary School', *Durham and Newcastle Research Review,* VII, 4, Autumn 1978.

Lawrence, J., Steed, D. and Young, P. (1978b) 'Non-Observational Monitoring of Disruptive Behaviour in a Secondary School, *Research Intelligence,* 4, 1.

Lawrence, J., Steed, D. and Young, P. (1981) *Dialogue on Disruptive Behaviour:* A study of a secondary school, PJD Press.

Lazarus, R.S. (1962) *Psychological Stress and the Coping Process,* McGraw-Hill.

Lefkowitz, M.M. *et al.* (1977) *Growing up to be Violent,* Pergamon Press.

Little, A.N. and Wiley, R. (1981) *Studies in the Multi-Ethnic Curriculim,* Schools Council, Multi-Ethnic Education.

Lowenstein, L.F. (1975) *Violent and Disruptive Behaviour in Schools,* NAS.

Lowndes, G.A.N. (1969) *The Silent Social Revolution,* Oxford University Press.

McNamara, D. (1970) *The Distribution and Incidence of Problem Children in an English County,* British Association for the Advancement of Science Paper, No.251.

Mandler, G. and Watson, D.L. (1966) 'Anxiety and the Interaction of Behaviour', in Spielberger, C.D. (ed.), *Anxiety and Behaviour,* Academic Press.

Marland, M. (1967) *The Craft of the Classroom,* Heinemann Educational.

Marshall, T. (1976) 'Vandalism: The Seeker of Destruction', *New Society,* 17.6.76.

Matza, D. (1969) *Becoming Deviant,* Prentice Hall.

Morrell, D. (1969) 'Happiness is not a meal ticket', *Times Educational Supplement,* No.2846. 19.12.69.

Mortimer, P., Davies, J., West, A. and Varlaam, M. (1984) *Behaviour Problems in Schools:* an Evaluation of Support Centres, Croom Helm.

Mungham, G. and Pearson, G. (eds.) (1975) *Working Class Cultures,* Routledge and Kegan Paul.

Musgrave, F. (1966) *Youth and the Social Order,* Routledge, and Kegan Paul.

National Association of Schoolmasters (1976) *Stress in Schools,* NAS.

Nottingham Class Management Observation Schedule, *Newsletter No.3* (1978) Teacher Education project, Nottingham University School of Education.

O'Hagan, F.S. (1977) 'Attitudes of offenders and non-offenders towards school', *Educational Research,* 19, 2, 142-146.

Olweus, D. (1978) *Aggression in the Schools: Bullies and Whipping Boys,* New York, London: Halsted Press.

Orme, N. (1973) *English Schools in the Middle Ages,* Methuen.

Parry-Jones, W.L. and Gay, B.M. (1980) 'The Anatomy of Disruption: A Preliminary Consideration of Interaction Sequences within Disruptive Incidents', *Oxford Review of Education,* Vol.6, No.3, Autumn 1980.

Parsons Talcott (1964) *Essays in Socilogical Theory,* Free Press.

Paul, L. (1973) 'Vandalism and Violence', *Spectrum,* 6, 1, September 1973.

Platt, A. (1969) *The Child Savers:* The Invention of Delinquency, University of Chicago.

Pile, W.D. (1979) *The Department of Education and Science,* The New Whitehall Series 16, Allen and Unwin.

Polyani, M. (1964) *The Tacit Dimension: Collected Papers,* Routledge and Kegan Paul.

Popper, K.R. (1964) *Conjectures and Refutations: The Growth of Scientific Knowledge,* Routledge and Kegan Paul.

Poteet, J.A. (1974) *Behaviour Modification: A Practical Guide for Teachers,* U.L.P.

Powers, M.J. *et al.* (1967) 'Delinquent Schools', *New Society,* 19.10.67.

Pritchard, C. and Taylor, R. (1975) 'Classroom Violence', *New Society,* 27.11.75.

Rafky, D.K. and Sealey, R.W. (1975) 'The Adolescent and the Law: A survey', *Crime and Delinquency,* 21. 2, 131-8.

Reimer, E. (1971) *School is Dead,* Penguin.

Reynolds, D. (1975) 'When Teachers Refuse a Truce', in Mungham, G. and Pearson, G. (eds.) *Working Class Culture,* Routledge and Kegan Paul.

Reynolds, D. (1976) 'The Delinquent School', in Hammersley, M. and Woods, P. (eds.) *The Process of Schooling,* Routledge and Kegan Paul and Open University Press.

Roberts, B. (1977) 'Treating Children in Secondary Schooling', *Educational Review,* 29, 3, 204-212.

Robins, L.N. (1966) *Deviant Children Grown Up: A Sociological and Psychiatric Study of Sociopathic Personality,* The Williams and Wilkins Co. Baltimore.

Rose, G. and Marshall, T.F. (1974) *Counselling and School Social Work,* Wiley.

Rosenthal, R. and Jacobson, L.P. (1968) *Pygmalion in the Classroom: Teacher Expectation and Pupils' Intellectual Development,* New York: Holt, Rinehart and Winston.

Rubington, E. and Weinberg, M.S. (1968) *Deviance: The Interactionist Perspective,* Collier McMillan.

Rutter, M. (1967) 'A Child's Behaviour Questionnaire for Completion by Teachers: Preliminary Findings', *Journal of Child Psychology and Psychiatry,* 8, 1-11.

Rutter, M. *et al.* (1974) 'Children of West Indian Immigrants: Rates of Behavioural Deviance and of Psychiatry', *Journal of Child Psychology and Psychiatry,* 15, 241-262.

Rutter, M. (1975) *Helping Troubled Children,* Pelican.

Rutter, M., Maugham, B., Mortimore, P. and Ouston, J. (1979) *Fifteen Thousand Hours,* Open Books.

Schools Council (1970) *Cross'd with Adversity,* Working Paper No.27.

Schur, E. (1971) *Labelling Deviant Behaviour: Its Sociological Implications,* Harper Row.

Schutz, A. (1964) *The Problem of Social Reality:* Collected papers, The Hague, Nijhoff.

Stebbins, R.A. 61975) *Teachers and Meaning: Definitions of Classroom Situations,* Leiden, E.J. Brill.

Steed, D. (1982) 'Tired of School: Danish Disruptives and Ours', *Cambridge Journal of Education,* 13, 1.

Shipman, M. (1975) *The Sociology of the School,* Longman.

Spielberg, C.D. (ed.) (1966) *Anxiety and Behaviour,* New York: Academic Press.

Staffordshire Education Committee (1977) *Disruptive Pupils in Schools,* Report of a working party.

Stenhouse, L. (ed.) (1980) *Curriculum Research and Development in Action,* Heinemann Educational.

Stone, J. and Taylor, F. (1977) *Vandalism in Schools,* Save the Children Fund.

Tattum, D. (1982) *Disruptive Pupils in Schools and Units,* John Wiley and Sons.

Thelen, H.A. (1967) *Classroom Grouping for Teachability,* John Wiley.

Times Educational Supplement (1975) 'New Trust Aims to Stop Lawlessness', 14.3.75.

Tizard, J. (1973) 'Maladjusted Children and the Child Guidance Service', *London Educational Review,* 2, 2.

Toffler, A. (1980) *The Third Wave,* London, Collins.

Topping, K.J. (1983) *Educational Systems for Disruptive Adolescents,* Croom Helm.

Upton, G. and Gobell, R. (eds.) (1980) *Behaviour Problems in the Comprehensive School,* Faculty of Education, University College, Cardiff.

Varlaam, A. (1974) 'Educational Attainment and Behaviour at School', *Greater London Intelligence Quarterly,* No.29.

Vernon, P.E. (1969) 'Intelligence and Cultural Environment', *Manuals of Modern Psychology,* Methuen and Co.

Ward, J. (1971) 'Modification of Deviant Classroom Behaviour', *British Journal of Educational Psychology,* 41, 3, 304-313.

Waetjen, W.B. (1970) 'The Teacher and Motivation', *Theory into Practice,* 9, 10-15.

West Macott, E.V.S. and Cameron, R.J. (1981) *Behaviour Can Change,* Globe Education.

Wilson, H. (1980) 'Parents Can Cut the Crime Rate', *New Society,* 4.12.80.

Wilson, M.D. and Evans, W. (1980) *Education of Disturbed Pupils,* Schools Council, Working Paper No.65, Evans, Methuen.

Wilson, P. (1971) *Interest and Discipline in Education,* Routledge.

Withall, J. (1975) 'An Objective Measure of a Teacher's Classroom Interactions', *Journal of Educational Psychology,* 47, 203-212.

Wolff, S. (1969) *Children Under Stress,* Allen Lane.

Wootton, B. (1978) *Crime and Penal Policy,* George Allen and Unwin.

Young, M.F.D. (ed.) (1976) *Knowledge and Control,* Collier, McMillan.

Young, P., Steed, D. and Lawrence, J. (1980) 'Local Education Authorities and autonomous off-site units for disruptive pupils in secondary schools', *Cambridge Journal of Education,* 10, 2, 55-70.

Zander, M. (1979) 'What is the evidence on law and order?', *New Society,* 13.12.79.

INDEX